De-Idealizing Relational Theory

Self-examination and self-critique: for psychoanalytic patients, this is the conduit to growth. Yet within the field, psychoanalysts haven't sufficiently utilized their own methodology or subjected their own preferred approaches to systematic and critical self-examination. Across theoretical divides, psychoanalytic writers and clinicians have too often responded to criticism with defensiveness rather than reflectivity.

De-Idealizing Relational Theory attempts to rectify this for the relational field. This book is a first in the history of psychoanalysis; it takes internal dissension and difference seriously rather than defensively. Rather than saying that the other's reading of relational theory is wrong, distorted, or a misrepresentation, this book is interested in querying how theory lends itself to such characterizations. How have psychoanalysts participated in conveying this portrayal to their critics? Might this dissension illuminate blind-spot(s) and highlight new areas of growth?

It's a challenge to engage in psychoanalytic self-critique. To do so requires that we move beyond our own assumptions and deeply held beliefs about what moves the treatment process and how we can best function within it. To step aside from ourselves, to question the assumed, to take the critiques of others seriously, demands more than an absence of defensive-ness. It requires that we step into the shoes of the psychoanalytic Other and suspend not only our theories, but our emotional investment in them. There are a range of ways in which our authors took up that challenge. Some revisited the assumptions that underlay early relational thinking and expanded their sources (Greenberg & Aron). Some took up specific aspects of relational technique and unpacked their roots and evolution

(Mark, Cooper). Some offered an expanded view of what constitutes relational theory and technique (Seligman, Corbett, Grossmark). Some more directly critiqued aspects of relational theory and technique (Berman, Stern). And some took on a broader critique of relational theory or technique (Layton, Slochower).

Unsurprisingly, no single essay examined the totality of relational thinking, its theoretical and clinical implications. This task would be herculean both practically and psychologically. We're all invested in aspects of what we think and what we do; at best, we examine some, but never all of our assumptions and ideas. We recognize, retrospectively, how very challenging a task this was; it asked writers to engage in what we might think of as a self-analysis of the countertransference. Taken together these essays represent a significant effort at self-critique and we are enormously proud of it.

Each chapter critically assesses and examines aspects of relational theory and technique, considers its current state and its relations to other psychoanalytic approaches. *De-Idealizing Relational Theory* will appeal to all relational psychoanalysts and psychoanalytic psychotherapists.

Lewis Aron, Ph.D., ABPP is the director of the New York University Postdoctoral Program in Psychotherapy and Psychoanalysis. He is the author and editor of numerous articles and books on psychotherapy and psychoanalysis and well known for his study and reading groups around the world. His most recent book, co-authored with Galit Atlas, is the Routledge title *Dramatic Dialogue: Contemporary Clinical Practice*.

Sue Grand, Ph.D., is faculty at the NYU Postdoctoral Program in Psychotherapy and Psychoanalysis. She is the author of *The Reproduction of Evil: A Clinical and Cultural Perspective* and *The Hero in the Mirror*, and has co-edited two books on the trans-generational transmission of trauma. She practices in NYC and in Teaneck, NJ.

Joyce Slochower, Ph.D., ABPP is Professor Emerita at Hunter College and the Graduate Center, the City University of New York. She is on the faculty of the New York University Postdoctoral Program, the Steven Mitchell Center, the National Training Program of NIP, the Philadelphia Center for Relational Studies, and the Psychoanalytic Institute of

Northern California in San Francisco. She is the author of *Holding and Psychoanalysis* and *Psychoanalytic Collisions*. Second editions of both books were released in 2014. She is in private practice in New York City, where she sees individuals and couples, and runs supervision and study groups.

RELATIONAL PERSPECTIVES BOOK SERIES

LEWIS ARON, ADRIENNE HARRIS,
STEVEN KUCHUCK & EYAL ROZMARIN
Series Editor

The Relational Perspectives Book Series (RPBS) publishes books that grow out of or contribute to the relational tradition in contemporary psychoanalysis. The term *relational psychoanalysis* was first used by Greenberg and Mitchell[1] to bridge the traditions of interpersonal relations, as developed within interpersonal psychoanalysis and object relations, as developed within contemporary British theory. But, under the seminal work of the late Stephen A. Mitchell, the term *relational psychoanalysis* grew and began to accrue to itself many other influences and developments. Various tributaries—interpersonal psychoanalysis, object relations theory, self psychology, empirical infancy research, and elements of contemporary Freudian and Kleinian thought—flow into this tradition, which understands relational configurations between self and others, both real and fantasied, as the primary subject of psychoanalytic investigation.

We refer to the relational tradition, rather than to a relational school, to highlight that we are identifying a trend, a tendency within contemporary psychoanalysis, not a more formally organized or coherent school or system of beliefs. Our use of the term *relational* signifies a dimension of theory and practice that has become salient across the wide spectrum of contemporary psychoanalysis. Now under the editorial supervision of Lewis Aron, Adrienne Harris, Steven Kuchuck and Eyal Rozmarin, the Relational Perspectives Book Series originated in 1990 under the editorial eye of the late Stephen A. Mitchell. Mitchell was the most prolific and influential of the originators of the relational tradition. Committed to dialogue among psychoanalysts, he abhorred the authoritarianism that dictated adherence to a rigid set of beliefs or technical restrictions. He championed open discussion, comparative and integrative approaches, and promoted new voices across the generations.

Included in the Relational Perspectives Book Series are authors and works that come from within the relational tradition, extend and develop that tradition, as well as works that critique relational approaches or compare and contrast it with alternative points of view. The series includes our most distinguished senior psychoanalysts, along with younger contributors who bring fresh vision. A full list of titles in this series is available at https://www.routledge.com/mentalhealth/series/LEARPBS

[1] Greenberg, J. & Mitchell, S. (1983). *Object relations in psychoanalytic theory.* Cambridge, MA: Harvard University

De-Idealizing
Relational Theory

A Critique From Within

Edited by
Lewis Aron, Sue Grand,
and Joyce Slochower

 Routledge
Taylor & Francis Group

LONDON AND NEW YORK

First published 2018
by Routledge
2 Park Square, Milton Park, Abingdon, Oxon OX14 4RN

and by Routledge
711 Third Avenue, New York, NY 10017

Routledge is an imprint of the Taylor & Francis Group, an informa business

British Library Cataloguing-in-Publication Data
A catalogue record for this book is available from the British Library

Library of Congress Cataloging-in-Publication Data
Names: Aron, Lewis, editor. | Grand, Sue, editor. | Slochower, Joyce
Anne, 1950– editor.
Title: De-idealizing relational theory : a critique from within / edited by
Lewis Aron, Sue Grand, and Joyce A. Slochower.
Description: Abingdon, Oxon ; New York, NY: Routledge, 2018. |
Series: Relational perspectives book series | Includes bibliographical
references and index.
Identifiers: LCCN 2017060368 (print) | LCCN 2018002926 (ebook) |
ISBN 9781315113623 (Master) | ISBN 9781351625593 (Web PDF) |
ISBN 9781351625586 (ePub) | ISBN 9781351625579 (Mobipocket/Kindle) |
ISBN 9781138080157 (hardback : alk. paper) | ISBN 9781138080164
(pbk. : alk. paper)
Subjects: LCSH: Object relations (Psychoanalysis) | Interpersonal relations. |
Psychoanalysis.
Classification: LCC BF175.5.O24 (ebook) | LCC BF175.5.O24 D42 2018
(print) | DDC 150.19/5—dc23LC record available at https://lccn.loc.gov/
2017060368

ISBN: 978-1-138-08015-7 (hbk)
ISBN: 978-1-138-08016-4 (pbk)
ISBN: 978-1-315-11362-3 (ebk)

Typeset in Times New Roman and Gill Sans
by Florence Production Ltd, Stoodleigh, Devon, UK

Contents

Author biographies

Lewis Aron, Ph.D., ABPP is the director of the New York University Postdoctoral Program in Psychotherapy and Psychoanalysis. He has served as president of the Division of Psychoanalysis (39) of the American Psychological Association; founding president of the International Association for Relational Psychoanalysis and Psychotherapy (IARPP); founding president of the Division of Psychologist-Psychoanalysts of the New York State Psychological Association. He is the cofounder and co-chair of the Sándor Ferenczi Center at the New School for Social Research; professor, Interdisciplinary Center (IDC), Herzliya, Israel. He was one of the founders of *Psychoanalytic Dialogues* and is the series co-editor of the *Relational Perspectives* book series (Routledge). He is the editor and author of numerous clinical and scholarly journal articles and books, including *A Meeting of Minds*, and most recently, with Galit Atlas, *Dramatic Dialogue: Contemporary Clinical Practice*. He is widely known for his study/reading groups in NYC and online.

Sue Grand, Ph.D., is faculty and supervisor at the NYU Postdoctoral program in psychotherapy and psychoanalysis; faculty, the trauma program at the National Institute for the Psychotherapies; faculty, the Mitchell Center for Relational Psychoanalysis, and fellow at the Institute for Psychology and the Other. She is an associated editor of *Psychoanalytic Dialogues* and *Psychoanalysis Culture and Society*. She is the author of: *The Reproduction of Evil: A Clinical and Cultural Perspective* and *The Hero in the Mirror: From Fear to Fortitude*. She is the co-editor, with Jill Salberg of *The Wounds of History: Repair and Resilience in the*

Trans-generational Transmission of Trauma and *Trans-generational Transmission and the Other: Dialogues across History and Difference.* She is in private practice in NYC and Teaneck, NJ.

Joyce Slochower, Ph.D., ABPP is Professor Emerita of Psychology at Hunter College & the Graduate Center, CUNY; faculty, NYU Postdoctoral Program, Steven Mitchell Center, National Training Program of NIP, Philadelphia Center for Relational Studies & and PINC in San Francisco. Second editions of her books, *Holding and Psychoanalysis: A Relational Perspective* (1996) and *Psychoanalytic Collisions* (2006) were released in 2014. She is co-editor, with Lewis Aron and Sue Grand, of the forthcoming volumes *De-Idealizing Relational Theory: A Critique from Within* and *Decentering Relational Theory: A Comparative Critique.* She is in private practice in New York City.

Emanuel Berman, Ph.D., is a training and supervising analyst at the Israel Psychoanalytic Society, and Professor Emeritus of Psychology at the University of Haifa. He is chief international editor of *Psychoanalytic Dialogues.* He received the Sigourney Award (2011); edited *Essential Papers on Literature and Psychoanalysis* (1993); and wrote *Impossible Training: A Relational View of Psychoanalytic Education* (2004). His papers on psychoanalytic history, the analytic and the supervisory relationship, the political context of psychoanalysis, film, and other topics appear in several journals and books. He has edited Hebrew translations of Freud, Ferenczi, Winnicott, Balint, Bowlby, Britton, Ogden, Aron and others, and belongs to the steering committee of the Israel Winnicott Center.

Steven H. Cooper is a training and supervising analyst at the Boston Psychonalytic Society and Institute, and clinical associate professor of Psychology at Harvard Medical School. Dr. Cooper is the author of three books, *Objects of Hope: Exploring Possibility and Limit in Psychoanalysis* (2000) published by The Analytic Press; *A Disturbance in the Field: Essays in Transference-Countertransference* (2010) published by Routledge and *The Melancholic Errand of Psychoanalysis: Exploring the Analyst's Relationship to the Depressive Position* (2016) also published by Routledge. In 1989 he won the JAPA prize from the *Journal of the American Psychoanalytic Association* for his paper examining defence. He served as joint chief editor of *Psychoanalytic Dialogues* from 2007–2012 and is now chief editor emeritus. He is currently on the editorial boards of the *International Journal of Psychoanalysis*, *Contemporary Psychoanalysis*, and *Psychoanalytic Dialogues*.

Ken Corbett, Ph.D., is assistant professor, New York University Postdoctoral Program in Psychoanalysis and Psychotherapy. He is the author of *A Murder over a Girl: Justice, Gender, Junior High*, and *Boyhoods: Rethinking Masculinities*.

Jay Greenberg, Ph.D., is Training and Supervising Analyst, William Alanson White Institute, Editor of *The Psychoanalytic Quarterly*, former Editor for North America of the *International Journal of Psychoanalysis*, and former Editor of *Contemporary Psychoanalysis*. He is co-author with Stephen Mitchell of *Object Relations in Psychoanalytic Theory* and author of *Oedipus and Beyond: A Clinical Theory*, and in 2015 received the Mary S. Sigourney Award for Outstanding Achievement in Psychoanalysis.

Robert Grossmark, Ph.D., ABPP is Adjunct Clinical Professor and consultant at the New York University Postdoctoral Program in Psychoanalysis. He teaches at The National Institute for the Psychotherapies, The Eastern Group Psychotherapy Society, the clinical psychology doctoral program at The City University of New York and the Minnesota Institute for Contemporary Psychotherapy and Psychoanalysis. He has authored a number of papers on psychoanalytic process and *The Unobtrusive relational analyst: Explorations in psychoanalytic companioning*. He co-edited *The One & the many: Relational approaches to group psychotherapy* and *Heterosexual masculinities: Contemporary perspectives from psychoanalytic gender theory*, all published by Routledge.

Lynne Layton is a psychoanalyst and part-time faculty at Harvard Medical School. She supervises at the Massachusetts Institute for Psychoanalysis and teaches at Pacifica Graduate Institute. She is the author of *Who's that Girl? Who's that Boy? Clinical Practice Meets Postmodern Gender Theory*, and co-editor of both *Bringing the Plague: Toward a Postmodern Psychoanalysis* and *Psychoanalysis, Class and Politics: Encounters in the Clinical Setting*. She is past editor of the journal *Psychoanalysis, Culture & Society*, is associate editor of *Studies in Gender and Sexuality*, and is co-founder of the Boston Psychosocial Work Group. She is Past-President of Section IX, Psychoanalysis for Social Responsibility, of Division 39, and co-founder of Reflective Spaces/Material Places-Boston.

David Mark, Ph.D., is co-director of The Institute for Relational Psychoanalysis of Philadelphia (IRPP). Among other work, in 1997, he co-authored with Jeffrey Faude, Ph.D., *The Psychotherapy of Cocaine Addiction: Entering the Interpersonal World of the Cocaine Addict*, published by Jason Aronson. He is in private practice in Philadelphia and Narberth, PA.

Stephen Seligman is clinical professor of Psychiatry at the University of California, San Francisco; joint editor-in-chief of *Psychoanalytic Dialogues;* training and supervising analyst at the San Francisco Center for Psychoanalysis and Psychoanalytic Institute of Northern California; and clinical professor at the New York University Postdoctoral Program in Psychoanalysis. He is the author of *Relationships in Development: Infancy, Intersubjectivity, Attachment* (Routledge), and co-editor of the American Psychiatric Press' *Infant and Early Childhood Mental Health: Core Concepts and Clinical Practice.*

Steven Stern, Psy.D., is a faculty member at the Massachusetts Institute for Psychoanalysis and clinical associate professor of Psychiatry at Maine Medical Center and Tufts University School of Medicine. He is a member of the International Council of the International Association of Psychoanalytic Self Psychology, and was Associate Editor of the *International Journal of Psychoanalytic Self Psychology* until 2015. A consistent advocate of a broadly integrative relational perspective, in his new book, *Needed Relationships and Psychoanalytic Healing: A Holistic Relational Perspective on the Therapeutic Process* (Routledge, 2017), he weaves together and expands many strands of his thinking over the past three decades. Steve practices in Portland, Maine with specializations in psychoanalysis, psychodynamic psychotherapy, couples therapy, and clinical supervision.

Acknowledgements

Every effort has been made to contact the copyright holders for their permission to reprint selections of this book. The publishers would be grateful to hear from any copyright holder who is not here acknowledged and will undertake to rectify any errors or omissions in future editions of this book.

Chapter 1 first published as Slochower, J. (2017), Going Too Far: Relational Heroines and Relational Excess. *Psychoanalytic Dialogues*, 27:3, pp. 282–299. Reprinted by permission of Taylor & Francis LLC.

Chapter 5 first published as Stern, S. (2002), Identification, repetition, and psychological growth: An expansion of relational theory. *Psychoanalytic Psychology*, 19:4, pp. 732–734. Reprinted by permission of American Psychological Association.

Chapter 6 first published as Seligman, S. (2014), Paying Attention and Feeling Puzzled: The Analytic Mindset as an Agent of Therapeutic Change. *Psychoanalytic Dialogues*, 24:6, pp. 648–662. Reprinted by permission of Taylor & Francis LLC.

Chapter 7 first published as Corbett, K. (2014), The Analyst's Private Space: Spontaneity, Ritual, Psychotherapeutic Action, and Self-Care. *Psychoanalytic Dialogues*, 24:6, pp. 637–647. Reprinted by permission of Taylor & Francis LLC.

Chapter 9 first published as Cooper, S.H. (2014), The Things We Carry: Finding/Creating the Object and the Analyst's Self-Reflective Participation.

Psychoanalytic Dialogues, 24:6, pp. 621–636. Reprinted by permission of Taylor & Francis LLC.

Part of Chapter 10 first published as Layton, L. (2013), Dialectical Constructivism in Historical Context: Expertise and the Subject of Late Modernity. *Psychoanalytic Dialogues*, 23:3, pp. 271–286. Reprinted by permission of Taylor & Francis LLC.

Introduction to De-Idealizing Relational Theory

A critique from within

Lewis Aron, Sue Grand, and Joyce Slochower

Here's a paradox: psychoanalysis is, above all, a process of self-reflection. We ask our patients to revisit their life narratives, to open them up to reflectivity, inquiry, dialogue, and new perspectives. Self-examination and self-critique: for our patients, this is the conduit to growth. Yet within the psychoanalytic field, we haven't used our own methodology. We haven't subjected our theories to self-examination. In fact, from its earliest beginnings, psychoanalysts have gathered protective circles around ourselves. Professional affiliation seems to require theoretical loyalty, and that loyalty oath seems opposed to critical self-examination. Inquiry, difference, and self-reflection: these have always percolated on the inside, but too often, they have been unwelcome. Eventually these inquiries yield theoretical schisms, which then occludes the ubiquity of theoretical mutual influence. Each subgroup (Freudian, Kleinian, Lacanian, Interpersonal, Self Psychology, Relational—to name a few) has positioned itself *against* the perspective of the psychoanalytic other. As we explicated/illustrated the "rightness" of our particular position, we also identified the gaps/ limitations, or naïveté of this alternative perspective.

As a result, much of our psychoanalytic literature is organized around two overlapping tropes. In the first, we find essays that provide clinical or theoretical support for the author's particular point of view. In the second, we find essays that critique the theory of the psychoanalytic other. Both tropes tend to extrude difference; they are oriented to an idealization of the self and the devaluation of the other. We have had long arguments about who owns depth; who are the true inheritors of Freud; who practices 'real' psychoanalysis; who has mapped the human psyche, and whose technique is most effective. As we recycle these tropes, we recycle the contest for dominance.

Psychoanalytic schools tend to have a possessive, guild-like investment in a particular theory. This investment has made us adversarial to difference and critique whether they originate from inside or from without. Marginalized or attacked, those who differed were either disappeared (Ferenczi, Rank) or expelled (e.g. Jung, Adler, Reich). Historically, self-critique was not viewed as the conduit to dialogic growth. Instead it was framed as rebellion, antagonism, and hostility. When new ideas developed, they usually resulted in schisms, furthering internal suppression and hostile separations.

The relational orientation was, like all new paradigms, born out of this adversarial milieu. Our ideas tended to be framed in contradistinction to the work of the non-relationalist; we borrowed from *and* repudiated our origins. We, too, failed to examine our own theory from the inside out. We didn't consider relational theory's contribution in tension with its limitations. Those who did, or did it very much, were themselves marginalized. Jay Greenberg is a prominent example, as will be discussed in the interview of him included in this volume.

Relational theory lends itself to internal critique in a particular way. Embracing a constructivist and perspectival reconceptualization of the therapeutic dyad meant that the analyst was no longer the arbiter of truth and falsehood. The patient's transference represents one—perhaps limited, but also potentially accurate—perspective on the analyst, rather than a distortion of truth. This recognition required the analyst to consider the patient's experience of the analyst's subjectivity as a legitimate perspective. This perspective was not to be dismissed as a displacement from the past.

In the tradition of Ferenczi, and borrowing from our Interpersonal roots, this re-conceptualization of transference means that the analyst must attend to and take seriously the patient's critique of the analyst. In relational analyses it has become *de rigueur* for the analyst to consider how they have lent themselves to the patient's criticism. The analyst asks: "What have I done that makes you view me in this way?" This query becomes a genuine expression of curiosity and interest. How has the analyst unconsciously participated in co-constructing the transference?

Bringing this clinical emphasis to bear on our inter-theoretical discussions and debates invites a more open point of entry for critiques of relational theory. We want, then, to ask the same questions about our *theory* that we ask of ourselves *clinically*. Rather than saying that the other's reading of relational theory is wrong or distorted or a misrepresentation, we are interested in querying how our theory lends itself to such a characterization; in what way does our writing invite such a reading? How have we participated in conveying such an understanding to our critics? And when we greet internal dissension and difference, we might ask ourselves: "How is this dissension illuminating our blind-spot? How is this difference highlighting new areas of growth?"

Relational theory embraces critique as the venue for growth. However, despite a theoretical perspective that ought to welcome self-critique, relational analysts are no more open or receptive to critique than those from other psychoanalytic schools. We are not any less defensive or rigid about our own ideas. Our perspectival emphasis notwithstanding, we have not readily engaged in, or even considered, self-critique. We have not engaged with the perceptions or critiques of others. It is the theory that is an improvement, not the character of the practitioner or the character of our psychoanalytic 'guild'.

The mission of this volume is to implement our own model of inquiry by turning an eye on ourselves. In so doing, we hope to depart from our field's adversarial construction of difference. We are seeking a more contructive cycle of inquiry and mutual dialogue. Rather than viewing self-critique as antagonistic and destructive, our intention is to be creative, respectful, and generative. Indeed, loving self-critique is essential to psychoanalysis' theoretical and clinical vitality. We aim to avoid further suppression and schisms that foreclose dialogue and mutuality.

To our knowledge, no psychoanalytic position has yet explored itself from the inside out. Here, we aim for a deepened understanding of our own theoretical position—both its limits and its potential. This kind of critique is not intended to represent a (partially defensive) justification or an elaboration of the rightness of our own position, nor to engage the other as an adversary or straw man.

We (Lewis Aron, Sue Grand, and Joyce Slochower) invited eminent relational thinkers to engage in this kind of internal critique. Where are our problems and limitations? How might we think about the critiques that have been made of us by other theoretical orientations? Where and how might we want to integrate the thinking of others? How might we want to recall our theories of origin?

Our authors responded enthusiastically to our invitation. The essays in this volume represent their accumulated scholarly, creative, and constructive wisdom, untainted by antagonistic opposition. This is, we believe a departure from our inherited ritual of difference.

Working together on these volumes has been enormously gratifying, collaborative, and fun. We thank all our authors for their rich contributions to these volumes and our Editors at Routledge for their support. We are especially grateful to Donna Bassin for her generosity in creating the beautiful images for each book cover. Finally, we want to thank Lily Swistel for her steady and expert editorial assistance.

This volume begins with two essays that take on and retrospectively critique our relational contribution to theory and practice. Joyce Slochower's expansive essay addresses the relational ideal, its implications, contributions, and clinical limits. Noting that the relational turn represented an overcorrection to traditional models lodged in notions of analytic asymmetry, certainty, and the baby metaphor, she explores the underbelly of this correction. Slochower suggests that our focus on the analysis of enactment and the mutative impact of analytic self-disclosure has created its own kind of clinical blindness. We sometimes fail to explore the problematic impact of self-disclosure and the mutual analysis of enactment. We are not always mindful of how the analyst's own need for privacy and self-protection skews mutual engagement. Relational work similarly may skip over patients' vulnerability and need for "alone" interiority, for an analyst who exercises restraint and comfortably owns her authority.

Slochower's relational holding model addressed much of this critique by introducing a more complex version of the baby metaphor into relational thinking while re-contextualizing holding as a co-constructed process. Contemporary relational ideas about self-state multiplicity, attachment theory, and relational co-shaping, have added to the complexity and layering of a relational holding model. Slochower reminds us that we remain (like all theories) vulnerable to caricaturing the other and obfuscating or sidestepping the limits of our own way of working.

Lewis Aron's interview of Jay Greenberg provides historical context for the development of relational ideas. In their conversation, Aron and Greenberg both reminisce about our early beginnings and describe how relational theory has developed. Aron probes the early collaboration between Greenberg and Mitchell, and explores their individual and differing perspectives and styles. As one of the original authors of the distinction between drive and relational approaches, what is Greenberg's assessment of the later development of relational theory and practice? Does he think that the arguments he and Mitchell made in the 1980s remain relevant in today's psychoanalytic world?

Emanuel Berman focuses on the press of party loyalty, inclusion, exclusion, and organizational divisions as they have played out in the psychoanalytic world and more particularly, within the relational orientation. Berman presents several cases, (one in considerable detail) that illustrate how these themes can shape (and skew) our clinical work. He examines how our relational ideals—egalitarianism, anti-authoritarianism, and our focus on interaction and intersubjectivity, may at times be counterproductive and even anti-therapeutic. Berman makes use of his deep knowledge of comparative psychoanalysis to question and challenge his own clinical work and use of himself as a relationally oriented clinician.

David Mark turns a lens on the relational theme of "radical" analytic equality. He explores how analytic self-disclosure can be misused in an attempt to mitigate a hierarchical analytic tilt. Self-disclosure can be used manipulatively *and* in a way that deepens and enriches the analytic relationship. Mark offers an incisive comparison and contrast of clinical cases by two leading relational contributors, Jody Davies and Philip Bromberg. He demonstrates how Davies, with her object relational leanings, highlights structural concepts, while Bromberg, with his interpersonal background, emphasizes a more phenomenological approach. Davies views enactments as generated in the heat of affective intensity in the transference-countertransference. Bromberg focuses on the immediate interpersonal relationship with self-states that are highly fluid and responsive to context. Mark shows that the analytic dyad achieves a momentary illusion of radical equality when they seem to step outside of the usual hierarchical structures of relating.

Steven Stern addresses the relational tendency to focus on repetitive clinical dynamics. He believes that this focus itself tends to create ongoing (though also useful) enactments. In Stern's view, our theoretical superstructure—with its emphasis on enactment, dissociation, and shifting self-states—doesn't sufficiently conceptualize our patients' emotional needs and how to address them. Stern urges us to further integrate "forward edge" thinking into the relational paradigm.

Steven Seligman, Ken Corbett, and Robert Grossmark share a focus on the limits of an interactive relational approach that tends to sideline quiet, reflective therapeutic space. Seligman notes that, like every analytic orientation, the relational turn tilts us in a particular direction, which may limit the impact of other dimensions of analytic process. He wonders whether relational work pulls us into an interactive mode at moments when watching and waiting might have more therapeutic efficacy. Seligman recognizes that the analyst's focus on countertransference, enactment, and self-disclosures can be transformative, but wonders whether we have tended to overlook the importance of "some of the more quotidian aspects of everyday analytic work." Seligman reminds us that disciplined observation and quiet focus can be enormously powerful therapeutic tools; they create a sense of safety and recognition that can deepen the work.

Ken Corbett also critiques the excessive idealization of analytic spontaneity and discusses the analyst's need for private, contemplative space. While there is no such thing as an isolated private mind, Corbett argues for private analytic space. Enactment, he agrees, is ubiquitous, but contemplative and containing modes are necessary for the analyst's self-care, and we need to be free to question the absolute values of spontaneity and authenticity. All this relatedness, Corbett pleads, is killing us. For both the patient's sake and our own we need private space for absorption, musing, reverie, dreaming, and silent listening.

Robert Grossmark builds on earlier relational writing on holding and regression with especially vulnerable patients by invoking the idea of "the unobtrusive relational analyst" as an alternative clinical position. With patients who suffer from psychic deadness and areas of unrelatedness, who lack mentalization and symbolization, the more dialogic aspects of relational technique (featuring enactment and self-disclosure) are problematic. Drawing on the clinical sensibility of the British Middle Group, Grossmark calls for a technical approach that emphasizes mutual-regression and unobtrusive presence.

Steven Cooper explores the overarching principles of relational theory as influenced by other theoretical perspectives. Cooper views relational theory not as a systematic metapsychology or theory of technique, but rather as a broad meta-theory on a different level of abstraction as compared to single schools such as self psychology. Cooper views Stephen Mitchell's unique sensibility to be his emphasis on the analyst's self-reflective participation. Cooper himself leans toward the use of object-relations theory concepts to understand the stability and consistency of behavior, in addition to the contextual emphasis on the interpersonal school. Cooper also underscores patient and analyst's need for privacy and a solitary space within the relational matrix.

Our volume closes with Lynne Layton's explication of the socio-historical context in which relational thinking and practice is embedded. She significantly broadens our relational lens by underscoring the role of cultural and power differentials (race, class, gender, and sexuality) that inform and sometimes shape relational experience. Layton brings in the work of sociologists and existentialists, and argues for an expansion of the relational perspective that includes its collective elements.

Layton proposes a "relational ontology" that grounds theory in the identity possibilities available to the individual. She calls for our theory to move beyond not only a one- and two-person psychology, but beyond a three-person psychology, to include our social hierarchies and power relations in our identifications and disidentifications regarding sex, race, class, gender, sexuality, and nationality. Layton makes the moving point that such work may not feel to us like legitimate psychoanalysis, but that it has the potential to make conscious aspects of our life choices of which we have not been aware. The problem that she pinpoints is that we as therapists are embedded in the same social system as our patients and so these relations may be difficult to identify.

Layton's essay locates clinical theory in a larger context and anticipates this series' second volume, *Decentering Relational Theory*. In it, we continue to explore the interface and collision between different theoretical positions as they have shaped—or failed to shape—the relational school. Like the present volume, it also aims to be a model of *growth in unity*, one in which difference strengthens our field rather than dividing it.

Chapter 1

Going too far
Relational heroines and relational excess

Joyce Slochower

Every psychoanalytic theory is organized around an implicit clinical ideal —a vision of the kind of analyst we want to be and the kind of change we hope psychoanalysis will effect (Slochower, 2006; 2014b). Implicit in our vision are corresponding notions of our ideal patient/process and of what's pathological/problematic.

Most often our ideal is formulated in conversation (actually, in argument) with its theoretical predecessors and competitors. While those conversations can deepen and enrich our thinking, they frequently don't. Instead, they become fighting words that generate a slide toward excess by exaggerating difference and rigidifying the core principles to which we adhere. We polarize, elevating the originality of our own contribution while minimizing, stereotyping, sometimes denigrating, the position of the psychoanalytic Other whose ideals collide—or overlap excessively—with our own. Each pendulum swing seems inevitably to provoke a counter-move that itself overcorrects. I think we always go a bit too far.

Perhaps it's only in hindsight that we can pause and moderate those over-corrections. This book marks a turning point in relational thinking. We've matured beyond our beginnings; we've got a history and so hindsight is possible. It's in this spirit that I consider the reactive excesses of early relational theory and practice—where we've been, where and how we may have gone too far, and where we can go now. In particular, I explore the shape of the relational ideal and its implications for our therapeutic goals, our patients, and for ourselves. Who do we aim to be in the consulting room? How do we view our patient—her potential and her limitations? What are the clinical goals of a relational analysis? What might those goals occlude?

This essay focuses on relational theory; however, the phenomenon I'm describing is more broadly relevant. Every psychoanalytic theory embodies its own ideals and is vulnerable to theoretical/clinical excess and limitations. No psychoanalytic theory—to my knowledge—has addressed either from the inside out.

Relational ideals

We embrace our therapeutic vision for good reason. Whatever its particulars, ideas about what psychoanalysis can do sustain us across the therapeutic long haul. They affirm fantasies/beliefs about our therapeutic capacity and generative potential. Countering a range of anxieties about who we are—and aren't—they support and steady us when the going gets rough.

We relationalists may be theoretically diverse, but we share an implicit and relatively distinct professional ideal. It first coalesced around a new perspective on analytic process as inevitably intersubjective. We emphasized the therapeutic potential inherent in mutually unpacking and working through what's enacted. Moving away from more authoritarian models and toward asymmetrical egalitarianism, we underscored the uncertainty accompanying this clinical point of entry (Aron, 1991). Moderating our power and omniscience, we affirmed our patient's capacity to see us, to function as an adult in the analytic context. We rejected sharply tilted authoritative clinical models lodged in beliefs about interpretive accuracy; some of us also rejected the developmental tilt (Mitchell, 1984) embedded in ideas of parental (analytic) repair.

In their stead, we turned toward what was unformulated and/or dissociated. We addressed how shifting self-states shaped analytic process for both patient *and* analyst. Unpacking these dynamics required mutual exploration because we were implicated along with our patients. By moving away from old analytic constrictions, we found new ways to be and to use ourselves with considerable therapeutic effect (e.g. Aron, 1991, 1992; Benjamin, 1995; 1998; Bromberg, 1993; 1995; 1998; 2011; Davies, 2004; Davies & Frawley, 1994; Harris, 2009; Hoffman, 1991; 1998; Mitchell,1984; 1988; 1991; 1993; D.B. Stern, 1992; 1997).

Although it isn't always acknowledged, the relational ideal has been strongly influenced both by Object Relations thinking and by the Interpersonal movement. Those groups had themselves reacted to their classical Freudian and Kleinian predecessors by moderating the ideal of an abstinent, paternal, rule-bound analyst and a drive-driven, pleasure-seeking patient.

Interpersonalists (e.g., Ehrenberg, 1974; Hirsch,1994; 2006; Levenson, 1972; Sullivan, 1954; Wolstein, 1959) rejected the traditional emphasis on drives (sexual and aggressive) along with ideas about interpretive purity and analytic neutrality. They reformulated therapeutic process by emphasizing its interactive element. This perspective anticipated central aspects of relational thinking, particularly the two-person nature of the analytic interaction, an interaction in which the analyst is a participant observer (Sullivan, 1954). This view would inform our rejection of interpretive certainty, our emphasis on co-construction and on the mutual analysis of enactment. But where interpersonalists saw two adults in interaction, the relational turn would expand this view to include a multiplicity of early, dissociated self-states. Relational trauma was reenacted in analytic space where it could be unpacked for the first time.

Object Relations theorists (especially Balint, 1968; Fairbairn, 1952; Ferenczi, 1952; Guntrip, 1961, and Winnicott, 1965; 1969a) and self psychologists (e.g. Kohut, 1984) also focused on early trauma (failure) and needed therapeutic provision. But unlike the Interpersonalists, they embraced the idea of therapeutic regression and the analyst's capacity to repair.

Winnicott's work (e.g.,1963) had a particularly powerful impact on relational thinking. He had pushed back against the classical ideal of abstinence and the interpretation of drive-based desire. Early experiences could, in fact, be re-found and then repaired within the analytic setting; the patient could be a baby again, but with a better, more responsive mother. The analyst's empathic, holding stance created a protected space and allowed the patient to turn over false self functioning to the analyst. As early (true self) experience was contacted, the patient would re-find and work through the original traumatic element within the analytic space, now *vis-a-vis* the analyst.

While some relationalists (including me) carried aspects of the object relations perspective with them, those coming from the interpersonal tradition reacted strongly—and negatively—to models organized around repetitive infantile object relations and analytic (parental) repair (Aron,

1991; Hirsch, 2014; Hoffman, 1991, 1992, 2009; Mitchell, 1984; D.B. Stern, 1992).[1, 2] Developmental tilt models seemed to lock the patient into a position of helpless dependence while encouraging the analyst's superiority and certainty.

But a careful reading of Winnicott complicates this view. For him, repair was not enough: in fact, it was crucial that the patient become angry at the analyst for the parents' original failure, now enacted in the consulting room. The analyst's non-retaliatory survival of the patient's attacks would facilitate a shift from object relating toward object usage (Winnicott, 1969a). This shift privileged the recognition of "otherness" in the developmental trajectory; in tandem with Winnicott's essay "The mother-infant experience of mutuality" (1969b) it anticipated the relational turn toward mutuality (see especially Benjamin, 1988; 1995).

Rejecting visions of a paternalistic, withholding, potentially shame-inducing (classical) analyst and of a benevolent, maternal, idealized (Winnicottian) one, relational (and especially feminist) writers underscored the analyst's ubiquitous—and flawed—subjectivity. Like the mother, she is a person first and last; her (non-ideal) subjecthood is to be celebrated rather than contained or excluded from the analytic dialogue. That subjectivity will be critical in the patient's development, and in particular, will facilitate her evolving capacity for mutuality (Bassin, 1997; 1999; Bassin, Honey, & Kaplan, 1994; Benjamin, 1986; 1988; 1995; 1998; Chodorow, 1978; Dimen, 1991; Dinnerstein, 1976; Fast, 1984; Goldner, 1991; Harris, 1991; 1997; Layton, 1998).

Perhaps, a bit drunk on the excitement of this new psychoanalytic vision, many relationists threw away the old book of analytic prescriptions and proscriptions (Hoffman 1996), or at least whole chapters of it. Interpretations were replaced by the concept of enactment (a term first coined by Jacobs (1986)—a Freudian influenced by self psychology). When unpacked, enactments were mutative; they would deepen the patient's capacity for intersubjectivity. Impasse didn't end analytic process, when mutually explored, it was central to therapeutic action.

Relationalists entered the clinical moment with an eye toward exploring our participation in it rather than interpreting the patient's fantasies about us as projection. This perspective turned classical Freudian and Kleinian theories on their respective heads. Where classical psychoanalytic essays had been replete with meta-psychology, relational writing was experience-near; analyst and patient came alive. (see, e.g., Grand's [2000; 2010] dramatic departure from academic writing style). Bringing the reader directly into the clinical moment without idealizing the analyst's capacity for self-reflectivity and honesty, Davies (2004), Grand (2000, 2010), and others illustrated how early, entrenched relational patterns could be shifted in the here-and-now (e.g. Aron, 1991, 1999; Hoffman, 1998; Mitchell, 1993; D.B. Stern, 1997). The analyst's ability to probe the intersection between her own and her patient's unconscious experience became the therapeutic lynchpin of relational theory. This was a new kind of analytic heroine—one who could save the day by virtue of her emotional accessibility.

Our relational heroine

Our relational heroine embodies nearly everything that other analytic theories rejected or disavowed. She's so different that she really is an anti-hero: she borrows old tropes, but then disrupts, rewrites, and reverses them (sometimes with an ahistorical sense of radical newness). An *analytic noir ideal* (Slochower, 2006; 2014b), the relational heroine is valorized for the very attributes that once represented flaws: her subjectivity, emotional responsiveness, even her reactivity, make her a better analyst rather than one needing more analysis herself. Like the interpersonalists before her, the relational analyst is real—open, responsive, non-defensive, able to self-disclose and use those disclosures to deepen the work. Like the object relationalists, she works with baby self-states along with adult ones; she recognizes the centrality of dissociation and relational trauma in analytic work.

But with inspiration came the potential for excess. And we were as guilty of this kind of excess as was/is every other psychoanalytic movement. Rebelling against, rejecting the therapeutic strictures of early analytic times, relationalists idealized much that prior models had sought to control.

Where classical analysts had been enslaved to abstinence, now we were free to be ourselves. Where once we concealed ourselves as much as possible, now we aimed to reveal; memoirs and essays organized around the therapeutic impact of self-disclosure proliferated. In our enthusiasm, we lost track of—or forgot—the cautionary wisdom about self-disclosure that our forbearers had sounded so loudly.

In delineating our differences with Freudian, Interpersonal, and Object Relations theories, our early writing also tended to overlook areas of convergence (for example, Sullivan's [1954] participant observation, Fiscalini's [1994] concept of analytic co-participation and Kohut's [1984] selfobject function). Our professional ancestors also included those Freudian writers (e.g. Jacobs, 1986; Loewald, 1960; Sandler, 1976) whose work humanized the analytic relationship, explored enactment and transference-countertransference dynamics (Mitchell, 2000). Writers who critiqued the object relational notion of regression to dependence ignored Winnicott's (1969) complex vision of the progression away from regression toward object usage and Balint's (1968) discussion of malignant regression—of the risks inherent in regression. Therapeutic regression was stereotyped as a simple corrective emotional experience and the selfobject function as a simple avoidance of patients' aggression.[3]

I was among those writers (including Benjamin, 1988; Bromberg, 1979; 1991, 1994; Davies, 1994; Ghent, 1992, and others) who identified with aspects of Object Relations theory as we confronted the relational critique. Responding to what I felt were the excesses of the early relational position—especially its near exclusive emphasis on mutuality, the joint exploration of enactments, and analytic self-disclosure—I suggested that we were idealizing explicit intersubjective exchange and had failed to make room for patients' need for holding when it collided with that ideal.

"Relationalizing" holding, I argued that analytic mutuality is a therapeutic goal but not a given, because some patients—and at certain moments all patients—cannot tolerate explicit evidence of the analyst's otherness without prolonged and serious derailment (I'll elaborate on this later). Underscoring the need for interior space and privacy (1993; 1994; 1998; 1999; 2004; 2013a), I invoked a relational holding metaphor to describe the creation of this kind of protected space. Holding supports an illusion of analytic attunement (variously shaped depending on the affective theme that dominates). Within that illusion, the analyst brackets her subjectivity as much as possible and privileges the patient's experience of both self and other.

My early writing expanded the Winnicottian metaphor beyond the arena of early need. Holding is a central element in work with states other than dependence (including hate, self-involvement, and ruthlessness); the need for holding makes itself felt across the developmental trajectory and also in adulthood, that is, outside the baby metaphor and beyond the consulting room (Slochower, 1991; 1992; 1993; 1994). While holding is most often organized around intense affect states—dependence, hate, self-involvement—the holding thread may also be found in humor (Slochower, 2013a).

Despite its different emotional forms, holding always limits explicit expressions of the analyst's separateness. It underscores the need for private experience and the development of a solid sense of interiority. Establishing conditions under which the patient can gradually assimilate and metabolize derailing aspects of affective experience, holding invites the patient to "create" the analyst in line with her own fantasies and needs, while excluding what would be excessively disturbing.

Whatever its particulars, the holding experience is embedded in a benign, generative idealization that heals, often without the kickback of devaluation. Like Sandler's (1960) background of safety, holding represents an underlying element across the analytic encounter that's also present as a silent background during explicitly interactive clinical work. An ongoing, non-pathological need for holding coexists with—and sometimes overrides —the need for intersubjective engagement. And while the need for a protected analytic space can represent a form of resistance or a problematic regression, it's sometimes therapeutically necessary.

Holding isn't something the analyst can do alone. Although we struggle to bracket (rather than delete) our disjunctive subjectivity, patients inevitably pick up aspects of our separate perspective. Holding "works"—when it does—because our patient participates in the holding experience by doing her own bracketing; she excludes from awareness those aspects of our subjectivity that would be excessively disruptive. In this sense, the holding experience (like all analytic interactions) is co-constructed, shaped by the participation of patient and analyst together. This vision of holding neither infantilizes the patient nor renders the analyst impervious and omniscient; it instead respects the shifting nature of subjective experience—including the patient's wish or need for an arena of protection and privacy within analytic space.

My early writing on holding emphasized the analyst's conscious attempts to hold and her struggle to bracket her disjunctive subjectivity (co-shaped by the patient's own bracketing process). Over time, however, I've become increasingly impressed by the unconscious relational dynamics that inform moves in and out of a holding stance. Increasingly, I underscore procedural aspects of holding our (and our patient's) spontaneous move toward, or away from active engagement.

Our holding response emerges out of a kind of non-verbal dance. The patient signals her intolerance of certain kinds of therapeutic exchanges via her explicit and non-verbal reactions to our input; we implicitly pick up on that intolerance and move toward a more containing position. But in a similar way, our patient also picks up on what we—or she—can't tolerate and partially brackets it. A mutually protective space emerges, one characterized not by dissociation but by a need/desire to keep the process going. Mutual bracketing buffers what could be derailing and the work deepens.

But analytic holding is always partial. Despite our best attempts at containment, we show plenty of ourselves by virtue both of how and when we hold and when we don't (Slochower, 1996a & 2014a; 1996b; 1996c; 1999; 2004; 2013a; 2013b)[4]. Of course, the obverse is true, too: even when we're engaged intersubjectively, there are ways in which we hold, both because we don't share everything with our patient and because we track her response to what we do say, implicitly holding her as we do so. So holding and explicit intersubjective exchange coexist as figure and ground in every treatment situation. Each has conscious and procedural elements; each shifts, often imperceptibly, as analyst and patient react and adjust to the other.

Despite my argument with the interpersonal edge of relational theory and my emphasis on interior experiencing within therapeutic space, my thinking was—and is—very much aligned with the relational emphasis on mutuality and intersubjective recognition. The need for holding may exist across the lifespan, but it represents an "earlier," less "mature" way of being in the world. Holding is especially useful when baby and child self-states emerge in (or outside) analytic space, but intersubjectivity remains the therapeutic goal. Holding is what helps our patient get there.

Developmental relationality in 2018

By the mid-1990s, the place of developmental tilt thinking had become the subject of active debate among relational writers.[5] A more nuanced portrait of both patient and analyst took shape. It included ideas about non-linear movement and shifting self-states; this developmental element makes itself known across the lifespan (Aron, 2001; Benjamin, 2009, 2010; Cooper, 2014; Davies, 2004; Grand, 2000, 2010; Harris, 2005; 2009; Mitchell, 1993; 2000; Pizer, 1998; Seligman, 2003; Stein, 1999; D.B. Stern, 2009).

Bromberg (2011) and Schore's (2011) work on relational co-shaping also underscores this non-verbal therapeutic element. Addressing something I see as a cousin to holding, Bromberg suggests that the analyst's continuous attention to dyadic process coalesces into a kind of procedural moderating response to the patient's emotional vulnerability and attachment needs. Ongoing relational co-shaping helps the patient develop a better capacity for affect regulation.

Relational co-shaping is the background element that's always there. Like holding (and like "e" enactments; Bass, 2003) it's informed by unconscious (procedural) factors—by continuous, subtle adjustments between analyst and patient. These adjustments easily go unnoticed against a noisier foreground of explicit interaction, except in moments of acute distress when they can morph into major enactments that break into the analytic dialogue.[6]

Micro-adjustments between analyst and patient occur in the "present moment" (D.N. Stern, 2004). They are the "something more" that the Boston Process Change Study Group (e.g., 1998) writes about. These shifts, subtle and often imperceptible, represent a therapeutic red thread at the core of clinical change. They help ease emotional reactivity and shift implicit relational knowing.

Relational shaping, then, overlaps with what I call holding, although relational shaping underscores the therapeutic value of sharing self-state experience with the patient. Still, the analytic holding function contributes to relational shaping and vice versa: our procedural—sometimes unconscious—response to the patient informs our conscious efforts to hold. Both operate behind the scene during active exploratory work; in moments of more acute distress, they dominate clinical process.

Enactments in a developmental context: the relational baby

Probably because much early relational writing rejected developmental tilt models, it tended to obfuscate the ways in which relational theory itself is lodged in an implicit model of therapeutic repair organized around the reparative power of the enacted moment.

Enactments, when worked through, represent a kind of relational do-over. We blunder and become the bad object (Davies, 2004). But we're really everything that the bad parent was not because we're willing to own our impact and say the unsayable— essentially, we're willing to change. In so doing we offer a powerful antidote to the relational configurations that traumatized; what had been dissociated reemerges in therapeutic space where it can be encompassed and metabolized. It's this process that strengthens affect regulation and reflective function.

Theories of affect regulation, attachment research, and dynamic systems theories have elaborated the staying power of early attachment and regulatory patterns (e.g., Ainsworth 1969; Beebe & Lachmann, 1994; 1998; 2012; Fonagy, Gyorgy, Jurist, & Target, 2004; Hess & Main, 2000; Stolorow, 1997; Warshaw, 1992). Because these patterns make themselves felt over time even as they transform, the relational baby remains an alive presence in the (adult) consulting room. Certainly, this empirical baby, formulated on the basis of infant research findings, is not the object relations theorists' passive recipient of good—or not good enough—maternal care. She's less a symbolic baby than one we've actually observed. She's more active—reactive to, *and* a participant in mother's own pulls and pushes.

Our increasingly sophisticated perspective on dissociation and shifting self-states (e.g., Bromberg, 2006; Davies, 2004; Grand, 2000; 2010; D.B. Stern, 2009) further supports that idea. Even when our patient feels like an adult, she has the capacity—perhaps disavowed, perhaps not—to access and temporarily move into an early self-state. So while at times we can speak to our patient *about* her more vulnerable self-states, at other times we need to speak *to* that baby because it's really she who's in the room.

I've recently suggested that holding facilitates affect regulation and deepens interior exploration (Slochower, 2013c) because it repairs—by buffering—shame states. By moving *toward* the patient and adapting to her (usually unconscious) self-state, the analyst implicitly limits the experience of being seen from the "outside in" and in so doing, softens the shame element.

So both holding and relational co-shaping, themselves corrective emotional experiences, are lodged in the realm of the intersubjective. They are less authoritarian; they coalesce in interaction with the patient rather than originating in an authoritative, diagnostic stance. Still, embodied therein is a reparative ideal that has resonance precisely because of the early experiences it reverses.

Psychoanalytic thinking has come a long way from a simple vision of patient-as-baby *or* as-adult. What still needs exploration is the way we understand patient need and its sources. When our patient needs holding, we view her as in a baby or child self-state. When she's engaged inter-subjectively, she's an adult. *It's always the baby (in the adult) whom we try to repair.* While there have been some discussions of the needs of the adult patient outside the baby metaphor (Boulanger, 2007; Slochower, 1993, 1996a; 2011a), we haven't developed an overarching view of this trajectory of early need. We've largely ignored models (e.g. Erikson, 1950; Kohut, 1984) that extend the developmental arc or developmental needs for attunement and repair beyond childhood (but see Seligman & Shanok, 1996). We haven't fully thought through a vision of development that fills in and complicates the gap between baby and adult. We haven't integrated the evolution of attachment needs as they are expressed across the lifespan. This remains a relational project worth undertaking.

Aloneness in relational space: pathologized or honored?

Pre-relational analytic models lodged in the ideal of neutrality demanded enormous containment on the analyst's part. Left to silently contend with our subjectivity, constrained from using it in the work, we were vulner-able to states of isolation and loneliness. Sharing our experience, using it directly, represented a problematic countertransference acting out that sent us back to analysis or at least for consultation.

The relational turn provided a creative solution to this problem. We could bring more of ourselves to the consulting room; we felt freer and more alive. We no longer needed to negate our subjectivity or remain in a self-abnegating position. We could express ourselves and engage in mutuality; both had therapeutic potential when used thoughtfully.

But there's always an underbelly. As we removed the constrictions of neutrality, we sometimes skipped over our own—and our patient's—need for private, 'alone' experience. We sometimes pathologized those patients who evaded or resisted a focus on our subjectivity and the reenactments occurring between us.

While the analysis of enactments is sometimes where it's at, it's also sometimes not. There are moments when our patients (and we) want or need to have the experience of being alone with an other who stays more or less "out of it". To move toward what's interior and private (Corbett,

2014; Slochower, 1993; 1994; 1998; 1999; 2004; 2013a). This desire is not always a resistance to engagement; it may represent *not* immaturity, but the capacity to engage with oneself (see Ogden's [1997] and Cooper's [2014] eloquent discussions of this dimension of analytic process.) Patients sometimes need to create the analyst more than they need to find her. It's here that a protected therapeutic space which privileges privacy more than mutuality becomes essential.

Winnicott (1958) reminded us that the capacity to be alone is first established when the baby can be alone in mother's presence. This capacity is the prerequisite for a vast number of adult experiences, including creative activity. Genuine (non-anxious) aloneness is an achievement that reflects the existence of the internalized good object. A witness more than a participant, the analyst who makes room for alone, private process helps re-create this early experience. She supports the elaboration of a solid sense of interiority while engaging intersubjectively.

Because a capacity to be alone and to sustain one's sense of interiority (Slochower, 2004) is a prerequisite for intersubjective engagement, we locate the need for aloneness as earlier on the developmental continuum. We tend to privilege, indeed idealize mutuality, and problematize what's *not* intersubjective. We assume that our "non-relational" (or, more accurately, apparently separate needs) are, if not pathological, then younger or earlier, reflective of a less developed relational capacity.

Yet the capacity to be alone, itself lodged in relational experience, has many facets that are no less mature than is mutual engagement. We carry both needs across the lifespan. Both are essential to relational work. When we exclusively privilege intersubjectivity, we lose track of the inherent value of privacy and aloneness *in adult self-states.* And we generate a new vision of pathology.

Despite her anxieties and defenses, the ideal relational patient can tolerate, and ultimately will welcome, expressions of our subjectivity. Even if she doesn't begin the treatment with this capacity, with our help she'll get there. When she does, we'll feel we've done what needed to be done (e.g., Slochower, 1996b; 2014a).

In many ways, I stand behind this vision and its developmental underpinnings. Keeping my eye on ways to help my patient deepen her capacity for intersubjective recognition is a focus that works for me. Still, it's a model with its own potentially problematic implications.

We've tended to pathologize those patients who cannot tolerate mutuality. We view them as undeveloped—or worse. We've regarded our patient's (and our own) wish—or need—for privacy, solitude, for non-interactive analytic experience, as inherently less "mature," less "developed" than intersubjective engagement.

There's nothing inherently "non-relational" about private, interior process. By including both privacy and mutuality in our clinical ideal, we move away from a problematic binary. But we need to further theorize the clinical meaning and value of aloneness and privacy if we are to avoid pathologizing it. We need to further explore the non-defensive—and defensive—dynamic functions of aloneness and deconstruct both. When is aloneness an evasion of intimacy and mutuality? When does it provide opportunities for self-exploration?

False dichotomies, false caricatures

Like every other psychoanalytic theory, relational theory has been the object of caricature. We've been depicted as clinically impulsive, self-referential, superficial, foreclosing, or sidestepping reflective space. These are caricatures that exaggerate and distort. But in the absence of clinical thoughtfulness, they're the doors we're vulnerable to walking through.

I think we've persuasively demonstrated that the analyst's willingness to explicitly explore her countertransference can open a dialogue with great therapeutic effect. By embracing what's shared and avoiding authoritarian interpretations, we collaborate with our patient to sculpt a historical narrative with considerable emotional power. That process can free up our patient's experience of self and other.

But when we idealize the mutative power of enactment, we run the risk of occluding its problematic edge and foreclosing what doesn't fit. Our investment in demonstrating the clinical power of the present moment and our participation in it can create its own blind spot(s).

Might we be, at moments, too anxious to relinquish our authority and relocate it within the relational matrix? Might we overlook our patient's need for us to *know,* to comfortably hold our authority? Do we sometimes leave unexamined her mixed feelings about moments of mutual exploration?

Clinical work is often enriched, and our patient often expresses gratitude, when we find a way to introduce our experience into analytic dialogue.

Still, I wonder whether there's sometimes more to these moments than meets the eye. Might some patients comply with what they perceive to be *our* wish that these moments be helpful? Might they sometimes say, "I'm so glad you told me how you feel" and shut down or fail to fully explore a sense of disturbance about our uncertain, mutual stance? Might they sometimes long for us to be more certain, more knowing, more authoritative than our theory seems to allow? And might we be a bit blind to this side of things because it collides with our professional ideal?

If we are to avoid the excesses of our theoretical position, we need to take these possibilities seriously. We need to move beyond an easy stereotype of relational work as located in loud impasse and explicit self-disclosure. I think it's especially important that we expose our students to a nuanced training that incorporates our Freudian, Kleinian, and Interpersonal ancestors' contributions and addresses the risks associated with every position, including our own.

Clinical blindness can be fueled by our professional vision *and* by the personal meanings it carries for us. Classical analysts may be given to interpreting a patient's denial as confirmation of the accuracy of their interpretation; they may sidestep or foreclose the possibility that they're just plain wrong. We relationalists are probably more vulnerable to the opposite risk—to taking a patient's explicit affirmation of what we say or do too much at face value—or too quickly accepting their criticism of us. There's a possibility that we will minimize the conflicted—and unconscious—dynamics that underlie her apparently un-conflicted affirmation or rejection of us, our theory, or our way of working.

No theory is immune to this kind of clinical blindness. It's further complicated by our patient's need to please us by "getting with" our clinical agenda, whatever its particulars. How this looks will depend on our theory. Patients in a classical or Kleinian analysis may too easily accept their analyst's interpretations or appear to appreciate a "no" in response to a request. Patients in a relational analysis are probably far freer to argue with us. But I wonder whether they may feel unconscious pressure to affirm the value of intersubjective exchange, to please *us* by engaging with us when really they'd rather not.

It can be tempting to turn a blind eye to this kind of dynamic because of the pleasure it affords us to be idealized (in whatever way we value), to see our theory confirmed. Can we parse our evaluation of the treatment's effectiveness from our pleasurable response to our patient's appreciation?

Analytic self-interest is implicated here. Whatever our theory, we're invested in having the treatment go the way we believe it should go and that investment can render us a bit deaf. We want something (whether self-affirmation, confirmation that we are "correct," closeness, authentic engagement, or a here-and-now interaction) and so we want our patient to want it too. We look for evidence that she does; we're tempted to accept things at face value when they fit our theory and/or our personal idiom. Will we become inattentive to the ways in which it derails or obfuscates?[7]

Relational ideals and the idealized dyad

Although caricatures are most often veiled attacks, it's also possible to caricature by exaggerating the positive and ignoring what's not. In addition to ignoring our wish and need for privacy and solitude, relational theory invites us to idealize the analyst's relational capacity.

The relational ideal envisions an analyst with considerable emotional depth, resilience, and self-reflectivity. She's both eager and able to examine herself, her process and reactions; when she hits a roadblock, she openly reflects on it and then moves past it. She does her best to hold herself to this ideal, and her patient moves toward it with her.

This is an ideal worth embracing and one worth aiming for. It invites us to work with ourselves, to examine our impact and consider the possibility that we're responsible for the current therapeutic roadblock. Yet it's not without an underbelly.

The relational ideal collides with an inconvenient clinical truth—that it's not only our patient who isn't always up for, open to, or capable of this level of emotional engagement or of reflectively considering why we're not. That we are not consistently capable of recognizing our limitations, flaws, and defenses. Despite our commitment to dyadic engagement and despite the considerable satisfaction we derive from the intimacy it allows, there are times when the shared analysis of enactments is the last thing we want. At moments (or longer), our need for self-protection and privacy surfaces and forecloses our wish or need for mutuality (Grand, 2010).

The relational ideal may exaggerate our intersubjective capacity and minimize the obstacles that stand between us (analyst *and* patient) and ongoing mutual engagement. Yet it's absolutely consistent with the relational ideal to acknowledge our limitations. In fact, our theory is so thoroughly grounded in the value of exploring our failings that we ought to be better at this than those who embrace a differently idealized analytic vision. And often we are—but not always.

As my work around the holding metaphor developed, I became increasingly interested in the tension between analytic ideals (including my own vulnerability to idealizing holding—and Winnicott) and the actuality of our more limited therapeutic functioning. Whatever its particulars, our vision represents our wish—and often also our need—to heal, to change, to make contact, to do something useful. Because our personhood limits our ability to meet that vision, it confronts us with a collision between wish and reality. In *Psychoanalytic Collisions* I explore the tension between analytic illusions and actuality and address how we negotiate them (Slochower, 2006; 2011b; 2014b).

Collisions emerge, independent of our theoretical allegiance, out of the space between the professional ideal to which we aspire and the reality of our human fallibility. Relational theory can invite us to idealize intersubjectivity and exclude its problematic edge; classical models can slide toward an idealized interpretive neutrality that masks an element of withholding or penetrating attack. Self psychology and holding models are vulnerable to sidestepping the negative transference-countertransference. You get the idea.

At its best, the relational ideal includes a recognition that it's elusive: even if we aim for ongoing mutual exploration, we know we can't ever quite get there. Full disclosure is impossible (because we analysts have our own unconscious—and unformulated—experience). It's also undesirable: no matter how much we value intersubjectivity, there will always be things—information, feelings, experiences—that we choose not to tell because of our own wish for privacy and/or because we suspect that it would be too disruptive, too disturbing, or too hurtful to do otherwise. We choose (partially unconsciously) how we engage and how we contain based on a mixture of our patient's and our own needs, wishes, and anxieties, along with our clinical ideas about what's therapeutic and what's not.

It's when we lose track of these complexities that we slide toward excess. Can we balance the ideal of analytic openness against the limits of our capacity to reach it *and* against the value of privacy?

Soft diagnosis within a relational perspective

The use of diagnosis, no matter how "soft," collides with relational theory —with ideas about co-construction, multiplicity, shifting self-states, and with our rejection of excessive analytic authority. When we hit a wall with a patient, we don't diagnose or blame her; we think about how we've been getting in the way and about what's being co-created. Shifting toward the intersubjective, we creatively revisit the impasse and examine our own contribution to it. This perspective has been enormously freeing and has greatly enriched clinical work.

Along the way, relationalists have moved beyond old visions of pathology; we've queried and rejected the concepts of resistance and perversion because they atomize the relational field and collide with our theory. We've challenged the idea of a patient's enduring dynamic style *outside* dyadic relatedness. What was thought of as resistance has been relocated in enactments, in our own countertransference, and sometimes in impasse.

Yet our move away from diagnosis runs the risk of minimizing the persistence and complexity of this individual element, of a particular patient's relatively consistent way of being in treatment and in life. That way of being makes itself felt across fluctuating self-states and multiple interpersonal relationships.

I want to invite this individual element and the use of "soft diagnosis" back into relational thinking. To revisit our earlier ideas about resistance, character style, the difficult or easy patient, and the like. Aren't some of our difficult patients just that—difficult—while others are far easier to work with? Not just because our subjectivities—or temperaments—collide or meld in a particularly problematic or facilitating way; not just because of an unusually fluid intersubjective dynamic or problematic countertransference, but because of who the patient is? Aren't some of our patients responsive and emotionally present, while others are quite unable to look at themselves or work with our input?

In part, our patient's way of being emerges in concert or in response to the impact of our own personhood and way of working. Yet I'm convinced that it's not all about us—our character or clinical style. It's sometimes also because of who the patient is, because of her dynamics, trauma history, degree of emotional difficulty or rigidity. Certainly, I—and you— will do better with some people than others, and this reflects the intersubjective element. But there's an individual element too.

In "Hate in the countertransference," Winnicott (1947) distinguished between what he called the subjective and objective countertransference. He asserted the existence of an:

> objective countertransference, or if this is difficult, the analyst's love and hate in reaction to the actual personality and behaviour of the patient, based on objective observation.
>
> (p. 195)

I wouldn't go this far; I don't believe there's such a thing as objective observation or assessment that resides outside the realm of the subjective. Still, I think Winnicott was reminding us of something important: the relatively enduring elements of personal style that we carry across relationships and interactions. While we will each react somewhat idiosyncratically to the other, there often is a consensual element—a widely shared 'take' that we regularly evoke in those who know us.

When a colleague refers a patient to me whom she describes as "difficult," I usually come to recognize what my colleague is talking about. Sometimes I find my way around that difficulty and the work gets going, but sometimes I experience what feels subjectively like an impasse. I've encountered, I think, someone who seems to need *not* to change, who's utterly locked into repetitive dynamic cycles. No matter how assiduously I address the co-constructed edge of that difficulty, I/we hit a wall. And while that wall may emerge out of my own resistances and/or the clash between our temperamental styles, sometimes it's really not me.

Historically, the labels we used to describe this kind of thing—the character disordered, concrete, or perseverative patient—are unappealing; they're too often used pejoratively and not dynamically. We have newer, richer languages today; we think about patients' difficulties with reflectivity, interiority, mentalization, a basic sense of intactness. We think about trauma, early failures in holding, or relational shaping. These concepts fill out and usefully complicate individual dynamics by locating them both developmentally and psychodynamically. They deepen our understanding of our patient's (and our own) particular inner roadblocks and developmental needs. They help us open a door where there seemed to be none. And address an element that resides partially outside the relational dyad.

Despite our move away from diagnostic labels, relational theory—like all psychoanalytic theories—embodies its own vision of psychological health and of its relative absence along with ideas about how best to move things toward that ideal. And while our vision guides us, it also leaves us vulnerable to a particular clinical blind spot. The classical analyst, for example, might respond to a patient's interest in the analyst's personhood as fantasy-driven, as something to be analyzed and interpreted. We're likely to do just the opposite by skipping over the dynamic, fantasy element embedded in her wish for mutuality.

When the patient in a relational treatment evades intersubjective dialogue —when she's avoidant of the other, when she cannot address what's going on between us and chronically seeks out solitude or relational disengagement, we view her as emotionally limited, perhaps schizoid. Certainly less healthy than her dyadically engaged counterpart. And while we don't diagnose her, our understanding emerges out of our (theoretically embedded) view of maturity or of its relative absence. It's a relational take on what represents pathology.

We need to make room for what's not explicitly intersubjective, to honor our patient's (and our own) need for alone experience outside the realm of the pathological. We need to welcome and honor her wish or need for privacy and interior experiencing. We need to consider the possibility that these wishes are appropriate, even desirable. We can do all this even as we keep an eye on her capacity to return to the relational world.

A call for some reflective self-restraint

In our enthusiastic embrace of what was previously forbidden, we sometimes fail to pay sufficient attention to the less-than-obvious impact of our freely speaking politics, sex, hate, love; in fact, of our freely speaking. We don't always teach new candidates the value of waiting, listening, and refraining from self-disclosure until they've gotten the lay of the emotional landscape. Or carefully investigating underlying dynamics before playfully introducing what might be disturbing.

I think some self-reflective restraint is in order (Slochower, 2014a). In its absence, we run the risk of doing harm in ways that are not necessarily analyzable. And no, I'm not suggesting that we return to a traditional treatment model; we'd lose far more than we'd gain by going that way. First of all, analytic restraint too often coalesces into a kind of holding back (Bass, 1996) that itself embodies a sado-masochistic enactment.

Second, even if we think restraint is desirable, we're well past believing that it's always achievable. There will be moments when our countertransference erupts—for better and for worse. To further complicate things, our restraint is no therapeutic panacea. Restraint—like analytic silence—can be gaslighting, mystifying, can demand compliance or trigger dissociation. There's no evading our impact, whether enacted or implicit.

But all these caveats can obfuscate the fact that we analysts sometimes do real harm by *doing*. In a recent paper, Csillag (2014) illustrates this: she became traumatically derailed by her analyst's engagement in political arguments about the Iraq war while he remained unaware of the toxic effect of what he said. His belief in openness resulted in a kind of oblivion to its excesses and a failure to consider the possibility that staying out would have been a far more productive analytic stance.

Just last week, I encountered a similar story. My new patient John described an experience that had "blown up" (his words) a previous treatment: his therapist had responded to John's impressive professional achievement by expressing and elaborating on his competitive feelings (his envy, wish to show John up, his own feelings of inadequacy). The therapist indicated that he would have felt it dishonest not to self-disclose. John, feeling both disturbed and unsafe, expressed appreciation for the analyst's honesty and refrained from articulating his upset reactions to the disclosure. The treatment went on, but John felt constrained and unable to talk openly about himself; eventually he quit, offering an excuse (a demanding new job) that his therapist accepted at face value. Because the analyst's self-disclosure fit his theory of therapeutic action, he didn't consider the possibility that something more lay beneath what had seemed so intimate and helpful. A clinical blind-spot with theoretical origins.

This kind of blind-spot can occlude our awareness of the disturbing impact of our attempt to engage the patient around our subjectivity and shared enactments. It pulls us *in*, and while rich clinical work can emerge as a result, at times we may miss its problematic underbelly. Allowing ourselves to look at our patient's dynamics *outside* the realm of the intersubjective offers an additional point of clinical entry that can coexist with an ongoing study of the co-created element. As Nancy McWilliams' (e.g., 2011) lucid work on psychoanalytic diagnosis makes clear, it's possible to think about diagnosis psychoanalytically *and* to include the intersubjective in our thinking. By addressing individual character style in interface and collision with our relational perspective, we further complicate our clinical perspective. We may find a place of self-holding that will help us sustain ourselves over the long haul. We may even consider the possibility that there are limits to the value of every clinical position: to interpretation, holding, confrontation, but also to mutually analyzed enactments.

We relationalists can engage, but we can also stay out. We can refrain from saying the unsayable, from jointly exploring our countertransference. We don't always need to break into our patient's process or into her illusions about us. We have a choice, albeit a partial one. That choice includes the possibility that some of our patients sometimes require a zone of deniability—an arena that allows them (and us) not to see what cannot be metabolized. It's here that analytic restraint may open therapeutic space rather than constricting it by making room for that need.

Of course, our move toward restraint isn't uniquely informed by our understanding of the patient; it's also shaped by our own need not to know, be known, or to challenge. In this sense, restraint is as dynamically complex as is intersubjectivity. It's here that the relational ideal of analytic uncertainty—of ongoing self-reflection—can stand us in good stead; it supports self-examination and openness to the ways that our clinical choice—whether to express or contain—has been influenced by our own dynamics.

So let's include the ideal of analytic restraint within the relational umbrella without elevating it to a primary or dominant place. Without it, we run the risk of disrupting things in ways that may not be analyzable. Certainly, most kinds of analytic harm can be worked through and repaired. But not all. Some enactments are boundary violations—sexual *and* nonsexual. They do lasting harm that cannot be worked through or analyzed successfully. This is an omnipresent danger for all of us, *no matter what our clinical theory*. We relationalists are no more vulnerable to committing major boundary violations than are those who adhere to a different theory. But we're also no less vulnerable.

In acknowledging all this, we invite a different kind of inter-theoretical dialogue, one that allows us to appreciate areas of commonality *and* difference rather than positioning ourselves as the second analytic coming. We've begun to engage in respectful—rather than competitive conversations with other models and to reflect on both relational theory's contributions and its limitations in the consulting room. The very existence of this volume—a self-critique that's neither defensive nor self-flagellating

—bears witness to how much we've matured as a psychoanalytic community. It's my hope that writers from other orientations will engage in a similar kind of self-critique. That we can continue to create meaningful inter-theoretical conversations, organized not in argument with our particular psychoanalytic other but with the aim of respectfully delineating our differences while also deepening areas of commonality.

Notes

1   Those early relational critiques of the maternal analytic ideal softened with time. Increasingly, some—though not all—relationalists recognized the importance of addressing child states in adult patients and considered ways of working that included a symbolic parental function. Mitchell's (2000) later writing anticipated that shift. Articulating four interactive modes through which patterns of connection become organized, he formulated a layered vision of an adult influenced by a range of relational modalities, at least some of which originate in infancy. The multiplicity of self-experience suggests that there are ways in which, at once or in rapid alternation, the adult moves between grownup, child, and baby states.

2   Interpersonalists also strongly critiqued the interpretive, drive-based emphasis of classical writers.

3   A very early exception was Bromberg's (1979) paper on the value of regression from an interpersonal perspective.

4   I recognize the influence of my own early Freudian and Object Relations training in my interest in this dimension of analytic work.

5   See the 1994 (v. 6) issue of *Psychoanalytic Dialogues* for a discussion of this issue.

6   Schore amplifies Bromberg's work by foregrounding the role of right brain, implicit processes in the quotidian psychoanalytic element.

7   One arena in which this dynamic becomes especially problematic—for all analysts, independent of their theory—is around our request of the patient to publish clinical material. Peripherally aware that self-interest is driving things, perhaps a bit guilty and anxious, we sideline what we'd rather not acknowledge. Perhaps our patient agreed because she's genuinely happy to help us and is comfortable with the inherent exposure. But perhaps other unexplored fantasies and anxieties underlie her apparent comfort. That she's our most special patient, or the opposite: that we really don't care about her, that we're engaged only because she contributes to our self-advancement. That she has no choice but to agree or we'll retaliate. And while we're no more vulnerable to this kind of dynamic than those coming from other theoretical orientations, we're also not immune.

References

Ainsworth, M.D.S. (1969), Object relations, dependency and attachment: A theoretical overview of the infant-mother relationship. *Child Development*, 40:969–1025.

Aron, L. (1991), The patient's experience of the analyst's subjectivity. *Psychoanal. Dial.*, 1:29–51.

Aron, L. (1992), Interpretation as expression of the analyst's subjectivity. *Psychoanal. Dial.* 2:475–508.

Aron, L. (2001), *A Meeting of Minds: Mutuality in Psychoanalysis*. Hillsdale, NJ: The Analytic Press.

Balint, M. (1968), *The Basic Fault*. London: Tavistock.

Bass, A. (1996), Holding, holding back, and holding on. Commentary on paper by Joyce Slochower. *Psychoanal. Dial.*, 6:361–378.

Bass, A. (2003), "E" Enactments in psychoanalysis: Another medium, another message. Psychoanal. Dial., 13:657–676.

Bassin, D. (1997), Beyond the he and she: Postoedipal transcendence of gender polarities. *J. Amer. Psychoanal. Assn.* Special Supplement: 1997.

Bassin, D. (1999), *Female Sexuality*. Northvale, NJ: Aronson.

Bassin, D., Honey, M. & Kaplan, M.M. (1994) (eds.), *Representations of Motherhood*. New Haven, CT: Yale Univ. Press.

Beebe, B. & Lachmann, F. (1994), Representation and internalization in infancy: Three principles of salience. *Psychoanal. Psych.*, 11:127–165.

Beebe, B. & Lachmann, F. (1998), Co-constructing inner and relational processes. *Psychoanal. Psychol.*, 15:480–516.

Beebe, B., Lachmann, F., Markese, S. & Bahrick, L. (2012), On the origins of disorganized attachment and internal working models: Paper 1. A dyadic systems approach. *Psychoanal. Dial.*, 22:253–272.

Benjamin, J. (1986), A desire of one's own: Psychoanalytic feminism and intersubjective space. In: *Feminist Studies/Critical Studies*. T. de Lauretis (Ed.). Bloomington: Univ. of Indiana Press, 78–101.

Benjamin, J. (1988), *The Bonds of Love: Psychoanalysis, Feminism and the Problem of Domination*. New York: Pantheon.

Benjamin, J. (1995), *Like Subjects, Love Objects*. New Haven, Yale Univ. Press.

Benjamin, J. (1998), *Shadow of the Other*. London: Routledge.

Benjamin, J. (2009), A relational psychoanalysis perspective on the necessity of acknowledging failure in order to restore the facilitating and containing features of the intersubjective relationship (the shared third). *Int. J. Psycho-Anal.*, 90:441–450.

Benjamin, J. (2010), Where's the gap and what's the difference?: The relational view of intersubjectivity, multiple selves, and enactments. *Contemp. Psychoanal.*, 46:112–119.

Boulanger, G. (2007), *Wounded by Reality: Understanding and Treating Adult-Onset Trauma*. Mahwah, NJ: The Analytic Press.

BPCSG (1998), Non-interpretive mechanisms in psychoanalytic therapy: the "something more" than interpretation. *Int. J. Psycho-Anal.*, 79:903–921.

Bromberg, P.M. (1979), Interpersonal psychoanalysis and regression. *Contemp. Psychoanal.*, 15:647–655.

Bromberg, P.M. (1991), On knowing one's patient inside out: The aesthetics of unconscious communication. *Psychoanal. Dial.*, 1:399–422.

Bromberg, P.M. (1993), Shadow and substance: A relational perspective on clinical process. *Psychoanal. Psych.*, 10:147–168.

Bromberg, P. (1995), Resistance, object-usage, and human relatedness. *Contemp. Psychoanal.*, 31:173–191.

Bromberg, P.M. (1998), *Standing in the Spaces. Essays on Clinical Process, Trauma and Dissociation.* Hillsdale, NJ: The Analytic Press.

Bromberg, P.M. (2006), *Awakening the dreamer.* Hillsdale, NJ: The Analytic Press.

Bromberg, P.M. (2011), *In the Shadow of the Tsunami.* Hillsdale, NJ: The Analytic Press.

Chodorow, N. (1978), *The Reproduction of Mothering.* Berkeley, CA: University of California Press.

Cooper, S. (2014), The things we carry: Finding/creating the object and the analyst's self-reflective participation. *Psychoanal. Dial.*, 24:621–636.

Corbett, K. (2014). The analyst's private space: Spontaneity, ritual, psycho-therapeutic action and self-care. *Psychoanal. Dial.*, 24:637–647.

Csillag, V. (2014), Ordinary sadism in the consulting room. *Psychoanal. Dial.*, 24:467–482.

Davies, J.M. (1994), Love in the afternoon: A relational reconsideration of desire and dread in the countertransference. *Psychoanal. Dial.*, 4:153–170.

Davies, J.M. (2004), Whose bad objects are we anyway? Repetition and our elusive love affair with evil. *Psychoanal. Dial.*, 14:711–732.

Davies, J.M. & Frawley, M.G. (1994), *Treating Adult Survivor of Childhood Sexual Abuse: A Psychoanalytical Perspective.* New York: Basic Books.

Dimen, M. (1991), Deconstructing difference: Gender splitting and transitional space. *Psychoanal. Dial.*, 1:335–353.

Dinnerstein, D. (1976), *The Mermaid and the Minotaur.* New York: Harper & Row.

Ehrenberg, D. (1974), The intimate edge in therapeutic relatedness. *Contemp. Psychoanal.*, 10:423–437.

Erikson, E.H. (1950), *Childhood and Society.* New York: Norton.

Fairbairn, W.R. (1952), *Psychoanalytic Studies of the Personality.* London: Tavistock.

Fast, I. (1984), *Gender Identity: A Differentiation Model.* Hillsdale, NJ: The Analytic Press.

Ferenczi, S. (1952), *First Contributions to Psycho-Analysis.* London: Hogarth Press & the Institute of Psycho-Analysis.

Fiscalini, J. (1994), Narcissism and coparticipant inquiry: Explorations in contemporary interpersonal psychoanalysis. *Contemp. Psychoanal.*, 30:747–776.

Fonagy, P., Gyorgy, G., Jurist, E.L., & Target, M. (2004), *Affect Regulation, Mentalization, and the Development of the Self.* New York: Other Press.

Ghent, E. (1992), Paradox and process. *Psychoanal. Dial.*, 2:135–159.

Goldner, V. (1991), Toward a critical relational theory of gender. *Psychoanal. Dial.*, 1:249–272.

Grand, S. (2000), *The Reproduction of Evil.* Hillsdale, NJ: The Analytic Press.

Grand, S. (2010), *The Hero in the Mirror.* New York: Routledge.

Guntrip, H. (1961), *Personality Structure and Human Interaction.* New York: Int. Univ. Press.

Harris, A. (1991), Gender as contradiction. *Psychoanal. Dial.*, 1:197–224.

Harris, A. (1997), Beyond/outside gender dichotomies. *Psychoanal. Dial.*, 7:363–366.

Harris, A. (2005), *Gender as Soft Assembly.* Hillsdale, NJ: The Analytic Press.

Harris, A. (2009), You must remember this. *Psychoanal. Dial.*, 19:2–21.

Hesse, E. & Main, M. (2000), Disorganized infant, child, and adult attachment: Collapse in behavioral and attentional strategies. *J. Amer. Psychoanal. Assn.*, 48:1097–1128.

Hirsch, I. (1994), Countertransference love and theoretical model. *Psychoanal. Dial.*, 4:171–192.

Hirsch, I. (2006), The interpersonal roots of relational thinking. *Contemp. Psychoanal.*, 42:551–556.

Hirsch, I. (2014), *The Interpersonal Tradition: The Origins of Psychoanalytic Subjectivity.* New York: Routledge.

Hoffman, I.Z. (1991), Discussion: Toward a social-constructivist view of the psychoanalytic situation. *Psychoanal. Dial.*, 1:74–105.

Hoffman, I.Z. (1992), Some practical implications of a social-constructivist view of the psychoanalytic situation. *Psychoanal. Dial.*, 1:74–105.

Hoffman, I.Z. (1998), *Ritual and Spontaneity in Psychoanalysis.* Hillsdale, NJ: The Analytic Press.

Hoffman, I.Z. (2009), Therapeutic passion in the countertransference. *Psychoanal. Dial.*, 19:617–637.

Jacobs, T.J. (1986), On countertransference enactments. *J. Amer. Psychoanal. Assn.*, 34:289–307.

Kohut, H. (1984), *How does Analysis Cure.* Chicago, IL: Univ. of Chicago Press.

Layton, L. (1998), *Who's that Girl? Who's that Boy? Clinical Practice Meets Post-Modern Gender Theory.* Northvale, NJ: Jason Aronson.

Levenson, E.A. (1972), *The Fallacy of Understanding.* New York: Basic Books.

Loewald, H.W. (1960), On the therapeutic action of psycho-analysis. *Int. J. Psychoanalysis.*, 41:16–33.

McWilliams, N. (2011), *Psychoanalytic Diagnosis.* New York: Guilford.

Mitchell, S. (1984), Object relations theories and the developmental tilt. *Contemp. Psychoanal.*, 20:473–499.

Mitchell, S. (1988), *Relational Concepts in Psychoanalysis*. Cambridge, MA: Harvard Univ. Press.

Mitchell, S. (1991), Wishes, needs and interpersonal negotiations. *Psychoanal. Inq.*, 11:147–170.

Mitchell, S. (1993), *Hope and Dread in Psychoanalysis*. New York: Basic Books.

Mitchell, S. (1997), *Influence and Autonomy in Psychoanalysis*. Hillsdale, NJ: The Analytic Press.

Mitchell, S. (2000), *Relationality*. Hillsdale, NJ: The Analytic Press.

Ogden, T. (1997), Reverie and metaphor: Some thoughts on how I work as a psychoanalyst. *Int. J. Psycho-Anal.*, 78:719–732.

Pizer, S.A. (1998), *Building Bridges*. Hillsdale, NJ: The Analytic Press.

Sandler, J. (1960), The background of safety. *Int. J. Psycho-Anal.*, 41:352–356.

Sandler, J. (1976), Countertransference and role-responsiveness. *Int. Rev. Psycho-Analy.*, 3:43–47.

Schore, A.N. (2011), The right brain implicit self lies at the core of psychoanalysis. *Psychoanal. Dial.*, 21:75–100.

Seligman, S. (2003), The developmental perspective in relational psychoanalysis. *Contemp. Psychoanal.*, 39:477–508.

Seligman, S. & Shanok, R.S. (1996), Erikson, our contemporary: His anticipation of an intersubjective perspective. *Psychoanal. Contemp. Thought*, 19:339–365.

Slochower, J. (1991), Variations in the analytic holding environment. *Int. J. Psycho-Anal.*, 72:709–718.

Slochower, J. (1992), A hateful borderline patient and the holding environment. *Contemp. Psychoanal.*, 28:72–88.

Slochower, J. (1993), Mourning and the holding function of *Shiva. Contemp. Psychoanal.*, 30:135–151.

Slochower, J. (1994), The evolution of object usage and the holding environment. *Contemp. Psychoanal.*, 30:135–151.

Slochower, J. (1996a & 2014a), *Holding and Psychoanalysis: A Relational Perspective*. Hillsdale, NJ: The Analytic Press.

Slochower, J. (1996b), Holding and the evolving maternal metaphor. *Psychoanal. Rev.*, 83:195–218.

Slochower, J. (1996c), The holding environment and the fate of the analyst's subjectivity. *Psychoanal. Dial.*, 6:323–353.

Slochower, J. (1999), Interior experience in analytic process. *Psychoanal. Dial.*, 9:789–809.

Slochower, J. (2004), But what do *you* want? The location of emotional experience. *Contemp. Psychoanal.*, 40:577–602.

Slochower, J. (2006; 2014b), *Psychoanalytic Collisions,* Hillsdale, N.J.: Analytic Press.

Slochower, J. (2011a), Out of the analytic shadow: On the dynamics of commemorative ritual. *Psychoanal. Dial.*, 21:676–690.

Slochower, J. (2011b), Analytic idealizations and the disavowed: Winnicott, his patients, and us. *Psychoanal. Dial.,* 21:3–21.

Slochower, J. (2013a), Psychoanalytic mommies and psychoanalytic babies: A long view. *Contemp. Psychoanal.*, 49:606–628.

Slochower, J. (2013b), Using Winnicott today: A relational perspective. *Revue Roumaine de Psychanalyse*, 2:13–41.

Slochower, J. (2013c), Analytic enclaves and analytic outcome: A clinical mystery. *Psychoanal. Dial.*, 23:243–258.

Slochower, J. (2014a), Analytic sadism and analytic restraint. *Psychoanal. Dial.*, 24:483–487.

Stein, R. (1999), Discussion of Joyce Slochower's Interior experience paper. *Psychoanal. Dial.*, 9:811–823.

Stern, D.B. (1992), Commentary on constructivism in clinical psychoanalysis. *Psychoanal. Dial.*, 3:331–364.

Stern, D.B. (1997), *Unformulated Experience: From Dissociation to Ima-gination in Psychoanalysis.* Hillsdale, NJ: The Analytic Press.

Stern, D.B. (2009), *Partners in Thought.* New York: Routledge/Analytic Press.

Stern, D.N. (2004), *The Present Moment in Psychotherapy and Everyday Life.* New York: Norton.

Stolorow, R.D. (1997), Dynamic, dyadic, intersubjective systems: An evolving paradigm for psychoanalysis. *Psychoanal. Psych.*, 14:337–346.

Sullivan, H.S. (1954), *The Psychiatric Interview.* New York: Norton.

Warshaw, S.C. (1992), Mutative factors in child psychoanalysis: A comparison of diverse relational perspectives. In: Skolnick, N. & Warshaw, S.C. (eds.) *Relational Perspectives in Psychoanalysis.* Hillsdale, NJ: The Analytic Press.

Winnicott, D.W. (1947), Hate in the countertransference. In: *Through Pediatrics to Psychoanalysis.* New York: Basic Books, 194–203.

Winnicott, D.W. (1958), The capacity to be alone. *Int. J. Psycho-Anal.*, 39:416–420.

Winnicott, D.W. (ed.) (1960), Ego distortions in terms of true and false self. In: *The Maturational Processes and the Facilitating Environment.* London: Hogarth Press, 140–152.

Winnicott, D.W. (1963), Dependence in infant care, in child care, and in the psycho-analytic setting. *Int. J. Psycho-Anal.*, 44:339–344.

Winnicott, D.W. (1965), *The Maturational Processes and the Facilitating Environment.* London: Hogarth Press.

Winnicott, D.W. (1969a), The use of an object. *Int. J. Psycho-Anal.*, 50:711–716.

Winnicott, D.W. (ed.) (1969b), The mother-infant experience of mutuality. In: *Psychoanalytic Explorations.* Cambridge, MA: Harvard University Press, 251–260.

Wolstein, B. (1959), *Countertransference.* New York: Grune & Stratton.

Chapter 2

The emergence of the relational tradition

Lewis Aron interviews Jay Greenberg

Interviews conducted on 8/7/2015 and 13/7/2015

Part 1 (8/7/15)

L: I want you to know that I have been looking forward to this interview for years. I think that the Relational school of thought had a huge impact on American psychoanalysis as well as worldwide psychoanalysis. Obviously, I think you hold a unique position in the field and that there are a lot of rumors, misconceptions, and misunderstandings about your role.

J: It's nice to be asked. (both laughing) I've been waiting for the right person to ask about this.

L: Let me start with the most basic topic. You and Steve were considered two of the important architects of the contemporary relational turn in America. Yet, in the minds of many relationalists, you are not associated with the current Relational School or movement.

J: Yes, but at the same time, some American and international thinkers do think I represent the relational point of view. This leaves me in a state of limbo, where I'm seen as the "other" by both sides.

L: Let me start by asking you a couple of questions about the very beginning. You wrote the '83 book with Steve. This book became an immediate classic and it remains so today. It seems, at least in '83, that you authored and agreed with the idea that there was a forced choice between the drive model and the relational model. You argued that there was a dichotomy between the two models due to their alternate premises. You suggested that both models would last forever and neither would become more dominant. Am I capturing this accurately?

J: Yes, it's all true.

L: Do you still believe that? If not, at what point did you stray?

J: Our stance in the book reflected the distance, at the time, between the two models, and the lack of integration of ideas. There was very little communication among adherents of the different models; the world was very different than it is now. When I talk to young graduates, for instance, it's as if I am speaking about something that happened around the Civil War Era. Nationally, there were the Ego Psychologists and the Self Psychologists. Internationally, there was virtually no communication between Anglophone and non-Anglophone analysts. The dividing lines were all extremely sharp, to the point where nobody bothered to think much about what went on over at the other side of the divide. That's the climate in which we wrote the book.

L: Given that these two models were so divided, could this idea have led you to argue that it was possible to combine them, rather than arguing that they would always remain inherently opposed?

J: We were more interested in establishing the integrity and legitimacy of the relational model as we defined it, and presenting it as an alternative to the orthodoxy that dominated the psychoanalytic climate in which we were living at the time. These ideas had been marginalized, certainly within mainstream North American psychoanalysis. We knew nothing of what was happening in continental Europe, and certainly nothing at all about Latin America. Thus, our point of view was very much shaped by our training as North American psychoanalysts, despite our interpersonal training at the White Institute. I've recently spoken about the influence of Hartmann and Ego Psychologists; they pretty much defined North American psychoanalysis from the late 1930s all the way through the 90s.

It's like the old wisecrack that "In Italy everybody is Catholic, even the Protestants." In the US at the time, everybody was an Ego Psychologist, even the interpersonalists, because the Ego Psychologists defined the discourse. I think this certainly contributed to the dichotomization of the two theories, given that you either agreed with Hartmann and the Ego Psychologists, or you disagreed. You talked about an average expectable environment, or thought, "No, what is interesting is not the average expectable environment, but rather the particulars of the environment." You talked about Mahler's ordinary devoted mother, or you thought, "No, mothers are not ordinary, they are all very different." In the 1940s, Hartmann, Kris, and Loewenstein revisited the idea of castration anxiety. They suggested that even though kids may not hear actual threats of castration, they may get a sense of veiled aggression in the family, which can have the same impact. This was a radical break – the idea that a child could detect an aggressive atmosphere, which they would register in the same way as castration, even long after people stopped debating whether or not castration was actually threatened. So, people were deterred from developing alternative points of view, due to the intellectual atmosphere of psychoanalysis at the time. If you did not agree with the accepted ideas of the time, you would be excluded from presenting at meetings, your papers wouldn't be published in mainstream journals, and so on. We set out to demonstrate that the relational model has its own integrity; it was not created as an emendation of something else.

L: Right, that the model can stand on its own.

J: Yes, it can and does stand on its own. Before the 1983 book, the relational model didn't exist. There were people working on their own, independently, not necessarily knowing one another. If they were alive, and we invited them to this 'club,' people like Melanie Klein and Harry Stack Sullivan would have fled in terror and outrage. Most of the theorists were dead, so they couldn't protest. Even so, some Kleinians did protest at the inclusion of Melanie Klein in the Relational group. But we were trying to establish the integrity of the relational model, which we essentially created. To do so, we had to prove that the model stood independently of the hegemonic drive model. What we didn't realize at the time was that this view was very specific to North America. There was a more developed relational sensibility in other parts of the world. Recently, many early Latin American papers by the Barangers, Bleger, Heinrich Racker and others, have been becoming quite popular in the United States. Compared to North America, the Latin Americans had much less trouble moving into a model that integrated a drive theoretical and relational point of view. Because this work was not translated, we were unaware of its existence.

L: Yes, I understand what you mean regarding the development of thought in Latin America. You mentioned Europe to be similar in this context.

J: I think European development occurred later. I'm specifically referring to the non-Anglo European development in relational ideas, predominantly in Italy.

L: But I was under the impression that there was a different interpretation of Freud between European and American psychologists.

J: Thank you for jogging my memory on that. I think the French, for instance, had their own anti-Ego Psychological beginnings, dating back to Lacan's analysis with Loewenstein. From then on, also in the offshoots of Lacanian thought, Laplanche, for instance, reads Freud in a much different way than we do and in a much more relational way than we do, although they would certainly bristle at my use of the term. Many of them read Freud on a daily basis. Their interpretation of Freud was nothing like the one in our object relation's book or the Freud we were taught.

L: It is interesting that both you and Steve had backgrounds in political thought. Particularly, because your writing posed the idea of a political intervention, right?

J: Well, it turned out to be. I am not sure if that was our intention at the start, but it certainly did have political effects to say the least. I know that John Gedo wrote that this book was political in its intent, but this was not true, at least to the best of my knowledge. I think our objectives were heuristic and educational. When we began, it was certainly not my intention to create a Relational movement, nor do I believe it was Steve's. That was the next step in Steve's 1988 book, of course. We've laid out the idea that these separate approaches had common conceptual underpinnings, which suggests they are capable of being integrated. Steve's subsequent idea was to go ahead and do so, even at the extremes of Klein and Kohut. When we were writing the book, however, our aim was more to clarify things and establish the integrity of an alternative line to an ego psychological approach.

L: I understand that you wrote this book without political intent nor an agenda to create a movement. Although, I think it was in fact political in a broader sense. You described theorists as having certain commonalities of which they were unaware and would have even rejected. In a sense, you created a political coalition of these people without their consent. Can you understand how this may be seen as a result of political interest?

J: That's an interesting question. After seeing the book's impact as time has passed, I can understand the thought, "well that must be true." Yet, when I reflect on the days during which Steve and I were putting the book together, I realize that your characterization holds more truth in the context of the relational half of the book. At that point, drive model theorists had already viewed themselves as politically and conceptually joined, although they had their own squabbles about various nuances. It was very different with the relational thinkers, who would have kicked and screamed at the suggestion that they fell to the same side regarding certain issues. So, when you say that the book brought them together and framed it as if they had a common inherently political cause, I certainly see your point.

L: Do you remember if you and Steve ever conversed about your shared political backgrounds and interests?

J: Yes, explicitly so. Steve came from a very political family, the most influential member being a radical uncle. My parents were left wing activists, working as Lawyers' Guild types. They were fellow travelers and activists, but they became a bit disenfranchised from politics by the time I was more aware of these things. However, I was very politically involved in college.

L: But neither one of you viewed your joint work as a continuation of that political sensibility?

J: No. I don't think either one of us felt empowered enough to have any political impact at that young age. We were in our early thirties, just a year or two out of the institute when we started writing the book.

L: However, Steve's very first article challenges the whole psychoanalytic world about homosexuality. You can certainly view this as taking a very strong and empowered political stance.

J: Well, I think Steve always had the sense that he could change the world. So, I suppose I'm speaking more for myself when I said that we did not feel empowered.

L: Even so, it seems like you two collaborated well. Your differences did not get in the way, but rather fostered a sense of creative tension.

J: Yes, it's interesting. I could never have written the book without Steve's energy, but I don't think the book would have been as strong without my caution.

L: Right. Even back then, it was clear that you were more cautious.

J: Yes, well one reason this book worked is that Steve and I were both writing about theorists we loved. I loved the more cautious theorists, while Steve loved the more radical theorists. Throughout the process, Steve was like the gas pedal and I was the brake.

L: That's fascinating. Your dynamic was similar to the conflict-defense model.

J: Yes, and this was both intellectually and character based. He was always ahead of me in terms of productivity, but our dynamic worked. I was eternally grateful to him for putting up with my procrastination. Only in later years did I realize that procrastination works sometimes.

L: Before moving forward to discuss events that occurred after the book was written, I have a few more questions. It has always struck me that the book came out in '83, because it was such a politically significant decade. So much happened in the 70s and 80s that led up to '83. I find it interesting that Division 39 was formed in '79/'80. If you had written the book before that time, there would not have been a natural audience or a place to present your work.

J: I think that's fascinating, because at the time of its formation, Division 39 was a fairly conservative group. So, the group didn't really capture our attention. Right after the book came out, the local chapters started creating institutes, like the Denver Institute and PINC. The timing was spectacular, given that we had just written a book addressing some of the larger themes in the field. It could not have been better for us.

They invited us to speak about and teach the book in person.

L: You two had established together that the relational could work as an independent model. So, by '88, Steve went in his own direction to pursue relational theory and shifted from the '83 argument that there was no basis to choose the relational model over the drive model. At this point, did you realize that you were moving in different directions? If so, was this discussed?

J: After the '88 book was written, we talked about our developing ideas, and we could easily agree to disagree and have productive conversations. Sometimes we felt that the other was deluding himself; we would laugh about it. I don't believe many people know about this, but we were planning to write another book together after the 1988 Relational Concepts book had already come out. We wanted the book to be modeled on the 1983 *Object Relations* book, but much more clinically based. For a period of time we would often meet to present cases to each other to find areas that we agreed or disagreed upon. We were trying to develop some of the salient implications of the conceptual divide. I remember a particular moment during one of our discussions when we realized that no matter how we thought about it, the common ground was the interaction. At the time, the word, "interaction," was not used on a particularly widespread level. We intended for this term to be an organizing principle of the book. We actually had a contract to write the book, but I could not follow through, largely due to developments in my personal life. It was a wrenching incident for Steve and me.

L: Did he consider continuing on his own?

J: No, because I think the book was intended to be *ours*.

L: You had a contract with Harvard?

J: We had a contract with Arthur Rosenthal, who had been at Harvard in previous years. We viewed him as the "Godfather" of the *Object Relations* book, as well as my second book and Steve's second.

L: So, by the time you wrote *Oedipus and Beyond* (Greenberg, 1991), it was clear that you had chosen to go in a different direction.

J: Yes.

L: Thinking back to those early years, at the start of the institutionalization of Relational Psychoanalysis as you went in your own direction – can you remember how you felt about the direction in which Steve was headed, as well as the fate of American Relational Psychoanalysis?

J: More than any of my conceptual concerns, I had a problem with the institutionalization of Relational Psychoanalysis. I don't know if anyone knows this, so perhaps this should be off the record. Did you know that when Paul Stepansky and Steve planned to start *Dialogues*, they asked me to be co-editor? I said no. I wasn't entirely sure whether it was a good idea to create a Relational journal. I thought we had arrived at a time conducive to very interesting conversations within the broader psychoanalytic community, and thus we had won; winning meant that we could go to any meeting we pleased and speak freely. We were tolerated and even admired. However, Steve was not as interested as I was in playing a role in these conversations. I think this was a fundamental area in which he and I disagreed. I remember coming across something Steve wrote in a letter. He used an example of people having a party in a house and there is a group outside that starts singing.

L: Yeah, it's from the *Round Robin* (Mitchell, 1999).

J: Yes, the *Round Robin*. Using this example was his way of saying, "Ok, now you like our song . . . oh fuck you. We are going to continue singing it for ourselves and by ourselves. We are not going to engage by raising our voices and then allowing you to join us." I thought this was wrong. Personally, I found it productive to have conversations with people who dramatically disagreed, even those who would go as far as to reject the fact that I was a real psychoanalyst. I felt that this kind of 'rough play' had a purpose; I think it's fine that these people now want to 'sing' with us, even if we never agree.

L: I would like to shift to the topic of *Oedipus and Beyond*. One could say that you and Steve wrote the first book establishing that you can be a drive theorist or a relational theorist, but not both. However, by *Oedipus and Beyond*, the argument became that all theories are drive theories. The argument suggests that there's an implicit drive theory in any theory. Aside from politics and institutionalization, is it correct to say that you had arrived at a different conceptual place?

J: Yes, I had come to a place where I interpreted these other theorists somewhat differently. I felt that it wasn't possible to excise something that is pre-experiential. The whole idea of drive or not drive is less interesting than making room for some kind of inner direction, that cannot be simply excised theoretically. You can read Fairbairn and Kohut and recognize that they don't talk about drive in the same way, similar to Sullivan. But they all have some sense of who we are and how we fit into the world.

L: It strikes me that you used the word 'pre-experiential' right away. I recently spent a year comprehensively teaching Steve's journal articles, because I noticed an interesting contrast between his books and earlier articles. There is more raw content in the articles than in the books, because certain points were smoothed over by the time he edited the books. It was an interesting exercise. I noticed a trend from beginning to end in regards to his main target. When he argued against drives, I found his real target to be the "pre." I think he took from Sullivan that drives were pre-experiential, which suggests that personality is interpersonal and therefore doesn't exist before pre-personal relations.

J: That was certainly a subject about which we both thought the other was deluded. I was baffled about how he did and did not think certain things, and the feeling was mutual. We talked about that disagreement for years after the *Object Relations* book. I couldn't shake the idea that something pre-experiential has to be built into the theory in some way.

L: So the question remains: Can relationalists also have some notion of drives? Can we be relational, but also assume that there are some preconceptions in terms of one's core personality from birth? I know Steve was radically opposed to that idea.

J: I don't see why you can't be relational and believe in that too. It is interesting to think about the direction Steve would have gone with this idea if he were still alive. It seems to me that the specter that haunts the idea of "pre-experiential," is the specter of the average expectable environment. If you believe in the pre-experiential idea, that everything else begins to lose its impact, it becomes more Hartmann. This raises concern about losing the nuances and elegances revealed by the relational theory. Considering that Steve has been gone for 15 years and the extent to which things have changed during this time, I wonder if he would be less focused on that at this point. As the voices in this conversation have become more diverse over the years, I think the issue has been redefined to a certain extent.

L: Let me shift our focus to your respectful criticism on the clinical direction in which relational theory went. You've published words of caution against relational ideas, including one I find to be very important, which is the idea that the interactional focus was meant to be a description, rather than a prescription (Greenberg, 1981, 2001). Let me start by asking – Do you have any other key criticisms on the directional shift of the relational over both recent and early years?

J: I'm most inclined to respond to certain ideas from the early years. There was a feeling of euphoria about interaction and enactment, from the idea that we could loosen up, unlike the typical Freudian analyst of the 50's. There was the idea that it was actually not so terrible to gratify a patient, even if we didn't know very much about what was gratifying or not. This involved responding to the patient as an individual and "throwing away the book." This was, sort of prima facie, viewed as courageous, generous and therapeutically efficacious. I don't know if relational thinking continues to valorize those ideas at this point. I haven't heard many clinical presentations recently displaying any conviction about these ideals. I certainly found this troubling when I wrote the "analyst's participation" paper around 2000 (Greenberg, 2001).

L: (laughs)

J: I'm always at risk of being labeled an outcast. I think about the line from the Barangers' paper, saying "psychoanalysis, by definition in psychoanalysis everything is also something else." It's a great line, conveying the importance in looking at everything from a different angle, and that's what we do.

L: The hermeneutics of suspicion.

J: Yes, and this remains true even if a particular intervention has a remarkably benign effect in the short run. It is our responsibility in this field to look at all results using multiple perspectives.

L: One of the most common criticisms about the relational, as you mentioned before, is that it has abandoned the idea of the unconscious, whether it is a result of not paying attention to sexuality, or criticizing drive theory and thus getting rid of the drives. How would you respond to this?

J: I think that's an unfair statement. I do find that some contemporary authors of all theoretical persuasions have a tendency to take things at face value; by doing so, they leave themselves open to the charge of not believing in the unconscious. But I also think it would be a fascinating exercise to ask a group of people to describe their individual definitions of the unconscious, and then ask what would constitute evidence that they do believe in the unconscious. Furthermore, how do they use the unconscious? There are people who would say that if you don't believe in the primacy of sexuality as a motivation that it is not the unconscious. I would love to have a conversation with them. I think there is a tendency in many psychoanalytic communities to think about transference in a different way than it was previously viewed. There is more of a focus on subjectivity. For example, let's say you have an impression of me. Rather than focusing on how you've created this impression of me, subjectivity encourages the question, "How did I contribute in creating that impression?" I think some of my papers have contributed to this area, given that one of our important discoveries is that we play a significant role in shaping the patient's experience. We were euphoric about this finding, because it raises the question of whether or not there is a need for a concept of transference.

L: By rushing to understand the patient's impression of you, do you interfere with other important areas of focus?

J: The patient needs to view you in a certain way, regardless of the origin of this need. So, returning to some extent to the organizational part, we need more constant dialogue. I'm not suggesting back and forth critiques on one another's thoughts about specific concepts, like sexuality, transference, the unconscious; this would lead both parties to ultimately challenge the other's role as a legitimate psychoanalysis. Instead, the focus of the dialogue should be on our neutrality. How does the exploration of acknowledgement, awareness, or ownership of that hinder our ability to explore transference?

L: Let me ask a more deeply personal question. You've previously said that you played a more conservative role, while Steve was a Pied Piper of leading people in this relational direction. You were the voice of caution, which the relational community didn't take very well. What was that like for you?

J: Well, you are deepening our discussion on transference (laughs). On one hand, Steve sensed that his place in the world was that of a

Pied Piper, which I believe he was. On the other hand, my place in the world tends to be that of an outsider; the one to be rejected and excluded. You can confirm that with my loved ones (laughs). I recognize that we both had a specific character, and I think this is central to the way things unfolded.

L: This brings us back to the first thing you told me. You are recognized as the 'other' in both communities. The classical community views you as more of a relationalist, whereas the relationalists think you lean more towards classical thought.

J: Right, that's not an accident. Like they say, character is destiny. I'm where I am today for good reasons, and I'm proud of my independence. But some of the ways I'm seen by some people do hurt my feelings and I don't want to overlook that. I think I felt excluded in some places, and most of all, I lost my best friend. Steve and I loved each other for a long time, and I feel like that's been taken away from me. It remains a very personal subject. I dream about it and I've talked about it within the last three weeks. To the extent that I have hurt feelings it is because that has been taken away.

L: That's very personal, not just about the movement.

J: No, it is not about the movement at all. As far as I'm concerned, I can hold my own against the movement, I have more than my share of commitments and involvements. The loss of some personal relationships is what hurts the most.

L: I want to address your 2001 paper on the analyst's participation, which was rejected by *Psychoanalytic Dialogues*. I know from discussing this with Steve, that he and I wanted the paper to appear in *Dialogues*. Steve believed that the criticism belonged in *Dialogues* and it was a debate for us to have among one another.

J: I didn't know I had friends on the other side. But I have a strong sense that people and institutions do what is necessary. My feelings were hurt, but I also told myself that they were not ready to publish the paper at the time. I wasn't aware of that particular twist regarding the decision. But, for whatever reason, whoever made that decision did not think *Dialogues* was on solid enough ground to publish a critique from the inside.

L: The rationalization was that, "We can handle the arguments, but this is too ad hominem and too personal and we have an obligation to protect contributors to the journal."

J: Yeah, like that Irwin Hoffman article.

L: Yes and it remains an important article.

J: I understood that. My first inclination wasn't to go "outside" the tent – to publish the paper in JAPA – but I didn't have any choice if I wanted to publish it, which I did.

L: There wasn't another suitable place?

J: Right, there wasn't another suitable place, and I also wanted it to be a target paper with discussions. The *Quarterly* didn't have discussions at the time and I wanted to hear relational voices criticizing and responding to the paper. *Contemporary Psychoanalysis* didn't seem like an option because I was the editor. So I couldn't think of any other good fit.

L: So, at first the White Institute and the interpersonalists were also not thrilled with your new direction with Steve. That's another place in which you became the 'other.'

J: Yes. The first thing that ruffled feathers was the idea of a relational model that included Sullivan and others. This was not viewed favorably. People disliked the notion that Fairbairn had ideas that were compatible with Sullivan's. The interpersonalists at White were very committed to seeing themselves as *sui generis*. When the book was published, senior people thought it was too balanced; they'd hoped that it would promote interpersonal thought. They thought this would inevitably tilt in favor of one model replacing the other, rather than keeping interpersonal thought in tension with the other.

Steve certainly gravitated quickly toward Fairbairn and to some extent Klein, but Fairbairn primarily. He felt that some of Fairbairn's ideas supplemented Sullivan's. By the time we were writing together, there were different threads of the interpersonal tradition . . .

L: I think the most basic point that Steve articulated was that interpersonal thinkers, specifically Sullivan, had a phobia of the internal world.

J: Yes, that would certainly be true pertaining to the idea of internal objects.

L: So, it wasn't the case that you two had a shared criticism of your past training.

J: No, I think we felt well-trained. We felt that we had gotten there, and we were in supervision with people who were more ego psychological, more Kleinian, and so on. It was quite diverse for that time.

J: I have to say, these questions have been fantastic.

L: I've been working on this for a long time.

J: I very much appreciate it. I've been interviewed a fair amount of times in the past and people often ask the wrong questions, but you're asking the questions I hoped you would.

Second part of the interview (13/7/15)

L: We were talking about drive theory and a bit about your book. I had asked you about your position by the time you wrote *Oedipus and Beyond.*

J: In the *Object Relations* book, we presented the conditions on the ground in a sense, in that certain theorists had rejected drive theory while others had maintained and supported it. As things stood at that time, both politically and conceptually, you did have to choose. But throughout writing *Oedipus and Beyond,* I realized that there is an implicit drive theory in the work of the theorists who had manifestly rejected drive theory. I hadn't realized this earlier. As I looked at Fairbairn's work – his work as we had presented it in the *Object Relations* book – and even at Sullivan, I saw that they shared an idea, that from the beginning of life, something moves people in a particular direction. Toward the object for Fairbairn, away from anxiety for Sullivan, that sort of thing. Why would we move toward objects? Or away from anxiety? For both theorists, and I think for all theorists, there is a directional thrust that is, to use the word we discussed last time, pre-experiential. For me, that is the essential meaning of "drive."

L: As I followed Steve's attempts to respond to your challenge, my sense was that he conceded about Sullivan. He couldn't resist your critique that the avoidance of anxiety served as drive. However, my sense was that he could not concede on Fairbairn. It seemed as though he actually tried giving you two different answers, because he knew the first didn't work, and the second was problematic for other reasons. His first answer was that it's not a drive in Fairbairn, because it's simply the way we are built. He differentiates between intent and structure. To paraphrase, he says something along the lines of, "No, we seek other people in the same way as leaves seek other leaves on a branch, and the way bees seek other bees. It's not a drive nor is it instinct, but rather it is just the way we are built." I think it was a strain to say that there was no motivation implicit in Fairbairn. In a 2002 paper on Fairbairn that was published after he died, he gives a different answer. He says, and again I am loosely paraphrasing from my memory, "No, Fairbairn says more than that. Yes, we are built that way, but we want to be loved and for others to accept our love from the very beginning." He then reads Fairbairn through Jessica Benjamin's theory of recognition, and says, "We really want to relate to the other as a separate subject." He suggests that this is what it means to love, be loved, and have our love accepted. It is to be an agent and to see the other as a subject. I think this answer is very close to where you came from, regarding both agency and relatedness as senses we are born with.

J: Yes, I agree. Now we're approaching the topic about the next argument I had with Steve over many lunches and dinners. I believed that if I could prove that Fairbairn and Sullivan did have drive theories, I could go on to show that they were also suggesting a single, unitary drive. And if there is only one drive, then conflict doesn't come on the scene until we encounter objects. In contrast, I believe that it is one of the strengths of

Freud's psychoanalysis, of his dual drive theory, that conflict is built into the organism, even before we meet our mothers. Regardless of the particular way you characterize the drives, the idea that there is conflict from the beginning seems essential to me.

L: It's very important in today's world, because various people are putting forth both neuropsychoanalytic research and infancy research about drives. I'm referring to Joe Lichtenburg, Mark Solms, and Jaak Panksepp. They say that there are seven, or really eight or nine drives, and Joe says there are five and now six or more drives. In Irwin Hoffman's review of your book, he said if you line them up like a star, you can have five or six motivations in each corner, and still emphasize conflict. In light of current research, it seems somewhat ironic that analysts wanted to get rid of drive theory for years, because it's no longer scientific to think in terms of drives. Neuropsychoanalysts and neurologists are saying that there are drives, while we want to get rid of them. How do you view the current scene? Are you satisfied with Hoffman's answer?

J: I'm not so interested in how many drives people have. If I remember correctly, when I wrote about dualism in *Oedipus and Beyond*, I thought it was parsimonious, elegant, and clinically useful, but it's not what interests me the most. I'm most interested in the topic Lacan calls the divided subject. It's the idea that we are not of a piece; there's not a unitary motivational force that causes interpersonal conflict. Take the idea that we unambivalently seek to be recognized by an other. With this mindset, problems arise when the desired recognition isn't forthcoming in a way that's adequate or satisfying. Thus, the conflict is interpersonal at the beginning. In my opinion, this doesn't seem to account for human nature.

L: That conflict just cannot be accidental or circumstantial.

J: Or avoidable.

It reminds me of Roy Schafer's idea that the romantic point of view promotes the idea that conflict can be avoided. That's why I wanted to talk about a fundamental motivational structure, in which we are divided from the beginning in certain ways. Again, if somebody wants to talk about five motivational systems or seven, it doesn't hugely trouble me. My feelings about any of those viewpoints are primarily based on their clinical relevance.

L: Let me dig into the critique of the romantic vision with you a bit more. A lot of the current relational thinkers are very much reconnected to traumatology, which is the focus on trauma. This may align with the idea that the problem is external. On the other hand, trauma was denied for a long time by the analytic world, so its rediscovery is important. Do you have any thoughts about that balance, or the tension between the recognition of trauma that we hadn't, and the dangers of making it all external?

J: Yes, I've been thinking about this for various reasons. I think Freud got it right at the beginning, in *Studies on Hysteria*, in which he discussed trauma. He didn't really distinguish between external and internal sources of trauma. For instance, the trauma could be that when you were a girl, your brothers threw dead animals at you. Or it could be that you were driving your kids in a wagon and the horses bolted. It could also be that your sister is suddenly on her death bed, and your first thought is "Oh, now I can marry my brother in law." The trauma is whatever it is that we find overwhelming. The source is less important than the process of simply trying to comprehend the sense of being overwhelmed. Of course, that idea went off the rails with the abandonment of the seduction hypothesis. I think this set psychoanalysis in a very bad direction. For a long time, we were dealing exclusively with repression directed against endogenous wishes, so the external trauma was marginalized ideologically. Of course, the pendulum had to eventually swing back, and it did with Ferenczi and Adler to some extent. We've been off in a sort of conceptual and political swamp, because you have to emphasize and come down on one side or the other.

L: Let me ask you pointedly. In today's analytic world, using the word relational in a broad sense, do you think that other schools of analysis pay adequate attention to the character of the family and the parents? Do they pay adequate attention to the analyst as a person, both of which are highlighted by the relational model? Or I should ask, do relationalists pay too much attention to that as another side of it?

J: That's a very good question and one that is almost impossible to answer. I think the relational literature tilts in the direction of "the other," but too much emphasis on one thing or another has always been characteristic of psychoanalytic writing, from the very beginning. There's a tremendous difference between the way cases are written up in literature, and the way analysis is practiced. If you spoke to the most doctrinaire Freudian of the old school, the 50s Freudian, you wouldn't talk to them about a case for very long before they would say, "Well, the father was this kind of guy and the mother was this kind of person," and it would even be hinted at in the case write ups. But when it comes to the more abstract formulation, conversation would always return to the intrapsychic conflict. For a while, you had to do this to get your paper published or to be certified. When Brenner talks about compromise formation, he talks about five components: drive, the defense, anxiety, depressive affect, and calamities of childhood. The calamities of childhood are the events that take place in the family. He said that you aren't likely to cover all five elements when analyzing a compromise formation. Sometimes you emphasize one element rather than another. So, a conversation with your patient in which you emphasize the calamities of childhood might not be so different than the conversation with an emphasis on a different element. But, if you are writing it up, you must present it in the framework of the received theory. I think the same is true for relational. All of us who do the work, who are decent at it, are pretty agile. I think there's a large contrast between the way things are practiced and the way they are written up. In my 2001 paper, I was alarmed, but I think I made it clear that I wasn't talking about the practice so much as about the literature.

L: You don't accept the usual relational critique of classical practice and ideology, that it is always the patient projecting onto the analyst. So, in classical practice it is not so much who the analyst is, but more so how the patient views them. You know the critique that it's about an empty container.

J: That would be true of some of the classical thought. I think that if you read Baranger's work from the 60s, you will notice that they use the idea of asymmetry, similar to you, but in a different manner. They certainly say that the analyst participation is real, but it is very muted. I think that's also true of the more conservative group of contemporary Kleinians and British. But in Latin America, at the same time as the Barangers were writing their version of field theory, Racker said that the greatest myth of the psychoanalytic solution was that it is a relationship between a sick person and a healthy one. So despite the asymmetry, if a session goes dead I'd certainly look at my current participation.

L: That would no longer differentiate the relationalists from everyone else.

J: Absolutely not. But there are subtle differences in how the analyst's participation is seen. I would say if you looked at the contemporary field theorists, the Latin Americans, the Italians, The Italian Bionion . . .

L: Ferro . . .

J: Ferro and Civitarese. That group certainly see the analyst as contributing more to the field than, let's say, Levenson did. Levenson felt that the patient set the tune and the analyst danced to it. There's very little in Levenson about self-disclosure; he notices that he is not himself, but there's nothing very much about what might have contributed to that.

L: Since you mentioned Levenson, I'm tempted to ask you whether he was an influence on you or Steve. If so, to what degree did he influence you two early on?

J: Early on, he was not so much an influence for me personally. I do not recall either one of us being in supervision with him. I think we came to appreciate how much ahead of his time he had been in certain ways. As I look back, however, I think he is an extremely important figure and his ideas were in the air as we were writing and certainly as we were growing analytically. Thus, I would say he influenced us in ways that we were not necessarily aware of at the time.

L: I want to shift our focus back to ego psychology. You made the point several times during our last session that one of the problems was Hartmann's average expectable environment. Can you elaborate on this?

What was it about ego psychology during this period that lent itself to the need for the relational to respond to it? Where did they go wrong?

J: I think the first major place they went wrong in a way that demanded the relational critique was in the idea of the average expectable environment. They knew they had to respond to those who believed that people live in families, that they live in a world in which families influence them. That was very much in the air, really from the time Freud abandoned the seduction hypothesis. And when the émigré analysts came here from Europe and took over American Psychoanalysis, they were very mindful of the need to preserve the explanatory power of the received model. Their problem was determining how to do so, while also acknowledging that there is an environmental influence. The idea of the average expectable environment was one way of doing this. This idea explains that the environment is influential, but outside of the extremes and the overtly traumatic experience, people will abandon their own inner dynamics. This would allow them to shape their own worlds, free from influence. The idea that the world is relatively average and expectable really ducked the question the critique raised, in terms of both analytic and developmental processes. There is a great line from Mahler in the early 40s, which I believe I quoted in the *Object Relations* book, when she talks about a sickly child. She says, "The environment, extremely overanxious, consulted one doctor after another."

(both laugh)

J: Even Mahler couldn't bring herself to say parents or mother. I think that begged for some kind of response.

L: During our last interview, I asked you about your experience with Roy Schafer. I noted that many critics of Ego Psychology were Rapaport's students. They were predominantly psychologists, with Schafer as the outstanding example and Gill as an exception. In some ways, I think ego psychology hasn't received credit for launching the critique.

J: By the 1970s, ego psychology, and more broadly the project of modeling the mind itself had become complex, unwieldy, and far removed from clinical practice; it had reached a dead end. Rapaport had a reputation as something of a taskmaster; it was important for his students to get away from the large shadow that he cast. Steve and I didn't pay too much attention to George Klein's (1975) critique, although I did in *Oedipus and Beyond*, but there's a striking parallel between his view and ours. When he argued that Freud had two, not necessarily compatible theories, he distinguished between metapsychology, which was based in concepts of force and structure, and clinical theory, which was based in the language of meaning. But interestingly, when he talked about Freud's clinical theory, he cited authors such as Fairbairn, who we viewed as offering a radical alternative to Freud.

So, while we shared a sense that things were moving in the direction of relational thinking, George Klein found that thinking in Freud while we found it in the dissents. I imagine this difference was due primarily to the different traditions within which we had been trained.

Schafer (1976) of course didn't go as far as Klein in arguing for this kind of clinical re-focusing. He was interested in recasting the language of psychoanalysis in terms of action, with an emphasis on personal agency; in the 1970s he was still arguing that classical Freudian narratives were the best psychoanalytic ways to understand the human experience. In retrospect, his focus on action did shift things; after all, our actions are directed toward others and we respond to the acts of others. In this connection, there's an interesting Latin American paper written by José Bleger. I believe it was in '67. In the paper, which wasn't translated into English until a couple of years ago, he makes a virtually identical critique of metapsychology to Klein's and Schafer's. His target was meta-psychology; the drive theory essentially.

Where Schafer came up with the action language, Bleger came up with what he called the dramatic point of view, which he believed should replace metapsychology. The similarity between a dramatic point of view and Schafer's action language is clear, although the dramatic point of view is much more inherently interactive and relational than the action language. Schafer wasn't fully ready to separate himself from some of the underlying assumptions of metapsychology and ego psychology. So, although his critique effectively addressed all of the major premises, some of the sensibilities were still there. He remained more of a one-person theorist than Bleger or even Klein.

L: When Mitchell writes about Schafer, he emphasizes the similarity between his critique of ego psychology and Sullivan's. Similarly to Sullivan, Schafer critiques the reifications and the mechanization of ego psychology.

J: Yes, I think that's true as far as it goes. However, what Sullivan put in place was an interpersonal point of view. As Sullivan continues to draw diagrams, they are similar to other pictures of the mind, but the diagram represents a two-person model. He shows an area of anxiety, as well as the manner in which a person interacts with other people's theories of anxiety. He used this as a spring board for his ideas of interpersonal thinking, rather than Schafer's.

L: In the years after Sullivan, is there anyone else in the analytic world similar to him in terms of developing a two-person perspective? Or, is Sullivan in some ways really *sui generis*?

J: Well, Sullivan certainly had great plans to be *sui generis*, and he colored the way the White Institute worked for many years.

L: I want to discuss a paper that you wrote a long time ago, that is very much cited in analytic literature. It was a critique, a re-examination of neutrality (Greenberg, 1986), and the re-definition of neutrality, which you re-worked into the neutrality between being an old and a new object. I want to run something by you and hear your reactions. My view on many dichotomies throughout the history of psychoanalysis is along those lines. There are some analysts who think it is necessary to lean in the direction of being a new object, a good object, and correct the past traumas and errors. However, there's another group in the analytic world who believe, "No, by doing so, you do not give the patient a chance to re-experience the trauma. You need to lean more on the side of being the bad old object who repeats the problem. This way, the patient is allowed the experience of repeating it in a different way." Is neutrality an option, or do we all just have proclivities to lean in one direction or another? Where do you lean?

J: You know, of course, that paper is now 30 years old. It was written in the context of the current time. I can't think of anyone these days who wouldn't agree with that statement about being an old object and a new one. The statement suggests that if you can't be a new object, the analysis will never be underway. I think it's worth noting that I pal around with some pretty old-fashioned types. I don't know anyone who wouldn't say, "Well I've certainly softened up over the years. I'm certainly more gentle, and not as austere." So, I think the battle is over to some extent. If your target adversary is the group of ego psychologists in the 50s, I cannot think of any who are still around today.

L: But doesn't this still shed light on the distinction between schools? The self-psychologists certainly lean in the direction of the leading edge; the new object. The Kleinians lean in the direction of the old object transference, or being the traumatizing object.

J: Yes, I think there are certainly people who are more comfortable in one place or another. There are people who consciously position themselves as good objects, whether it is a self-psychologist or a relational analyst. But these days, it is not exclusive to people who identify with one specific theoretical point of view. I recently went to a discussion of a clinical presentation, and it was difficult to determine how the speaker would have defined herself. She was certainly from a classical institute, but she was clearly working hard to position herself as a good object in contradistinction to a bad object, which she believed populated the patient's history. Personally, I would like to think that I am pretty comfortable welcoming negative transference, and I think that's important.

L: Maybe in a way that contemporary relational theory leans away from . . .

J: Again there's the distinction between what has been written versus what has been practiced. So, I have to preface that exactly by saying again, I think there's an inclination or tilt in the literature, suggesting that it's important that we be experienced as good and new objects.

L: This relates to my recent book. This year, I've been doing a lot of work on Harold Searles. I've been looking at his world and life in depth, working with his family, and studying manuscripts and videotapes. I mention him, because he repeatedly said that when people would watch his interviews, they thought he was both crazy and sadistic.

His counterclaim was that analysts were so desperate to be liked (1965, 1979). They strove to be viewed in a nice, caring and helpful manner – in a benevolent position. He tries to demonstrate the other side of this, being the bad, traumatizing, even inhumane monster. He feels that the patient experiences their parents in those ways. Without providing this source, the patient will never learn to deal with their inner turmoil. Thus, the analyst needs to fill that role. Reading about him has spurred my thoughts about this. I think I've learned a lot from him, particularly about tolerating the inhumane parts of myself.

J: I think Winnicott (1949) is very insightful on this subject. I think it's fair to say his position is, "Whether we want to be bad objects or not, we are: we end the session, we go on vacations, and we say no to the patients in a variety of ways all the time." He was very clear about that. It's interesting, because he is often quoted on the other side of this, which is really a partial understanding of his idea. So in my view we don't have to go out of our way to be bad objects. My interpretation of the question is – Can we find the part of who we are through our patient's experience, or do we in some way collude with them to deny? I think Winnicott is fairly clear that not just limits, but also sadism and hatred, are involved in maintaining the frame. At the same time, we create a holding environment.

L: I'm thinking of my last questions for you, as we wrap this interview up. What do you find most exciting on the horizon? What are you hopeful or excited about in the field?

J: For close to eight or nine years, I've been involved in the developing international conversations in the field. It is interesting to observe the mix of what is shared and what separates us, while trying to explore the implications of this. It resonates in my mind on a couple different levels. What about psychoanalysis is universal and generalizable, and what is local? Another noteworthy observation is that a lot of people are arriving at similar destinations via very different routes. This raises the question: Are we arriving, or are we at the same destination? How are we different? How does an Italian Bionian field theorist differ from a relational analyst? What can these conversations help us learn? This is certainly one area about which I'm quite excited. I tend to gravitate towards topics that focus on unpacking our clinical work. This is an affirmative way of saying that I'm not so excited by neuropsychoanalysis, or infant research, but I'm rather more intrigued by methods we use to work with patients, as well as the conversations surrounding this topic.

L: Do you think there is a method that is most effective to do so? Do you think the best research will come from a more rigorous method?

J: I'm not sure if I would use the word rigorous, at least not in the sense that it's usually used. I think what I find to be the most generative is the data that comes from our work, as opposed to neuroimaging or baby watching. I think there's a lot that's very exciting about the process of finding more about what we think and who we are in the psychoanalytic situation. This might involve questioning ourselves and wondering, "Why did I say that? Why did I do that? Why didn't I pick up on that one?"

L: Does that seem new or different from the way in which traditional analysts were reflective and thoughtful? What makes this different?

J: I think it's different, because we're talking to people from a wider range of traditions.

L: So, you actually see the pluralism of contemporary psychoanalysis as a potential great advantage?

J: Yes, that's what I had forgotten to say, since the question seemed to be more aimed at the scientific aspect. In this regard, I do not think there have to be convergences and in some ways I hope not.

L: There are some people in the field, like Paul Stepansky (2009), who feel that all the pluralism is a sign of deterioration of the field. They believe pluralism reflects negative splintering. However, others view the pluralism, or multiplicity, as a positive thing. They view it as a sign that we're thriving. It sounds like you are on that side.

J: It's hard to make a case that we are thriving in certain respects, but pluralism is healthy from an intellectual point of view. It creates a cacophony of conversations. There are some people who are more likely to take on the role of a good object, some people more likely to allow, and some who even take on or encourage the role of the bad object. There are different kinds of people involved in the field as well as different fundamental assumptions that go into the work.

L: That's your 1995 paper on the interactive matrix.

J: Yes, exactly. I think we all have the potential to contribute.

L: It's funny that we are ending on the subject of the interactive matrix paper. I have to tell you that it's one of the most important papers I've read in my life. Many of your papers are very important, but I find this one particularly so.

J: Well thank you.

L: Thank you for the interview.

J: I appreciate it, I appreciate the interview.

References

Baranger, M. & Baranger, W. (2008). The Analytic Situation as a Dynamic Field. *Int. J. Psycho-Anal.*, 89, 4:795–826.

Greenberg, J. R. (1981). Prescription or Description: The Therapeutic Action of Psychoanalysis. *Contemp. Psychoanal.*, 17:239–257

——, (1986). The Problem of Analytic Neutrality. *Contemp. Psychoanal.*, 22:76–86.

——, (1991). *Oedipus and Beyond: A Clinical Theory*. Cambridge, MA: Harvard University Press.

——, (1995). Psychoanalytic Technique and The Interactive Matrix. *Psychoanal. Q.*, 64:1–22

——, (2001). The Analyst's Participation. *J. Amer. Psychoanal. Assn.*, 49:359–381

Greenberg, J. & Mitchell, S. (1983). *Object Regions in Psychoanalytic Theory*. Cambridge, MA: Harvard University Press.

Klein, G. S. (1975). *Psychoanalytic Theory: An Exploration of Essentials*. New York: International Universities Press.

Mitchell, S. (1988). *Relational Concepts in Psychoanalysis*. Cambridge, MA: Harvard University Press.

Mitchell, S. A. (1999). Reply to Richards. *The Round Robin, Newsletter of Section I, Division 39, American Psychological Association*, Winter, 1999, 14, 1:10–14.

Mitchell, S. A. (2002). Fairbairn and the problem of agency. In: F. Pereira and D. E. Scharff (Eds.) *Fairbairn and Relational Theory*. London: Karnac, pp. 212–230.

Schafer, R. (1976). *A New Language for Psychoanalysis*. New Haven, CT and London: Yale University Press.

Searles, H. (1965) *Collected Papers on Schizophrenia and Related Subjects*, New York: International Universities Press.

Searles, H. F. (1979). *Countertransference and Related Subjects-Selected Papers*. New York: International Universities Press.

Stepansky, P. E. (2009). *Psychoanalysis at the Margins*. New York: Other Press.

Winnicott, D. W. (1949). Hate in the Counter-Transference. *Int. J. Psycho-Anal.*, 30:69–74.

Chapter 3

Relational psychoanalysis and its discontents

Emanuel Berman

I was intrigued to hear of the plan to publish this book, as it reverberated with an old concern of mine. Psychoanalysts are often critical, and their criticism is the sharpest and most elaborate when discussing the work of other analysts who identify with a different school of psychoanalytic thought and practice. Of course, I have also experienced the pleasure of exposing the weaknesses of an approach I disagree with. With the years I reached the conclusion, however, that such polemics do not contribute a lot, especially when it comes to clinical practice. After all, if I have basic disagreements with – let us say – Melanie Klein's method of conducting analysis, this means that its impact on the way I treat my patients is not great; so exploring its shortcomings is not going to make me into a better analyst. On the other hand, exploring the problematic sides of theorists who I do feel more deeply influenced by – in my case, for example, Ferenczi or Winnicott – may be much more relevant for improving my own clinical skills (Berman, 2017).

So it seems to me an important challenge to develop a critical view of relational psychoanalysis, which has influenced me considerably for many decades. Although my studies at the NYU Postdoctoral Program (1972–1976) took place before the concept "relational" came into being, many of the courses I took in the tracks existing then lay the foundations for an analytic world view emphasizing relationships; my three supervisors (Mannie Ghent who belonged at that time to the Interpersonal-Humanistic track, and Ruth Jean Eisenbud and Mark Grunes who belonged to the Freudian track) all emphasized object relations and transference-counter-transference issues; and my simultaneous studies of family therapy at the

Albert Einstein College of Medicine also sensitized me to the subtlety of interpersonal interaction.

My subsequent training at the Israel Psychoanalytic Institute, while exposing me to more classical views, also expanded my knowledge of British object relations models and of Self Psychology, and my theoretical emphases further crystallized (Berman, 2010).

No wonder, therefore, that when invited by Ghent – who became my close friend – to join the faculty of the newly formed Relational Orientation at NYU (in which I started teaching during my 1986–1987 sabbatical), I gladly accepted. Subsequently I joined the editorial board of *Psychoanalytic Dialogues*, worked with Steve Mitchell and afterwards with Lewis Aron on planning my book on training (Berman, 2004a), and during my 2000 sabbatical (shortly before Steve's untimely death) became enthusiastically involved with the founding of the International Association for Relational Psychoanalysis and Psychotherapy (IARPP) and served on its first board.

Still, I always had some concerns. One episode in 2000 stuck in my mind. One of my tasks was recruiting non-US analysts to serve on the IARPP council, to give more substance to its international nature. I proposed a prominent analyst whose work, in my view, was quite close to the relational spirit, even though he belonged to a classically oriented IPA society. I was quite upset when an objection was raised to inviting that colleague, because "he believes in drives". Steve and Mannie supported my proposal, and that analyst was indeed invited, but I became sensitized to the danger that the relational movement may develop its own orthodoxy and its own criteria as to "who really belongs".[1]

These concerns were later expressed by me in writing:

> The relational tradition . . . is not immune from some of the risks of 'party lines' and 'school loyalties' . . . Although relational psychoanalysis now has its journals, its organizations, and its conferences, I still hope it will not evolve into a school in the traditional sense but, rather, will help to mold a professional and intellectual climate free of the constraining impact of 'schools' . . . 'schools' have made positive contributions, by allowing a multiplicity of voices, safeguarding against a repressive global uniformity, and offering analysts a friendly, facilitating environment of like-minded colleagues. Yet,

at the same time, these schools have produced inbred groups whose members espouse a single point of view (often that of a particular founding father or mother), created their own vocabulary, read mostly their own journals, and have become involved mostly in their own training programs.

(Berman, 2004a, pp. 6–7)

Another way to formulate my thinking about psychoanalytic schools is that they originate from an understandable wish of many analysts to find a theoretical home, but easily degenerate into theoretical fortresses, surrounded by impenetrable walls blocking real communication between "us" and "them", which are often designated as "true psychoanalysis" vs. "false psychoanalysis", or else "dated analysis" vs. "up-to-date analysis".

If I were to evaluate the situation at present, my feeling is that the relational movement managed on the whole to remain pluralistic and open-minded, but my concerns were not completely unfounded. I feel that from the beginning relational authors wavered between inclusive and exclusionary trends. The wish to guarantee the survival of innovative ideas in a climate dominated by more traditional views (in the U.S. during the 1980s mostly Freud seen through an Ego Psychology prism) led to a polemical style which at times simplified classical models in order to emphasize their shortcomings and make a case for a necessary revolution. At the same time, Mitchell and many of his collaborators did acknowledge a multiplicity of useful ideas stemming from numerous theoretical traditions, and this was clearly expressed in the title *Psychoanalytic Dialogues* and in the subtitle referring to "relational perspectives" in the plural.

Let me give a simple example of the wavering between exclusion and inclusion. Aron (1996), in his groundbreaking *A Meeting of Minds* (which I got to know very well by recently editing its Hebrew edition), emphasized that Freudian interactionists are *not* relational analysts. One of his examples of Freudian interactionists was Ted Jacobs, though he placed Jacobs and McLaughlin "toward the more radical pole of the Freudian interactionists" (p. 200). Nine years later Aron and Harris (2005) invited Jacobs to contribute to volume 2 of the "Relational Psychoanalysis" series, where (in my personal view) he fit quite well. Indeed, the description of the Relational Perspectives series in the Routledge website states:

We refer to the relational tradition, rather than to a relational school, to highlight that we are identifying a trend, a tendency within contemporary psychoanalysis, not a more formally organized or coherent school or system of beliefs. Our use of the term relational signifies a dimension of theory and practice that has become salient across the wide spectrum of contemporary psychoanalysis.

The issue of "who really belongs" led to a crisis in *Psychoanalytic Dialogues* in 1996. A paper submitted by a British Independent author, Paul Williams, was initially turned down, after some of the editors viewed it as insufficiently suitable for a relational journal. Christopher Bollas, who had been a member of the Editorial Board since the journal was established in 1991, resigned in protest. The paper was eventually published and thoroughly discussed (Williams, 1998), but Bollas remained critical of the relational approach. Williams became Joint Editor-in-chief (with Glen Gabbard) of the *International Journal of Psychoanalysis* between 2001–2007, and is an Associate Editor of *Psychoanalytic Dialogues* since 2006.

The more exclusionary direction was expressed at times in polemical debates with a message of "no one else can offer what we have to offer". This tone was probably adopted in response to equally exclusionary attacks against relational views from the more classical establishment (and at times from traditional interpersonal circles as well). Both sides used at times symbols of belonging; for example, whereas some classical authors would claim that an analyst not using the couch is not a real analyst, in a recent IARPP internet colloquium a participant claimed that a relational approach should negate the use of the couch. (I think both positions are dogmatic and absurd; the couch can contribute to a richer intrapsychic and intersubjective exploration in some dyads [Ogden, 1996], and may block it in other cases; its use or avoidance should be a matter of clinical judgment).

I suspect that the sharper splitting between theoretical models was strengthened by concurrent institutional rivalries; as we know, relational trends flourished within Division 39 of the American Psychological Association (many of whose members were barred for decades from joining the IPA because of the fanatical medical domination of the U.S. psychoanalytic establishment), and at the independent NYU Postdoctoral Program; whereas most institutes and societies of the IPA-affiliated American

Psychoanalytic Association historically emphasized classical, ego psychological (and more recently also Kleinian) views.

This organizational division markedly differs from the situation in Israel, for example, where many relational analysts belong to the IPA-affiliated Israel Psychoanalytic Society, and maintain a daily dialogue (stormy at times, friendly at other times) with colleagues who are more influenced by Freud, Klein, Bion and so on. Moreover, in the Israeli analytic scene the sharpest divisions seem to be between followers of Klein and of Kohut, whereas relational analysts at times represent a "middle group", acknowledging a broader spectrum of influences (Berman, 2014).

In the newer (non-IPA) Tel Aviv Institute of Contemporary Psychoanalysis one may also find colleagues with classical and Kleinian views, others more invested in the heritage of Winnicott and Kohut, and also analysts with relational views – the differences between the two competing organizations are more marked in their organizational structure (the IPS is more traditional, in TAICP trainees are listed as members and participate in committees) rather than in theoretical views, which are heterogeneous in both (Berman, 2004a).[2] I suspect that my own viewpoint, which emphasizes the development of relational aspects and intersubjective nuances in many psychoanalytic traditions throughout the years, seeking common elements rather than sharp contradictions, is influenced by this pluralistic organizational structure in which I function daily, and by feeling identified with both the IPA and the IARPP.

Belonging to both organizations made me aware of certain paradoxes. The IPA had a long tradition of strong authority; Ernest Jones served as its president between 1920–1924 and again between 1934–1948. Since the late 1950s, however, all IPA presidents serve for four years and then step down and are no longer part of its administration. The same rule of rotation applies to all office holders and board members of the IPA. On the other hand, several board members of the IARPP have served on the board continuously since its establishment in 2000 till now. In other words, the "anti-establishment" may become more of an actual establishment than "the establishment". Sociologists call this a process of institutionalization.

Finally, let me return to the issue of clinical usefulness, with which I started. Overall, I feel that the relational components in my clinical work serve me well in most analyses and psychotherapies. But with closer scrutiny I can notice instances in which the same components did not work so well. One example that illustrates such a risk is a case I presented at the IARPP conference in Los Angeles (Berman, 2004b), under the title "Fear of relating". The following case material originates from that unpublished presentation.

A few weeks after the beginning of his analysis, Ofer expressed his disappointment that he does not know me at all. When I suggested that he may have some observations and impressions, he denied that. I reminded him of some impressions he reported a week earlier, when he accidentally saw me in the street – I appeared to walk fast and be preoccupied – but it turned out he forgot that incident. He said that he actually doesn't want to know too much about me, as I should remain above him. Moreover, my own personality and private life are none of his business, being unrelated to my function as his analyst: "what difference does it make if you like your eggs sunny-side-up, or scrambled?" I pointed to his conflict about seeing me and getting to know me, and suggested that not seeing too much and not knowing too much were survival tactics developed in his childhood, when some things he saw were too painful.

In the following session he arrived five minutes late, and hesitated if he should tell me why – he actually went swimming. Maybe telling me is unneeded, apologetic? – it's his time, and it won't interest me how he spends it. I said that he perceived me as either critical or as indifferent, but not as curious or as attentive to him. He confirmed that such options didn't even occur to him. My talk of analysis as a partnership, he added, made him anxious. He wanted me wise and knowledgeable, so I could reach his unconscious, which is hidden behind a wall that must be broken.

I said that my image was more of a hedge, in which one can push some branches aside and see through. This reminded him of the hedge that actually surrounded his childhood home, and of peeking into a striptease show in a nightclub as a child. When I connected these associations to his curiosity about me, he said it was true – he was curious, for example, about what I did in the second room adjacent to my consulting room – but he often forgot this curiosity.

In our subsequent meeting he reported that the discussion was upsetting, he became fearful that he was in conflict with me, that our harmony was destroyed, and if so our work together was doomed. In his more harmonious professional relationships, he explained, he suppresses any criticism he might have, feeling that if it were expressed all would be destroyed.

Conflicts are lethal – he never experienced resolving a conflict in a way that increased closeness.

As that analysis went on, it became clear to me that attempting a fuller intersubjective exploration would be premature. Unlike some other analyses, I could not utilize my countertransference and complementary identifications much, or experiment with self disclosure (Berman, 2001), until a much later stage. In the first few years of Ofer's analysis I found myself "less relational". To some degree the early stage of this analysis brought to my mind:

> . . . instances of severely traumatized individuals, who are so painfully involved in fighting for their lives that their object relations are severely impoverished. In such cases, it is possible that a longer period of staying inside the (joint) cocoon is crucial, requiring the analyst's tolerance for the analysand's avoidance of the other – that is, avoidance both of outside figures as meaningful others, and of the analyst as an other. This may lead to a purer 'mirror transference' of the kind Kohut described, or to a use of the analyst mostly 'as a provider of time and of milieu'.
>
> (Berman, 2001, p. 60)

A case where I came to realize that my rather uninhibited relational style may backfire was that of a woman analysand, Maya, whose family history included painful early losses. Having myself lost my mother at age seven, this background aroused intense identification in me. When the news came one day that another member of her family was diagnosed with a terminal illness, Maya was in great pain, and at the end of the session I spontaneously hugged her. I knew that for me this was not a seductive act at all, and was reassured by Ferenczi's (1932) and by McLaughlin's (1995) thinking that such physical expressions of compassion may be important.

I was surprised and saddened when Maya told me subsequently that she did experience my embrace as erotic, and it embarrassed her. I thanked her for sharing this feeling openly, and after further exploration avoided any physical gestures with her. This experience helped me to understand that Ferenczi was naïve when he assumed that physical closeness seen by him as fatherly and non-sexual was necessarily experienced the same way by his patients.

Whereas the two analyses I mentioned were overall successful, my final example comes from an analysis interrupted one-sidedly by the patient, and experienced by me as a failure. Here is an abridged version of my case study (Berman, 2002), emphasizing the way in which my relational approach may have contributed to this disappointing outcome.

In the second session Alice lay on the couch, telling me how conflicted she became about it. I had mentioned it is customary to start with a few sessions face to face, and although I left her the choice, she feared I would be mad at her if she lay down too soon. I commented that she was not sure I was honest with her about my feelings, and she said that if it was just my personal wish, it did not belong. (Now I realize how early she expressed the need to keep my personal feelings out of the analysis). Her associations went to her mother's violent outbursts, which used to calm down instantly if an outsider rang their doorbell, because facades were very important in their family. I interpreted how little space was left in-between the outbursts and the facades. (What I better understand in retrospect is her wish for an impersonal analyst, related to how frightening her mother was when "being personal").

Several stories about various relationships – past and present – made me reflect that she fluctuated between rage at the other and total identification with the other, with difficulty in integrating these phases. She opened the following session by saying I had spoken too much and had left her confused. When I responded by saying that apparently my pace had been too fast for her, she was surprised, being sure I would tell her she was resisting the analysis. I noted her expectation that I'd require an adjustment to myself, rather than striving to adjust to her. She then spoke of her fear of insulting me, as she insults mother when constantly telling her that all she gives her never fits. (In retrospect, was I busy reassuring her I was not insulted, and missed the ominous signs that eventually she would tell me, too, that all I give her doesn't fit?). Subsequently, she connected her unease about my taking responsibility for confusing her with her need for me to be perfect.

A meeting outside my office with another analysand, whom she knew, was experienced by Alice as painful. She spoke of an envelope that broke down, introducing foreign experiences: a fear of boring me, a need to impress me. I raised the question whether these new experiences were really foreign, or perhaps were present all along but cast aside. My question aroused shame and sadness: how could she be so dumb, denying these feelings? I commented that first she perfectionistically attempted to avoid "dirty" and petty feelings, and when they came to the surface she perfectionistically scolded herself for daring to deny them.

Her associations led to a childhood event: she made noise and a neighbor threatened to tell her parents; she said she didn't mind, they would not punish her; then her mother came out and contradicted her. She felt horribly shamed, "caught with her panties down". When I said she chose a metaphor of sexual humiliation, she was taken aback, but then agreed. I emphasized her pain that her mother spoiled her confidence that they were on her side. She said that with many people she is not sure, and agreed with me when I added there is a part of her which is not on her side, and I had a feeling that if I were to be too much on her side, she may turn against me.

Shortly afterwards she started a session announcing she had complaints: I don't focus on her resistance, I let things go; am I weak like her father? I noted that she appeared to assume that she was only trying to evade things, and only I could make her look at them; perhaps, I wondered, she was conflicted herself between wishing to see and wishing to avoid? She responded saying she needs me to be up, and herself to be down; I must be in a tall watch-tower, from which everything can be observed, even if this implies that the territory is fenced up. (In retrospect, this was a clear early expression of a value conflict between us – I have been always critical of hierarchical structures [Berman, 1998, 2000, 2004a] – and it could have alerted me to the danger that I may have been trying to make her accept my egalitarian values, lacking empathy for her deep need for a powerful guardian; one may wonder whether a relational approach may confound authority and authoritarianism?)

Other themes that came up during that period were her fear of being flooded if she knew too much about me; her turning me in her mind into a severe judge, rather than an ally; the way analysis quickly shifted for her from a choice into a chore, as happens to her often; and associations to her father as disconnected, confused, untrustworthy as a protector. Still she listed me as one of the good fathers she was able to find in her life.

Later on, however, she expressed humiliation at "having to buy empathy from me". When she brought up intense feelings of envy, and I wondered about their relevance to us, she said she didn't envy me, because all I had could contribute to her; but envy may still appear later on. She was hurt that I did not congratulate her on a professional achievement, but had a hard time expressing her disappointment, being fearful I'd experience it as burdensome demandingness. In the following session she said she was reluctant to come, because my acceptance of her disappointment made her feel close to me. Exposing her neediness, she said, was so embarrassing. She wanted someone who could meet her needs accurately, Alice continued the following time; explanations or subsequent corrections were no good.

On one occasion, she asked to shift a particular session to an earlier time, but then failed to show up. It crossed my mind she may have forgotten the change, and may show up at her regular hour, which I had already filled. I therefore called her, and it turned out she had indeed forgotten. A week later, she brought up my call as a confusing boundary violation, "bursting the bubble". She would have preferred to come at the usual time and be sent away, she said; my call strengthened her guilt for forgetting. She needs the analysis to be conducted in sterile conditions, she added. (I made an effort to be empathic with her need, but in retrospect I see that her reaction irritated me. Having to send her away when she comes would have been most unpleasant for me, and I experienced her preference as both masochistic and coercive, trying to turn me into a rigidly formal person, which I never wished to become). Later on she said it was a relief that I wasn't intimidated by her anger, and did not surrender to her pressure.

When I spoke about moments in which I hurt her inadvertently, and my need to know about it so I understand better her experience and take it into account, she interpreted me as saying she was problematic and in need of special consideration. She would have preferred an analyst who could foresee her sensitivities, while seeing them as universal, not as unique to her. I interpreted her repeated fear of being scolded for her sensitivity and neediness. Alice started weeping, saying it was so difficult to cry while lying down, so painful to consider that being humiliated may have been her fantasy (and not my intention).

The following time she described a difficulty to come; we became close, and my empathy aroused erotic feelings in her, she explained. In general, she found sexual themes quite embarrassing to discuss with me. Her ambivalent attitude towards male sexuality came up very hesitantly, later on, and she laughed and agreed when I said that she responds to my encouragement to discuss sexuality as a threatening masculine penetration in itself, or as a form of voyeurism.

Once more, Alice expressed disappointment: the benefits of analysis are not clear, she hasn't changed much. She brought up again fears of boring me, relating them to her parents' impatience, their self-absorbed difficulty to listen to her. She also mentioned things she had to discover for herself as a child due to her parents' neglect; for example she learned from reading a book of fiction that it's good to wash every day. I related this to her difficulty to internalize anything from relationships, including the one with me. I mentioned her preference to come at the wrong time and discover on her own that she had forgotten the change, rather than get a phone call from me. Alice added that at some times her parents were intrusive as well. (While I consciously felt empathic with her, in retrospect I notice an aggressive element in my interpretation, as if I were telling her, "you see, it's your problem after all"; and her response can be understood in this context to mean, "you may not be neglectful like my parents were, but you do remind me of them in your intrusiveness".)

In the following session she said she had felt remote when we had discussed her determined self-sufficiency. I suggested that she was quite conflicted about achieving greater intimacy with people, and she said forcefully that she doesn't want to be helpless and dependent. (Again, I notice now how fearful she was about some goals that I consider central in analysis, such as a better capacity for intimacy).

Alice recalled moments in which she had felt hurt or misunderstood by me. My repeated emphasis on analysis as a continuous process of disappointments and reparations was difficult for her, she added, because of her wish for a perfect, omniscient analyst, and because of her doubt that I could care about her at all. (Here she really disarmed me, I notice now: I feel that caring and a capacity for reparation are among my best qualities as an analyst, while various shortcomings I am aware of would stop me from making any claim for perfection . . .) Later on I brought up her constant fear of the analysis unsettling her long-established survival strategies, which she had experienced as vital when growing up; she felt this was indeed so.

I also pointed out passive aggressive elements in her way of dealing with me, the combination of feeling weak, "playing dumb" at times, watching to see if I'd notice things – coming late and testing me, will I respond, for example – while inwardly knowing exactly what I should have done. (This interpretation, I see now, also expressed my frustration and anger at her growing criticism; I described the pattern accurately, but I was not empathic to its possible sources, such as distrust that I would really take care of her, leading her to secretly take control, in spite of her yearning to be childlike and passive and allow me to raise her).

There were many tensions with her parents, and Alice insisted that her refusal to contain their madness is what allows her to maintain her own sanity. She mentioned her feeling that her parents drive her crazy by denying things she perceives.

Eventually Alice expressed her wishes to leave analysis, listing numerous disappointments with my being, in her experience, either too rigid or too weak. I shared with her my feeling that my own needs indeed may have influenced me in ways that became confusing for her, but in addition I may have been responding to unresolved conflicts of hers – her rage at my rigidity, her fear and guilt vis-a-vis my flexibility/weakness – which combine to create a situation of "damned if you do and damned if you don't". Understanding this cycle, I suggested, may be a crucial part of our analytic work. To this she reacted by saying that she didn't wish to treat me so that I could treat her.

Alice added that I seemed enamored of my flexibility, that she was afraid that I was more invested in my ideological "baby" than in her needs as a baby. This was damaging to her basic needs, so the issue was not individual fine tuning, as I believed.

We continued the dialogue, with her elaborating her fear that I work with her as a parent/friend dealing with an adolescent, while she experiences herself as much smaller; and my sense that she was fearful I would reject her if she failed the role I offered her, and expressed her more infantile needs. I suggested that we had reached a most crucial stage in the analysis, in which the rage and bitterness she used to describe in other relationships actually became experienced in the room, and though this was enormously painful, it could also become a springboard for deeper work, and eventually for change. She said she was happy we finally saw things eye to eye, but soon also expressed annoyance that I offered hope while she was enraged.

Shortly afterwards Alice decided to terminate, and suggested we meet one more time. I interpreted that she was afraid to stay in the room with me, after being aggressive towards me, and she confirmed this. After some discussion she accepted my preference to meet for two more months.

In childhood, she recalled, father's "rigid" compulsive rules saved her from chaos. In this context, she experienced my insistence on a termination period as helpful.

Among the themes that came up during the termination process were her tendency to devalue the other, and to disconnect inwardly, in order to make separations possible; her need to depart triumphantly, while actually feeling small inside; her reluctance to acknowledge her mother's craziness because this meant giving mother "allowances", and her fear that when I tried to show her how she often provoked her mother to re-traumatize her, this implied justifying mother, or else – once more asking her to be grown up, as daddy always did, and "understand" that mom is so vulnerable.

In one of the most moving sessions of that period, Alice spoke of her mother, who for years had been practically absent from family life because of her professional aspirations, until she suddenly "returned home" due to a physical and emotional breakdown. Mother wanted then to become close again to Alice, but Alice couldn't meet this need, having given up on mother, unable to forgive her betrayal. I related her pain during her mother's absence to her fear that I was more committed to my professional values than to her "baby" needs; and her reluctance to become newly involved with mother to her disbelief in reparation between me and her, possibly colored by a suspicion that I was still motivated by my own needs, maybe protecting my self-image and reputation.

Following that session, Alice said I had touched her the way she needed, and paradoxically this made it easier to leave, knowing that she did get something here, and better understandood what went wrong. But she felt more invested in a potential new analysis in the future; reparation, she commented, carries with it the rupture. I spoke of her fantasy wish for a relationship with no ruptures. We parted in a guardedly friendly manner.

I can well imagine analyzing this failure with an emphasis on Alice's pathology. It would not be completely wrong. I could also well imagine analyzing it in terms of the shortcomings of my analytic technique. But both of these directions seem to me insufficient. I prefer to view the failure of my work with Alice neither as her personal failure, nor as my own (personal or theoretical) failure, but as *a failure of the two of us as a team, based on a transference/countertransference entanglement which we did not manage to disentangle early enough.*

Paradoxically, a relational perspective is helpful now in my attempt to decipher in retrospect what was the difficulty, even if the same perspective may have played a part in creating the difficulty in the first place. Some of my belated insights are quite personal and unique to me but it is possible that tracing the emotional sources of my insistence on some relational ideals (Slochower, 2017) may contribute to the understanding of "relational countertransference patterns" which are more general.

What was my countertransference in this analysis? I was quite fond of Alice all along, even though at times I felt hurt by her or mad at her. Still, from an early stage on I experienced us as enormously different individuals. I had reasons to identify with some of Alice's biographical background, but our solutions to our childhood traumata were almost opposite. I suspect this variance took its toll on my empathic attunement with her.

To give one example: like Alice, I also grew up with a very disturbed parent, my stepmother. My father also frequently begged of me to understand her vulnerability and forgive her excesses. However, unlike Alice, what in my experience helped me keep my sanity was accepting his wish, rarely confronting my stepmother, disidentifying with her by fully acknowledging her craziness, and learning to avoid painful clashes by understanding and predicting her behavior. I assume this was easier for me because she was not my biological mother, and I had an internalized sane mother to hold on to.

Another major difference between Alice's childhood and my own was that in my family, unlike in hers, the compulsive parent – in terms of demands for "law and order" – was also the crazier one, while my father was generally quite permissive. It is not surprising that Alice identifies strict authority with sanity, while for me it is usually something negative. My father did treat me as a grown up from early on, and unlike Alice I liked this attitude very much, and it must have contributed to my rebelliousness whenever I later felt infantilized (in school, in the army, or during my analytic training; Berman, 1998, 2004a, 2010, 2013).

I now realize, that when I offered her an "adult to adult" contact in some situations, in my mind it brought up a supportive father respectful of me, and in her mind a disappointing father, not allowing her to remain a child, and trying to mobilize her to forgive her destructive mother, with whom he was deeply aligned. On the other hand, my expressing personal feelings at some points made me identified in her mind with her mother's lack of boundaries, and both these transferential connotations were negative.

Alice was right in sensing my commitment to certain values, to my "ideological babies". Being involved in the development of relational and intersubjective models in psychoanalysis has been a source of excitement for me. On the other hand, she was wrong in her fear that I cared less about her personally. A more accurate formulation would be to say that my commitment to egalitarian relational models (which, as must be evident, has early personal sources in my life), as well as my own excitement about openness and intimacy, may have made me too confident that my caring for her would be best expressed through helping her to reduce her rigidity and need for control, to become less dominated by her punitive superego, and to allow herself a freer personal and intimate involvement, with me and with others.

In this respect, I may have tried to mold our analytic goals in my own direction, not sufficiently taking to heart her protests that these are not her own goals (Berman, 2001). A power struggle evolved between us, each of us forcefully attempting to bring the other to a particular emotional position. Alice, in some ways, "became the crazy mother" in the transference, but I couldn't stay with her in that regressive world patiently enough, and found myself searching my way out, offering her my own solutions, which she couldn't use.

Alice correctly perceived my reluctance to assume the role of a perfectly containing guardian, of an ideal father/mother, for which she yearned. My personal history, culminating in adopting a relational approach, may have made me suspect that being an authority figure will lead to an authoritarian position; we may tend to idealize the "not knowing" position, and pay insufficient theoretical attention to the crucial difference between authority and authoritarianism. On this background I may have blocked an idealizing transference which could have been helpful in her analysis at that developmental stage.

It is true that Alice also often undermined and sabotaged my authority; but I may have overreacted to these aggressive sides, losing contact with the desperately needy regressive wishes clouded by them. We locked each other out.

I feel considerably responsible for the development of this process, though Alice's distrust of interpersonal negotiation and of reparation also played an important role in our inability to eventually put our budding awareness of this transference/countertransference entanglement to constructive analytic use, and to reach a different phase in our joint endeavor (Berman, 2002, pp. 272–287).

I believe that relational psychoanalysis creates unique risks for the analytic or therapeutic process, just as a classical, Kleinian or Kohutian analysis create different sets of risks; such risks may be expressed through a generalized countertransference pattern, which each theoretical viewpoint may encourage and legitimize, relating to patients in general rather than to the unique personality of an individual patient. These patterns may relate to the analyst's initial fantasies about analytic work, which may have played a role both in choosing our profession and in feeling attracted to a particular theoretical model.

Among the specific risks of a relational approach (some of which are expressed or implied in my three case examples) are the danger that an emphasis on intersubjectivity and interaction may be premature for a particular highly defended or regressed patient, and may be experienced as intrusive and as narcissistically motivated; the danger that an image of analyst and analysand as mutually involved adults may block or cloud more regressive needs of the patient, whereas the egalitarian relational ideal may deprive a patient of experiencing the analyst as a strong dependable authority; and the dangers that the analyst's personal involvement and openness may be experienced as flooding or as seductive, self-disclosure may be felt to be exhibitionistic or as requiring of the patient to be the analyst's therapist, and the analyst's willingness to acknowledge and explore errors may be seen as a sign of weakness, as a way to rationalize empathic failures, or as a subtle method of avoiding the patient's anger.

Notes

1   So I was not completely surprised when, after my book on training appeared in the Relational Perspectives series, one of the reviewers in *Psychoanalytic Dialogues* commented: "Although Berman maintains that the outlook on the problems and solutions he is offering is a 'relational' one, I was not persuaded that he made that case" (Slavin, 2007, p 604).

2   This heterogeneity naturally has its drawbacks, too, which can be seen as "the perils of diversity" (Berman, 2003, 2004a, 2014).

References

Aron, L. (1996). *A Meeting of Minds: Mutuality in Psychoanalysis*. Hillsdale, NJ: Analytic Press.

Aron, L. and A. Harris (eds.). *Relational Psychoanalysis, v. 2: Innovation and Expansion*. Hillsdale, NJ: Analytic Press.

Balint, M. (1969). *The Basic Fault: Therapeutic Aspects of Regression*. London: Tavistock.

Berman, E. (1998). Structure and individuality in psychoanalytic training: The Israeli controversial discussions. *American Journal of Psychoanalysis*, 58, 117–133.

Berman, E. (2000). The utopian fantasy of a New Person and the danger of a false analytic self. *Psychoanalytic Psychology*, 17, 38–60.

Berman, E. (2001). Psychoanalysis and life. *Psychoanalytic Quarterly*, 70, 35–65.

Berman, E. (2002). Others' failures – and one's own. In J. Reppen and M. A. Schulman (eds.). *Failures in Psychoanalytic Treatment*. Madison, CT: IUP.

Berman, E. (2003). Contribution to a panel: The future of psychoanalytic training. *Psychoanalytic Dialogues*, 13, 419–427 & 445–449.

Berman, E. (2004a). *Impossible Training: A Relational View of Psychoanalytic Education*. Hillsdale, NJ: Analytic Press.

Berman, E. (2004b). *Fear of relating*. Paper presented at IARPP conference, Los Angeles.

Berman, E. (2010). My way. *Psychoanalytic Inquiry*, 30, 116–132.

Berman, E. (2013). Bullying in psychoanalytic life: A few episodes and some thoughts. *Psychoanalytic Inquiry*, 33, 124–129.

Berman, E. (2014). Psychoanalytic supervision in a heterogeneous theoretical context: Benefits and complications. *Psychoanalytic Dialogues*, 24, 525–531.

Berman, E. (2017). Pitfalls on our "New royal road": Commentary on paper by Joyce Slochower. *Psychoanalytic Dialogues*, 27, 307–312.

Ferenczi, S. (1932). *The Clinical Diary* (ed., J. Dupont). Cambridge, MA: Harvard University Press, 1988.

McLaughlin, J.T. (1995). Touching limits in the analytic dyad. *Psychoanalytic Quarterly*, 64, 433–465.

Ogden, T. (1996). Reconsidering three aspects of psychoanalytic technique. *International Journal of Psychoanalysis*, 77, 883–899.

Slavin, J. (2007). Psychoanalytic training: The absence of thirdness. *Psychoanalytic Dialogues*, 17, 595–609.

Slochower, J. (2017). Going too far: Relational heroines and relational excess. *Psychoanalytic Dialogues*, 27, 282–299.

Williams, P. (1998). Psychotic developments in a sexually abused borderline patient. *Psychoanalytic Dialogues*, 8, 459–491.

Chapter 4

Forms of equality in relational psychoanalysis

David Mark

The English analyst, Paul Williams, observed:

> there is a commonly reproduced, probably received idea that the inter-
> personal approach denotes 'equality between patient and analyst,'
> with the implication that the therapist must self-disclose in order to
> create a more equal therapeutic relationship. I do not know whether
> this idea is true or not, or to what degree . . .
>
> (2001, p. 712)

Williams, who sounded as if he suspected as much, was passing along a
half-truth, a kind of psychoanalytic "urban legend." Legends require a
certain ambiguity to flourish and this one is no exception. How does self-
disclosure "create a more equal therapeutic relationship?" It might be
argued that the analyst's self-disclosure is what J.L. Austin (1962), the
English ordinary language philosopher, called a "performative utterance";
regardless of the specific content, by doing what the patient is encouraged
to do—openly sharing one's thoughts, feelings, and experiences—the
analyst creates a sense of equality. But, the idea of creating a more equal
relationship by self-disclosing would seem to be less a performative
utterance than a "performative contradiction" (Havens, 1997); only a
person in a position of power could bestow equality to another, which
thereby reinforces that power and unequal status. In relational terms, the
analyst's self-disclosure as a means to create a more equal relationship
will often come across as condescending and manipulative. Thus, the use
of self-disclosure to create a more equal relationship would not only strike

some as ill-advised insofar as it would undercut the authority of the analyst, and inhibit the development of necessary transferences, but ineffective.

Legends aren't true, at least not verifiably so, but they do often have a germ of truth in them. This legend, often expressed in more pungent form than Williams' mild version, exists for a reason: Once self-disclosure becomes permissible, as it has for most relational[1] analysts, it inevitably becomes employed as an unconscious strategy. The analyst's self-disclosure defensively creates the appearance of equality to disclaim authority and power thereby defusing the patient's anger and grievance. This is a serious critique; certainly self-disclosure is often used defensively in this way. Nevertheless, the relationship between self-disclosure, equality, and the expression of conflict between people is quite complex. At times, equality leads to the expression of conflict. At other times—*even* when self-disclosure is, from one perspective, functioning defensively— something else very valuable is also occurring. Arrived at "naturally" (i.e., without conscious intent but via enactment), a quality of relatedness characterized as "radical equality" generates a powerful and potentially healing experience.

I intend to illustrate this by discussing cases from two prominent papers in the relational literature from the first decade of this century. Bromberg and Davies, two of the most well-known relational analysts and authors, are from different wings of the relational school. Bromberg trained in the interpersonal school, while Davies has been most influenced by object-relations theory. Their papers *Potholes on the royal road: Or is it an abyss?* (2000) and *Whose bad objects are we anyway? Repetition and our elusive love affair with evil* (2004) contain a central enactment with a remarkably similar structure. My primary purpose in writing this chapter is to describe this enactment, it's structure and phenomenology. In so doing, I will emphasize a specific way in which patient and analyst are functioning as equals, though this is often hidden just beneath the surface, as well as highlight a particular quality of relatedness— "radical equality"—that emerges with the resolution of the enactment. This quality of relatedness plays a central role in the therapeutic action of these enactments. I also intend to draw out theoretical and clinical differences between more interpersonal and more object-relational relational analysts.

The therapist's shifting personifications during these enactments

I find Sullivan's personifications of the self (good-me and bad-me), as well as not-me (frightening, dreadful affective experience too intense to be contained "within" it), helpful in describing the analyst's experience during the kind of enactments described in this chapter. In many circumstances, one's self-experience can easily move between, or be comprised by both, bad-me and good-me, which are ordinary, everyday states of being.[2] Bad-me, like good-me, is a conscious aspect of many self-states and refers to those times I feel I am bad; it was originally, and—in certain states—still is, associated with increases in bad feeling in the other. When working in areas of trauma, the patient's intense and awful feelings—e.g., of pain, hopelessness, and distrust—will often rapidly flood both patient and analyst. In such circumstances, it is particularly difficult for the therapist to tolerate being "bad" (bad-me). This is because, in the face of the traumatized patient's expression of overwhelming vulnerability and need, our failures and our own needs, which from outside the immediate emotional field are completely ordinary and inevitable (albeit often part of bad-me), are experienced as unimaginably awful. If we were capable of verbalizing it, we might say to ourselves, "It is not possible that I can inflict so much pain and damage. *That* is not-me" (Stern, 2010, p. 13).

In this charged atmosphere in which bad-me states are so difficult to inhabit, a multi-faceted spiraling process is initiated, in which the analyst's experiential freedom narrows. The analyst tries harder and harder to be "understanding" and "helpful." Increasingly, there becomes only room for the analyst's good-me. From this perch of goodness, it becomes impossible to recognize the patient's experience, which, of course, increases the patient's pain, rage, and despair, accelerating the process. The analyst undergoes a "simplifying of consciousness" (Bollas, 1992, p. 167), progressively scrubbing away pangs of conscience and all other threats to one's self-esteem, intensifying the enactment. Without realizing it, we have participated in the transformation of ourselves into only good-me as bad-me has disappeared (even as awful, uncanny not-me experience looms and threatens ever more frequently near consciousness).

While the analyst's transformation into only good-me has clearly occurred in interaction with the patient, the analyst's self-experience is, in a very important respect, familiar, albeit "strangely familiar". For most of us, the "innocence" that comes with being only good-me has a long history ("what a good, little boy!"); even if the innocence is "strangely familiar" since the context is so incongruent with it, the analyst's self experience does not feel like something or someone foreign has been forcibly placed within (as the notion of projective-identification might arguably suggest). Indeed, under the conditions described here, it is a way of feeling about ourselves we are motived to maintain. Furthermore, even the painful affective experience too intense to contain in one's self—the not-me experience—is paradoxically, our own. However much we wish it were, it is not simply experienced as foreign, the way an internalization of a bad parent might be. Indeed, Sullivan (1953) stressed that not-me experience was uncanny, unsettling in a strangely familiar way[3]. Because of these reasons, when the enactment resolves and a mutual unpacking of it occurs, there might be less the note (however subtly present) of blame, of shifting responsibility, attached to the analyst's acknowledgment of having harmed the patient (Benjamin, 2018).

Equality and radical equality[4]

Those who worked with Sullivan say he was extraordinarily sensitive to ongoing shifts in his patient's self-esteem. In his lectures, he emphasized that therapists must pay close attention to it. But what of the analyst's? We are equally prone, every bit as much as our patients, to shape our interactions with them in such a way as to maximize our experience of good-me, and—as will inevitably occur in any significant relationship—we are also equally prone to dissociate those aspects of ourselves that are too awful to accept.

We each need the other to regulate, to validate, to serve as "affirming witness" and "durable respondent" "to the best that we hope we are" and the "worse aspects of ourselves that we fear we are" (McLaughlin, 1995, p. 434). Furthermore, as the relationship between patient and analyst deepens, as each gets under the other's skin, patient and analyst appreciate that co-creation is not merely an abstract philosophical concept, but a specific empowering and intimate experience; patient and analyst are equally dependent on the other to realize their best, and are equally vulnerable to the other to shape their worst.

These aspects of equality—always present—are largely obscured because our role provides narcissistic protection by placing us in the less vulnerable position. When an emotionally intense enactment begins to resolve, this equality becomes not only visible but experientially significant to both participants. Another form of equality is created at such moments. Differences in power and responsibility seem to wash away. It is as if the hierarchical, asymmetrical context of the analytic situation has been temporarily suspended; this makes the experience of equality feel "radical."

Radical equality is a highly desired experience. As a wish for a particular quality of relatedness, it is basic and primary, and not merely a denial of authority, power differences, envy, or dependency. This wish is not "basic and primary" in the sense that a baby could experience it; it cannot form until the child is out in the larger world and gathers something about what it's like to live within social structure. Only then, does the desire to live outside it take on meaning.[5]

Furthermore, while radical equality generates a spirit of communion, this does not imply an absence of conflict. Indeed, there are times that a fully inhabited anger only occurs after patient and analyst discover just how alike they are; the experience of equality opens up the possibility of conflict that had previously been muffled or evaded. In Bromberg's case (see below), it seems that he needed to discover his own anger before his patient would feel safe with his. In Davies' case, which follows Bromberg's, her patients' anger was defused, but for this person it was the expression of love, not hate, that was difficult and that was enabled by the experience of radical equality.

Bromberg's "potholes"

Stephen Mitchell compared the psychoanalytic process to driving a dual-control car (1997), the kind used in driver's ed classes. Bromberg (2000) all but straps us in the back seat of such a vehicle. From the rear passenger seats–with Bromberg and his patient, Alec, in the front, each at their own steering wheels–we feel what it's like to have an enactment gain momentum during an ongoing analytic inquiry. The more we get hurled about as the potholes deepen and proliferate, the more fervently do we wish the wheels would come off, just so we can get out of the car.

For months, Alec, a four-times-a-week analytic patient, increasingly openly expressed dissatisfaction "that the treatment is not moving fast enough" (p. 19). Something is amiss; a subtle impersonal quality permeates the air, indicating a mutual dissociation is circulating. For Alec, it's the "treatment" that's moving too slowly, not a problem between the drivers. Bromberg meets this with an equally impersonal response. This is a humdrum, everyday clinical occurrence about which he does "not feel consciously uncomfortable" (p. 19). The enactment has begun without being announced by as much as a speed bump.

Hoping it will accelerate the analysis, Alec, displaying "more enthusiasm than he's shown in months" (p. 20), next informs Bromberg that he joined a rational-emotive therapy group. *Now* we can feel some bumps in the road as Bromberg registers emanations from his "bad me," feelings of irritation signaling a threat to his self-esteem. By keeping his reaction "in a professionally containable framework of meaning" (p. 20), Bromberg maintains a version of his "good me." The more competent Bromberg feels, the more he firmly grasps the wheel, the more he unwittingly communicates to Alec he is unshakeable, beyond reach; in this way, Bromberg frightens and shames Alec.

What happens next really rattles things. Due to the expense of the group, Alec announces he can no longer afford four sessions per week. From the back seat, we see one of the drivers getting really "hot under the collar" (p. 20). The enactment races on. Alec, sensing Bromberg's anger, declares he'd be more comfortable sitting up (from the couch, not the passenger's seat!). The more Bromberg attempts to "explore" what is going on, the more he exacerbates the situation. Bromberg, the person who we have presumed has more command over the vehicle, soon reports "feeling totally 'possessed' by the out-of-control quality of [his] own feelings" (p. 21). With Bromberg's not-me "in control," we are desperate to get out of the car.

How does this enactment resolve? Bromberg does not tell us specifically, but the following is clear: (a) Bromberg had been reached in such an intensely (he says "overly") personal way that his emotional expressiveness ("self-revelation") as well as whatever was said and done was purged of his therapeutic zeal, and (b) there was some subsequent sharing of "our respective experiences, including the extent of our undisclosed anger toward one another and the warded-off shame it masked" (p. 22).

During the resolution of enactment, Bromberg surrendered (Ghent, 1990)[6] his good-me; he stopped trying to do the "right" thing. At this point, Bromberg became with, and to, Alec more fully the person he is. This is one aspect of what makes this moment intensely personal. It could be said that Bromberg's anger and hate emerged from repression. But, more than that, a secret and very personal "possession," a version of himself that now includes that which he had been unable to be (not-me)—characterized in this particular instance by fear, incompetence, anger, hate and shame about it all—moved from being dissociatively enacted to becoming him, that is, a version of "me".

While the notion of "unconscious experience" might well be an oxymoron (what is unconscious is inferred from the absence of experience), not-me *is* experience, albeit unformulated (Stern, 1997). It is weirdly paradoxical experience that is both disowned and yet "mine," ("invariably connected with the sentience of *my body*," italics in original, Sullivan, 1953, p. 161). Another paradox: however much not-me is activated by, embedded in, and shaped by, a particular field, it feels dreadfully familiar and has an individual history that reaches back long before analyst and patient met. In the kind of extended enactments that are the focus of this chapter, not-me is not only experience, but manifests itself as behavior, as "dissociated behavior" in which people do "things which may be quite meaningful to other people but are unknown to them" (Sullivan, 1953, p. 163). Thus, Bromberg's acceptance of his not-me not only permits the deepest kind of resonance with Alec's experience, he can see his responsibility for it. When not-me experience becomes absorbed as "me," I can own responsibility for what I have done. This is another reason why the resolution of enactment feels so personal.

From one perspective, Alec's role in the enactment might be seen as an effort to get beneath Bromberg's professional exterior, a form of probing (Aron, 1991, p. 37): How will Bromberg respond to Alec's rejection and criticism? From a different self-state, Alec is simply frantic to get out of the car. The enactment spirals out of control as Bromberg's expanding hate and anger—which Alec sees and knows but Bromberg cannot—pushes Alec to regard his own feelings and behavior as frightened and mollifying but that Bromberg cannot help but experience as frustrating and hostile. When Bromberg surrenders his good-me, Alec discovers how Bromberg tolerates feelings that Alec himself is struggling with.

We don't know Alec's history, but might expect that Bromberg's out-of-touch hate and anger terrified Alec—and caused him to detach from his own anger—in much the way some figure from his past did. As the enactment resolves, both Bromberg and Alec are in a position to see that Alec is not the only one who fears the other's power to make him feel inadequate, and how, under such circumstances, anger and hate are inevitable. In all of this—the vulnerability to feelings of inadequacy, the defensive anger and hate—Bromberg and Alec are revealed to each other to be, in a profound sense, equals.

While Bromberg characterized, in the aftermath of surrender, their anger toward one another as previously "undisclosed," I assume that until Bromberg was in touch with his own, their anger was not merely "undisclosed" but dissociated. If Alec's anger had been consciously withheld or repressed, empathy with respect to, or an interpretation of, anger would have struck a chord with Alec, and, as this case reads, that does not seem to be at all likely. This moment is consistent with at least an aspect of Williams' impression: Bromberg's "self-disclosure" led to an experience of radical equality (see following paragraph). On the other hand, the analyst's disclosure did not assuage the patient's anger (as it arguably did later) but facilitated it.

The postscript is dominated by the spirit of radical equality. Bromberg "spontaneously thanked Alec" for his "willingness to hang in while forcing me to see what I could not before acknowledge." Alec was able to simply, "undramatically and straightforwardly" accept Bromberg's gratitude, something that in turn was nurturing for him. "At that moment Alec revealed that he felt deserving of being acknowledged for having just given me something valuable, his help, and that I was not above being personally enriched by his acknowledgment in the same way that Alec felt enriched by my thanks" (p. 23).

I would argue that this experience of radical equality is inherently therapeutic, but that does not mean it is necessarily the enactment's "final act". The resolution may only be temporary. Bromberg's expression of gratitude, now experienced as a part of a mutually enriching authentic moment, might later come to be seen in a very different light. Or, to put the matter in terms of multiple self-states, radical equality to one self-state might be something very different to another (Grand, personal communication, 12/1/14). Alec might experience Bromberg's gratitude as an effort to seduce him out of feeling injured and aggrieved. Additionally, much the way therapist self-disclosure in a general way has a paradoxical performative effect of asserting power while disclaiming it, expressions of gratitude from the person with more power, carry with them a paradoxical message. Help given by the person with less power is usually dissociated by both parties. The expression of gratitude, with its implicit acknowledgment of help, from the person with more power both de-stabilizes the power arrangement and reinforces it (only a person secure in his power can give it away).

Davies' "bad objects"

In the first of two consecutive sessions that she describes, Davies, ill and in a vulnerable state, needs an "easy" patient. Perhaps most fundamentally, an "easy" patient is a person who affirms us in a version of our good-me. For Davies, this meant "patients who saw me as warmer, more caring, more therapeutically helpful than Karen did . . ." (p. 713). Unfortunately, Karen "was never easy!" (p. 712). In response to Karen's "stare" with its "gleam" of "energy and excitement" (p. 712), Davies' "stomach churned and . . . muscles stiffened . . . it seemed as if my body knew that *something* was coming, and my body told me it wasn't good" (italics in original, p. 712). If Bromberg's excerpt begins with an impersonal quality of relatedness between himself and Alec, the atmosphere in Davies' report is highly charged right from the start. One gets the sense that both Karen's and Davies' internal objects—vague, but intense affective presences—are stirred up. With all this circulating, Davies hears Karen demand an earlier hour for a future session with "the heat of her disowned rage penetrating" the air (p. 712).

This angry, humiliated, needy demand functions both as a probe and a quasi-hypnotic suggestion. Karen probes: "I need to find reality, an emotional truth. Let's see if you are as loving and caring as you take yourself to be." At the same time, it narrows Davies' focus as she becomes increasingly only good-me. She tells herself "Ah, yes, here it was: the impossible demand, the necessity of the moment that I simply could not provide. Why did Karen never ask me for things that I could give her?" (p. 712). This inner dialogue is not merely a defense. The dialogue both reflects and sustains Davies' good-me. In the glow of this all-good, nurturing self-state, things are simple: Davies would provide if only Karen would ask for something in the realm of possibility. Davies explains, "I do know how important it is for you . . . and I so wish that I had the time. But you know how impossible my Monday morning schedule is . . ." (p. 712). To which Karen replies, "You're such a bitch . . . You're cold and unfeeling and ungiving. You've never been there for me—not ever. I mean sometimes you pretend, but it's just skin deep. Down deep inside you where I can see . . . it's just ice. The least you could do is admit it" (p. 715). Davies is "stunned" by the intensity of Karen's "hatred." She is particularly stunned, I would imagine, because, from the innocence and simple purity of all good-me, it must have felt especially undeserved and unexpected.

Mutual understanding is foreclosed. From good-me, Davies cannot see how hateful the specific form of her refusal was to Karen. What to Davies' good-me is tact, is to Karen a familiar form of dishonesty. After all, even before Karen's searing reply, "a small and unwanted voice" (p. 713) inside Davies realized that Karen had not demanded the impossible. Davies had rearranged her schedule for other patients. This voice, a momentary breach in defense, revealed to herself a previously hidden version of her bad-me. Yes, she realized she's inconsistent, and she's a bit guilty too, but these qualities are not truly awful; unlike not-me, they are not shrouded in Sullivan's "uncanny emotion." In Davies' apparently regretful and empathic claim that she simply could not switch the hour, she was "provoking, seeking, and engaging with the worst that the other has to offer [which thereby] unconsciously secures [her] own internal sense of goodness, righteousness, and innocence" (p. 723).

In this charged interpersonal field—with Davies inwardly "seething" over Karen's perception of her—Davies surrenders. In so doing, she accepts her not-me. "I hate the self that I have become with her. I AM the bitch she describes (p. 715)." Davies' surrender marks the end of the impasse and dramatically alters the charge in the field. A direct, personal, intimate relatedness is enabled. The following exchange, it is true, can be said to strengthen affect tolerance as well as the therapeutic alliance, but, to my mind, these are almost unintentional consequences of an embrace of, and participation in, a very human, personal relationship. As with Bromberg's "postscript" of gratitude and acknowledgement, in both form (the style is just plain talk) and content, Davies conveys a responsiveness to the spirit of radical equality. She writes:

Our session draws to an end, and it has become quiet. Then, 'You hate me,' says Karen . . . 'Mhmm,' I tell her. 'Sometimes we hate each other, I think. Not always, not even usually, but sometimes we can get to this place together. I guess we're gonna have to see where we can get to from here. Neither of us likes it much; it just is.' 'Yeah,' says Karen, 'It sucks.' 'Yea, it does,' I answer.

(p. 716)

The effect of Davies' extraordinary—though simultaneously simple and ordinary—exchange at the end of the session can hardly be exaggerated. Still sick the next day, Davies braces herself for another rough time. But Karen surprises her, bringing her a thermos of milky tea. The spirit of radical equality, having surfaced at the end of the previous session, persists into this one. It would certainly have been shattered had Davies refused, or explicitly interpreted, the offering. If Davies showed Karen in the previous session that she, too, can hate, in this one, Karen demonstrates that she, too, can love (p. 727).

In the "milky goodness" of the tea exchange, Davies decides to bring up a thought from the day before. Telling Karen that the "worst part of yesterday" was that she hated herself, Karen can, at first, barely believe it: "Really? . . . you really hated yourself more than me? I mean, you sometimes hate yourself? . . . [Karen continues] The only time I feel good is when I find the evil parts of other people . . . like with you. It makes me feel less alone" (p. 728–729). This exchange beautifully captures the experience of radical equality. Davies writes, "[f]or this very brief moment, we have become coconspirators, coconstructors of alternative selves too toxic to be owned independently but now held, sustained, even tentatively enjoyed as a moment of commonality between us" (p. 728).

Even though "self-disclosure" is a term that makes more sense with reference to an analyst who intends, and maintains, a minimally expressive stance (since something is more likely to actually be disclosed under such circumstances), I will continue to use the term below. Both Bromberg's and Davies' cases contain effective self-disclosures of anger, hate, and shame. In the following, I both describe the conditions that made the disclosure of hate and anger so effective for Bromberg and Davies, and suggest that other self-states of Alec and Karen might have experienced these events very differently.

I will consider two moments: the first occurs at the end of the first session in which Davies agrees that she hates Karen; the second occurs in the following session when Davies tells Karen that, even more than hating Karen, she hates, and is ashamed of, herself. With respect to the internal world, Davies' first disclosure works much like interpretation in terms of therapeutic action (in a Racker, 1968, or earlier, Strachey, 1934, model). By acknowledging she, too, hates (much like a contained, benignly offered interpretation), Davies disconfirms her patient's unconscious fantasy (alters the internal object relations situation) and becomes a good object. With respect to the therapeutic relationship, this first disclosure, a quiet, reluctant acknowledgement that "[s]ometimes we hate each other," perfectly conveys, in tone and word, the feeling of surrender that had occurred earlier in the session and that marked the onset of radical equality.

Her second disclosure (of her own self-hate), much like Bromberg's expression of gratitude, is responsive to, sustains, and deepens the experience of radical equality. Yet, just as in Bromberg's example, Davies second disclosure might well be heard by different self-states of Karen in a way that undermines that very equality. When Karen hears that Davies hates herself, it has the impact it does precisely because it is coming from someone who implicitly loves herself; it isn't coming from another self-hating person. The therapist's explicit disclosure of self-hate turns out to contain another performative contradiction. The same might be said for the therapist's disclosure of hatred toward his or her patient. Obviously, a therapist cannot verbally disclose a hatred that is too unacceptable to own; such hatred is dissociated and can only be enacted. Bromberg and Davies spoke of their hatred (or anger) for their patients when it had was no longer "too unacceptable." Their disclosure made explicit an affective state whose intensity, though still palpable, had largely passed. The words that constituted the disclosure were not an expression of the feeling—that had happened earlier—it was an acknowledgement of it. When a therapist chooses to be explicit about his hatred, it paradoxically carries with it the implication of one's lovingness and self-acceptance.

There's a relief in the air after Davies openly acknowledges the mutual hatred pervading the therapeutic space. I imagine much the same occurred when Bromberg and Alec spoke of their anger (p. 22). Karen could tell that Davies trusted her enough to own what had previously been her not-me in Karen's presence. And she could tell that Davies cared about her (and her need not to be endlessly mystified) to risk speaking of the hatred that had been palpable, yet unverbalized. When such trust and care do not appear to be present, it feels—and might actually be—impossible for analysts to speak of their hate without being purely destructive. (For an example of where there is "no apparent space to speak to the mutual hatred that is occurring," see Grand, 2003[7]). In Bromberg's and Davies' cases, there is another reason for relief when the analyst speaks of hating. They discovered, with their patients' help, part of their not-me; prior to that, they had been unaware of their hatred. All along, Alec and Karen had known, even if they hadn't known they knew, of their analyst's negative feelings. This was a dangerous state of affairs and helped to escalate the enactment. The atmosphere becomes less dangerous, not more so, when the analyst, now alive to what is going on, acknowledges hate under these conditions.

Evolution or revolution?

Steven Mitchell (1993) argued that the changes that were occurring, in those early years of relational psychoanalysis, could be described as either evolutionary or revolutionary. If Davies and Bromberg were to offer a critique of each other's work, they might, perhaps, use these same terms. Davies might think that, in more than one sense, Bromberg, in his revolutionary fervor, has thrown the baby out with the bathwater. She might be concerned that Bromberg's stance is too essentially egalitarian and that he lets himself go too much (e.g., his "over-personal" hatred with Alec, or his lengthy, "sadistic" tale with Roseanne, in Bromberg, 2011, pp. 60–65). These qualities, she might fear, would drive the baby in the patient out of the room. If that "baby" is more or less a literal one, there is also the metaphorical baby of highly valued psychoanalytic concepts and methods (e.g., unconscious fantasy, projection, identification, the past, interpretation), which Bromberg appears to discard. Bromberg might argue that many of these traditional analytic concepts and methods have the effect of minimizing the significance of what is happening in the immediate interpersonal relationship between patient and analyst. In this way, he might feel that Davies' more evolutionary approach has not altered practice, and the very way in which one thinks about the analytic relationship, as much as he'd like.

In both stance and in their understanding of *dissociation, self, object* and *enactment*, the primary influence of object-relations theory and interpersonal theory on Davies and Bromberg respectively is evident. That the interpersonal-object relational difference leaves a theoretical and clinical stamp on their work is particularly striking given the fact that Bromberg and Davies do not provide the sharpest possible contrast between these two positions. In the first place, Davies—more like Interpersonalists —has throughout her career written about moments where, with much struggle, she put into words difficult to share experiences with her patients (e.g., with Karen, it was hate; with Mr. M, 1994, it was her erotic feelings). In the second place, Bromberg has himself been heavily influenced by object-relations theory,[8] and unlike many Interpersonalists, uses developmental theory extensively. Bromberg and Davies have another theoretical similarity; along with Mitchell and Stern, they share the distinction of bringing the notion of multiple selves into the relational model.

What they emphasize about the (multiple) self is, however, somewhat different. While both Bromberg and Davies speak of "self-states" and of "self-other configurations", the former—a phenomenological term—is more central to Bromberg's work, while the latter—a structural concept— is more central to Davies' thought.[9] Perhaps Davies might think that if Bromberg held his hand a bit more tightly to the "steering wheel" of a theory of internal structure, he would not become so completely undone by Alec. Would Bromberg's affect have been "so disturbingly overpersonal (2000, p. 21)", if he held onto the idea of a self-other configuration in which one person's overt shame and covert anger link with the other's overt anger and covert shame? On the other hand, perhaps Bromberg might think that if Davies held her own theory (i.e., the "inverse" of Klein's theory of envy, 2004, p. 723) more loosely, she might paradoxically appreciate its truth in the moment more fully. Did Davies regard her refusal to accommodate Karen's demand for an earlier hour as an instance of "provoking, seeking, and engaging with the worst that the other has to offer" to establish her "internal sense of goodness, righteousness, and innocence" (p. 723)?

Aside from this more general difference (phenomenological versus structural), Davies and Bromberg think about self-states differently in a much more specific sense. In Davies' model, much as in Fairbairn's, there are a finite number of sharply drawn self-states; the same self and object (e.g., the "bitch" or the "psychotic mother") can be evoked at different times. Bromberg's self-states are more numerous and have less structural "solidity" or consistency, insofar as they are inseparable from the context in which they emerge. This difference—Davies' *evocation* of self-states (or even, in some of her most poetic moments, a more explicit *invitation* of them[10]) versus Bromberg's unpredictable *creation-discovery* of self-states—is at the heart of their most distinctive clinical moments throughout their writing.

Davies and Bromberg, as do all multiple-self theorists, assign dissociation a pre-eminent role in structuring the mind, but their conception of it differs. For Davies, dissociation follows overwhelming affective intensity generated by *transference-countertransference enactments.* Her conception of dissociation follows Janet insofar as she contrasts it with associative processes.[11] Like leaves that catch fire when placed under a magnifying glass, the heat of the immediate interpersonal relationship is brought to a flash point as it is seen through the lens of fantasy, the experienced past parent-child relationship, sparking off dissociated selves. The transference-countertransference is her overarching context.[12] In effect, the psyche breaks apart along (Fairbairnian dissociated) self-state boundaries when affectively overwhelmed.

Sometimes, as with Karen where "a psychotic parent . . . hovers around" tormenting each of them (2004, p. 719), Davies confronts a dissociated self of her own ("I AM the bitch she describes"). At other times, she suddenly encounters a dissociated self-state of her patient (e.g., 1996, p. 570). At such moments, the affect in the room needs to calm down before reflection can take place. Davies' use of "therapeutic dissociation" (1996) makes sense in this theoretical context.

Dissociation is an unlinking process—this much is true for both Davies and Bromberg—but for Bromberg, the fundamental unlinking is "a defensive detachment of mind from self" (1998, p. 277). The fear of becoming affectively overwhelmed leads to dissociation; affective aliveness follows the collision of subjectivities that breaks up *dissociated enactments.* Rather than making its appearance when affectively overwhelmed, dissociation is in the interpersonal (Sullivanian) tradition a "proactive solution" (Bromberg, 2011, p. 15). The dissociated self-state that is created following collision is also discovered in that it has already been enacted (but not known, recognized or validated).

Bromberg contrasts dissociation, not with association, but with mentalization[13] (the capacity for self-reflection as well as the ability to think about what the other thinks of you without concretizing it).[14] One can see how from this theoretical perspective, the immediate interpersonal relationship is Bromberg's "overarching context" (see Bromberg, 2011, chapter 6) and bears more therapeutic weight for him than it does for Davies. Rather than being understood through the transference, Bromberg regards enactments as highly dense, concentrated, affectively intense (too intense, hence dissociation) segments of life. For him, the here-and-now relationship itself (or aspects of it) is dissociated; for Davies, the transferential relationship is the context for dissociation. This difference has consequences for how they understand therapeutic action and how they work as analysts.

While Davies has always been willing to immerse herself in powerful enactments, she advocates a balance, by way of "therapeutic dissociation" between being inside and outside the enactment and, closely related, between enactments and interpretation of the transference-countertransference phenomena that (for her) frame them (e.g., 1994, p. 168 and 2004, p. 726). Her interest in interpreting the transference meanings of the enactment, her concern with insight, and interest in understanding the patient's past are part of Davies' more evolutionary approach. For Bromberg, it is the enactment—and its transformation via affective elaboration, and participation in a mutual unpacking from within the enactment that is therapeutic. Specifically, Bromberg's description of clinical process, and what largely defines his listening framework, concerns changes in "I-feeling" from: (a) A dissociated state in which there is an impairment in mentalization; through, (b) A potentially creative period of destabilization in which all the old patterns of relatedness feel inescapably inadequate and inauthentic following a spontaneous, interpersonal collision; to, (c) If all goes well enough, mutual recognition. These different ways of participating in enactments reflects their overall difference in clinical stance.

Stance "captures . . . a basic sense and way of being in the hour with our patients" (Foehl, 2014, p. 30). A key difference between a traditional object-relations and Davies' relational-object-relational approach is the latter's fuller acceptance of the inevitability of enactments (e.g., contrast with Racker, 1968, p. 144). That greater acceptance is congruent with her further development of a stance characteristic of the British middle school; i.e., her work represents a freer expression of a developmental approach—i.e., a parent-child stance—in the analytic situation. This coordinates perfectly with the more reactive, conception of dissociation from which Davies works.

From early in his career, Bromberg advocated a stance of *participant observation* but filled in this sparse term with various (sometimes Sullivanian) developmental concepts. These developmental ideas helped to define qualities of relatedness that were important throughout the life cycle (e.g., "a feeling of deep communion" occurring in a "global matrix" of "tenderness," 1998, p. 42).[15] His interest in multiple self-selves has led Bromberg to essentially argue for an equal right to recognition for each self-state. His clinical examples often illustrate that this is hardest and yet most essential to accomplish with the most vulnerable and difficult selves (e.g., see the case of Roseanne, 2011, pp. 60–65). What is required is a keen eye for the fleeting appearance of the former and an honest, if not entirely happy, welcoming of the latter. Beyond that, Bromberg's conception of dissociation, as a proactive defensive detachment of mind from self that guards against shock—by managing relationships, keeping others at arm's length, suppressing surprise, unpredictability, and spontaneity—calls for a messier stance, one that encourages "safe surprises" and moments of nearly startling personal openness.

The notion that Davies' stance represents an evolutionary shift from a traditional analytic approach is particularly clear when we consider the fate of her "therapeutic self," a central part of her stance. She never loses sight of this self-state. It is "parallel" to her intensely personal "seeth[ing]" and "struggl[ing]" over Karen's powerfully hateful description of her (2004, p. 715).[16] At very different moments—moments when she is engaging very much in the spirit of radical equality—her "therapeutic self" is nevertheless present. For example, toward the end of the first session with Karen, Davies writes:

> A comment takes shape in my mind [that Davies hates herself]. It buzzes around, and I struggle with whether to say it. *It feels right, but it has appeared suddenly and I haven't had time to think about it.* I decide to hold the thought, not to share it at this moment with Karen.
>
> (p. 716, italics added)

As we shall see, it isn't that she decides not to say something that differentiates her from Bromberg. To be sure, her developmental stance is a relatively more cautious approach than Bromberg's. Her caution as well as thoughtfulness are evident in the amount of time she believes she needs before giving expression to a thought that "appeared suddenly," even one that "feels right." More importantly, this degree of care and thoughtfulness, which both gains and loses therapeutic opportunities—much like using the transference-countertransference as one's dominant framework for listening— both reflects and creates a "therapeutic self."

Bromberg's "therapist self" (his term) is significantly different from Davies' "therapeutic self". Bromberg's therapist self is simply himself as he functions as a psychoanalyst. One might say that when Bromberg's therapist self degenerates into a "therapeutic self", it becomes part of the problem—not, as for Davies—part of the solution. During a spiraling enactment, Bromberg's therapeutic self occludes the fact that for him, it is not the transference-countertransference, but "the dimension of a human encounter" (Klauber in Bromberg, 2000, p. 6) that is at the center. This aspect of his stance is evident throughout. For example, even when he exercises restraint, there is a quality of directness and spontaneity about Bromberg's way of being and thinking in the room. With feelings his guide, he also tells us of a moment he decides not to speak: "I realize that it would be useful to have my own feelings under better control before saying anything further, and decide to wait and remain silent as I think about what is happening" (2000, pp. 20 21).

This difference in clinical approach comes into focus when we consider Davies' internal response to Karen's elixir: Davies was surprised, not simply because the offer was outside the ordinary frame, but because Davies was anticipating further conflict. "My patient is attempting to feed me warm milk. There must be an incredible interpretation in this somewhere!" She continues, "Who was I at this moment in the transference?" Numerous transference hypotheses follow (see 2004, pp. 725–726). These musings function as a form of affect regulation for Davies, facilitating her ability to delay and respond thoughtfully to Karen. One imagines that if Bromberg were to have found himself caught off guard by Karen's offer of tea and thinking in terms of its transferential meanings as Davies did, he would not regard it as affect regulation. It would get in the way, not facilitate, his response.

In this last section, I have tried to draw out Davies' and Bromberg's differences as clearly and sharply as possible, but I do not wish to lose sight of their similarities. It isn't only that the central enactments in Bromberg's (2000) and Davies' (2004) papers are very similar. Both of them are willing to allow themselves an intense personal participation in which they get far more discomposed ("not me" experience) than had previously been considered permissible. Both of them have a commitment to put into words what is difficult to say about what is going on within and between them and their patients during the resolution of the enactment. They each see mutual recognition as central to therapeutic action during the resolution of the enactment. And, I would add, each allows an experience of radical equality to take root, in which they offer their patients an egalitarian kind of participation, characterized by an everyday plainspokenness. It is at times such as these that patient and analyst have the momentary illusion that they have stepped outside ordinary, hierarchical social structure altogether. When the illusion fades, both participants return to the familiar asymmetry, but richer for the experience. The paradox is that these experiences are, like all deeply personal experiences, not at all instrumental and yet they form the heart of the work itself.

Notes

1 I had the impression that when Williams used the term "interpersonal approach" he meant the American relational school more generally.
2 In the following description, I am borrowing from Stern's (2010) multiple self model. For good reasons, Sullivan is not usually classified as a "multiple self" theorist. He explicitly wrote of a singular "self-system," and of how the initially separate good-me and bad-me "fuse" into a unitary "self" (1953, p. 201); whereas, following Stern, good-me and bad-me unlink from each other under emotional pressure. Perhaps the closest Sullivan came to expressing the idea of multiple selves was in a 1943 lecture in which he described "specious ideals" as "*almost* like a second self" (1956, p. 102, italics mine). For Sullivan, "personality" included not only that which was "phenomenologically describable" (1950, p. 221), i.e., the self, but that which was not "readily accessible to awareness" (1956, p. 4). Like the self, he tended to describe personality in unitary terms—the "whole personality" —as well. Nevertheless, in a 1944 lecture (1950), Sullivan commented, "for all I know every human being has as many personalities as he has interpersonal relations (p. 221)." In Sullivan's terms, the idea of many

    personalities but a single self comes close to Bromberg's (1998) definition of "health" as "the capacity to feel like one self while being many" (p. 186).

3 I suspect that Sullivan borrowed the term, "uncanny," from Freud for his specific, paradoxical implication of strangeness and familiarity. Freud (1919/2003), too, regarded the uncanny as a harbinger of "the unconscious" (Sullivan's not-me): "the uncanny is that species of the frightening that goes back to what was *once well known and had long been familiar*" (italics mine, p. 124). I italicized the end of this passage to starkly contrast Freud's notion of unconscious experience with Sullivan's, who regarded the "very early experiences" that provided the original source of the uncanny as "largely truncated, so that what they are really about is not clearly known" (1953, p. 163). This difference in thinking about unconscious experience ("once well known" versus "largely truncated . . . not clearly known") will be reflected in the last section of this chapter where I contrast the work of Davies and Bromberg.

4 I wish to thank Dr. Rachel McKay, who on an earlier version of this paper commented that I had not clearly enough distinguished between two different senses in which I was using the term "equality"; an ongoing characteristic, referred to now simply as "equality", and a second sense, "radical equality", which is a temporary phenomenon.

5 Radical equality is the psychoanalytic and dyadic expression of V. Turner's "communitas" (see Hoffman, 1998).

6 Ghent, who introduced surrender to the analytic literature, almost always used the term to refer to the patient's surrender. Benjamin's (2018) uses it to refer to the analyst's surrender to the third. For my purposes, the analyst surrenders to his not-me or Badness.

7 Grand, email 12/1/14

8 But, see the following paragraph. Bromberg borrows from the middle school object-relations theorists, in particular those who are more interested in phenomenological description than theoretical explanation (e.g., Winnicott and the Balints). Davies has been most influenced by Klein and Fairbairn. The latter, while generally grouped with the middle school, is something of an anomaly for that school in that his theory is more "structural" than phenomenological.

9 Similarly, for Davies, object has a structural, explanatory role it lacks for Bromberg. He uses object to capture an aspect of subjective experience, not to explain it.

10 See, e.g., 1996, pp. 569–570, or in the second session with Karen, see pp. 727–728. By contrast, even when Bromberg "invites" a self-state into the session, the emphasis is on creation, the immediate affective experience between the two of them (see 2011, pp. 78–80).

11 Fairbairn, whose work has in many respects influenced Davies, disagreed with this conceptualization of dissociation. For him, it "is an essentially

active process. This fact has been largely obscured as a result of Janet's formulation" (in Birtles & Scharff [eds.]1929/1994, p. 52).

12 For the exception that proves the rule see 2004, p. 715. We hear the voice of an American relational analyst—not a British object-relations theorist—in her description of this immediate and deeply personal moment. Notions like the "bad object" and "negative transference," Davies writes, "seems somehow unequal to th[is] moment."

13 He most frequently contrasts dissociation with conflict, but that opposition refers to dissociation as a structural concept, and here I am contrasting Davies and Bromberg with respect to dissociation as a process.

14 Sullivan's version of participant-observation (in which he stressed how vital it was for the therapist to anticipate how he comes across to the patient and to grasp what the patient thought the therapist thought of him) and Levenson's (1983) "semiotic skills" perhaps influenced Bromberg's contrast of dissociation and mentalization.

15 S. Pizer (2014) has recently written a moving and important paper on stance, also using Sullivan's "tension of tenderness."

16 Contrast this with Bromberg: "At this point I am feeling totally 'possessed' by the out-of-control quality of my own feelings . . . The affect I was feeling here . . . was so disturbingly over-personal . . ." (2000, p. 21).

References

Aron, L. (1991). The patient's experience of the analyst's subjectivity. *Psychoanalytic Dialogues*, *1*, 29–51.

Austin, J. L. (1962). *How to do things with words: The William James Lectures delivered at Harvard University in 1955*. Oxford, UK: Clarendon Press.

Benjamin, J. (2018). *Beyond doer and done to: Recognition theory, inter-subjectivity and the third*. London: Routledge.

Bollas, C. (1992). *Being a character: Psychoanalysis and self experience*. New York: Farrar, Straus, & Girous.

Bromberg, P. (1998). *Standing in the spaces: Essays on clinical process, trauma and dissociation*. Hillsdale, NJ: The Analytic Press.

Bromberg, P. (2000). Potholes on the royal road: Or is it an abyss? *Contemporary Psychoanalysis*, *36*, 5–28.

Bromberg, P. (2011). *The Shadow of the tsunami: And the growth of the relational mind*. New York: Routledge.

Davies, J. M. (1994). Love in the afternoon: A relational reconsideration of desire and dread in the countertransference. *Psychoanalytic Dialogues*, *4*, 153–170.

Davies, J. M. (1996). Linking the "pre-analytic" with the postclassical: Integration, dissociation, and the multiplicity of unconscious process. *Contemporary Psychoanalysis*, *32*, 553–576.

Davies, J. M. (2004). Whose bad objects are we anyway? Repetition and our elusive love affair with evil. *Psychoanalytic Dialogues*, *14*, 711–732.

Davies, J. M. and Frawley, M. G. (1994). *Treating the adult survivor of childhood sexual abuse: A psychoanalytic perspective*. New York: Basic Books.

Foehl, J. (2014). Affective relatedness in stance and process: Commentary on papers by Stuart A. Pizer and Barbara Pizer. *Psychoanalytic Dialogues*, *24*, 29–36.

Freud, S. (2003). *The Uncanny*. New York: Penguin Classics.

Ghent, E. (1990). Masochism, submission, surrender—masochism as a perversion of surrender. *Contemporary Psychoanalysis*, *26*, 108–136.

Grand, S. (2003). Lies and body cruelties in the analytic hour. *Psychoanalytic Dialogues*, *13*, 471–500.

Havens, L. (1997). A linguistic contribution to psychoanalysis: The concept of performative contradictions. *Psychoanalytic Dialogues*, *7*, 523–534.

Hoffman, I. Z. (1998). *Ritual and spontaneity in the psychoanalytic process: A dialectical-constructivist view*. Hillsdale, NJ: The Analytic Press.

Levenson E. (1983/1995). *The ambiguity of change: An inquiry into the nature of psychoanalytic reality*. Northvale, NJ: Jason Aronson.

McLaughlin, J. (1995). Touching limits in the analytic dyad. *Psychoanalytic Quarterly*, *64*, 433–465.

Mitchell, S. (1993). Reply to Bachant and Richards, *Psychoanalytic Dialogues*, *3*, 461–480.

Mitchell, S. (1997). Influence and autonomy in psychoanalysis. Hillsdale, NJ: Analytic Press.

Pizer, S. (2014). The analyst's generous involvement: Recognition and the "tension of tenderness." *Psychoanalytic Dialogues*, *24*, 1–13.

Racker, H. (1968). *Transference and countertransference*. Madison, CN: International Universities Press

Stern, D. B. (1997). *Unformulated experience: From dissociation to imagination in psychoanalysis*. Hillsdale, NJ: Analytic Press.

Stern, D. B. (2010). *Partners in thought: Working with unformulated experience, dissociation, and enactment*. New York: Routledge.

Strachey, J. (1934). The nature of the therapeutic action of psychoanalysis. *International Journal of Psychoanalysis*, *13*, 117–126.

Sullivan, H. S. (1950). The illusion of personal individuality. *Psychiatry*, *13*, 317–332.

Sullivan, H. S. (1953). *The interpersonal theory of psychiatry*. New York: Norton.

Sullivan, H. S. (1956). *Clinical studies in psychiatry*. New York: Norton.

Williams, P. (2001). Object relationships—symmetry and asymmetry; Commentary on paper by Anthony Bass. *Psychoanalytic Dialogues*, *11*: 711–716.

Chapter 5

Needed analytic relationships and the disproportionate relational focus on enactments[1]

Steven Stern

Introduction

I begin with an extended excerpt from my 2017 book, *Needed Relationships and Psychoanalytic Healing: A Holistic Relational Perspective on the Therapeutic Process*. This quote provides the orienting framework for my more specific critique of enactment theory, which is the focus of the present chapter.

> In my 1994 paper, "Needed Relationships and Repeated Relationships: An Integrated Relational Perspective," one of my major points was that the unconscious communications and countertransference pulls of patients in psychoanalytic treatment are not only in the direction of enacting old problematic patterns of relational engagement (e.g., Mitchell, 1988, 1997); patients also unconsciously pull for or signal (directly or indirectly) the kinds of responses they long for or need from the analyst. Accordingly, analysts, unconsciously (and/or consciously) responding to *this* kind of pressure, may find themselves engaging in more positive forms of enactment.
>
> I still believe this to be the case, but find that this understanding remains insufficiently incorporated into contemporary Relational theory, which continues to focus disproportionately on problematic enactments. In this book I am still advocating for more of a balance in how we think about the analytic process and therapeutic action. However, in the present book the phrase "needed relationship," while retaining some of its meaning from the original paper, has expanded

to refer to *the healing aspects of the analytic relationship in all of its therapeutic complexity.*

The contemporary Relational focus on repetition (Mitchell, 1988, 1997), enactments (Levenson, 1972, 1983; Bromberg, 1998, 2011; D.B. Stern, 2010), impasses (Stolorow & Atwood, 1992), doer/done-to complementarities (Benjamin, 2004), subjugating thirds (Ogden, 1994); crunches (Russell, 2006), and other forms of difficulty caused by conflicts and disjunctions between and within the patient's and the analyst's subjectivities, has been critical to the development of power-ful new understandings and clinical approaches within the Relational paradigm. At the same time, it has, in my view, given Relational psy-choanalysis a pathology-oriented cast—a disproportionate emphasis on what Tolpin (2002) termed "the trailing edge" as opposed to "the forward edge" of the patient's moment-to-moment states and self-presentation, and the analytic process as a whole. One might glean from the mainstream Relational literature (with many notable excep-tions) that the needed analytic relationship is primarily defined as a set of strategies for recognizing, withstanding, and recovering from or transforming enactments and other forms of relational turbulence, rather than a more balanced view in which recognizing and coping with enactments is only part of a broader conception of what our patients need from us in the service of their treatment aims and psy-chological growth. In my experience, while working with enactments may be the hardest part of analysis (thus warranting the attention they have received), it is not the biggest or, necessarily, the most import-ant part. The concept of needed relationship is intended as a more balanced overall conceptual and therapeutic frame for Relational psychoanalysis.

I agree with Levenson (1972, 1983) that enactment is constant in analysis. I would even say that an analysis, from beginning to end, is essentially a long, complex "developmental enactment" (Orange, 2012) in the sense that it is primarily a *lived experience*, and that what is transformative is a function of the unique forms of lived experience that analysis potentially offers (co-creates). Where I disagree with Levenson is with the assumption that *what* is enacted is always a transform of the problems under consideration at the level of verbal inquiry, or even problems of any kind. That is simply not my experi-

ence, and I believe that examining analytic interaction through a lens
that is biased in the direction of seeing "the difficulty," rather than a
totality that includes "the remedy" as well as the difficulty, runs the
risk of interfering with an unfolding connectedness (Geist, 2009),
thereby potentially retraumatizing the patient in ways that *are* enactive
in the problematic sense.

I would argue that both the nature and the experienced quality of
analytic interaction are so entangled with the ways that the analyst is
holding, perceiving, interpreting, and participating in the interaction,
that Levenson's (1983) extremely useful question, "What's going on
around here?" (i.e., what is being enacted even as we speak), becomes
a Zen-like *koan* that cannot be answered from any single frame of
reference or "vertex" (Bion, 1962). For example, if I approach the
unfolding analytic engagement with the implicit question, "What does
the patient need from me?" and am experiencing, and participating
in, the analytic exchange through that vertex, the nature of "what's
going on here" must now include whatever effects my participating in
this way have on what's going on. Similarly, if one's dominant
approach to the ongoing interaction is through the vertex of the
question, "What's going on around here?" (as opposed to "What does
the patient need from me?"), this also will have a particular effect
on the nature of what *is* going on.

To state this issue more generally, the question I am raising is
how the analyst's intentional orientation to the process interacts with
and affects the unintentional dimensions of the process implied in the
question, "What's going on around here?"—recognizing that the question, "What's going on around here?" is itself an intentional orientation
to the process. My own current solution to the koan is that, while there
are extreme, unresolvable paradoxes involved, overall the question,
"What does the patient need from me?" is superordinate to the question, "What's going on around here?" but that part (though by no
means all) of what the patient needs from me is to be asking the
question, "What's going on here?" and employing that question to
better approach the question of what the patient needs. This hierarchy
tilts the analyst's primary "hermeneutic" from one of "suspicion"
(Ricoeur, 1970) to one of relatively greater "faith" or "trust" (Orange,
2011) in so far as it assumes that, no matter what's going on, there is

always an underlying forward edge need (Tolpin, 2002) that is being implicitly expressed in whatever is going on.

(S. Stern, 2017, 20–23)

Fundamental theoretical challenge

In this chapter I broaden the implications of the issues addressed in my book by questioning whether the whole theoretical super-structure—including (a) the centrality of enactments (and technical approaches to transforming them), (b) the positioning of dissociation as the fundamental organizing principle of the psyche, and (c) a view of the psyche as constituted by multiple selves or self-states—provides a sufficient conceptual foundation for understanding the minds, struggles, and therapeutic needs of our patients, and for orienting analytic clinicians to their core therapeutic aims and functions. Presuming that the overarching *telos* of the relational turn is to provide analytic patients with the relational experiences they need in order to work through their struggles and achieve their therapeutic/developmental aims, does this core set of theoretical constructs offer a sufficiently comprehensive model of mental functioning and therapeutic action to guide relational analytic practice? I know that contemporary relational theory is multidimensional, with many (and ever-proliferating) theoretical frames of reference offering important insights into our patients' minds and struggles, and into the nature of what we need to offer them. Many of these do not explicitly adhere to what I'm calling the "super-structure of relational theory." But as I read much of the relational literature, it seems to me that many authors return to this core theoretical constellation as an implicit center of gravity for understanding and characterizing analytic interaction and therapeutic action.

I have always felt this to be a limitation of relational theory (Stern, 1994, 2002b, 2015). The way I would put it now is that this set of theoretical constructs and metaphors cannot serve as an adequate bedrock of relational theory because it is really a theory about "cracks" and "warps" in the bedrock of the psyche—the scars and defense organizations that mark the "sites" of early relational trauma—rather than the bedrock of the psyche itself. I know that dissociation theorists posit the "normal" multiplicity of self-experience *as* the bedrock of the psyche, with roots in

Sullivanian theory (Bromberg, 1998, 2011; Davies, 1996; Mitchell, 1993; Pizer, 1998; D.B. Stern, 1997, 2010). But it is the theory of trauma-based *pathological* dissociation, not normal dissociation, which underwrites the relational theory of enactments and therapeutic action.

Bromberg (1998, 2006, 2011), arguably the most influential relational dissociation theorist, summarizes his view of the mind as follows:

> Self-states are what the mind comprises. Dissociation is what the mind does. The relationship between self-states and dissociation is what the mind is.
>
> (2006, p. 2)

And later in the same chapter:

> Through the creative use of dissociation, the mind selects whichever self-state configuration is most adaptive at a given moment without compromising affective safety. The need to preserve affective safety organizes the mind's responsiveness to novelty. The heart of mental functioning is a complex interface between what is experienced as safe enough and what is potentially traumatic.
>
> (p. 4)

I'm looking closely at Bromberg's rich and always nuanced language for his view of the core motivations of the psyche. The word "adaptive" here could be interpreted to cover any motivational impetus that a reader might privilege, including, hypothetically, the *forward edge motivations* I am foregrounding in this chapter. But I read Bromberg's overall position as viewing the human psyche as motivated primarily (1) to maintain the sense or illusion of self-continuity, and (2) to preserve safety. The two, in combination, amount to a defensive (or at least, reactive) rather than a prospective, proactive motivational core.

Once developmental trauma is added to Bromberg's picture, a more rigid and extreme form of dissociation takes over as "a proactive defense against the repetition of what has already happened" (2006, p. 6), and, at the same time, as an unconscious strategy for maintaining an acceptable experience of "me," while warding off the traumatic consequences of consciously experiencing "not-me" states. On this view, enactments become the primary vehicle of therapeutic action because they are what make possible an intersubjective experience and re-integration of the sequestered not-me self-state configurations. As the patient's dissociated not-me self-states provoke and encounter the analyst's not-me states, enactments arise, and thus the opportunity for the essential therapeutic action: the arrival of the capacity for reflective awareness of these dissociated states, usually first in the analyst. In this model, the telos of therapy is the development of new capacities to reflect on the formerly dissociated, allowing one to "stand in the spaces between different self-states" (Bromberg, 1998), and forward movement relies on the analyst's active work to notice self-state (and accompanying affective) shifts and to find ways to facilitate "self-state sharing" in the dialogue.

Bromberg's insights are profound, and have illuminated much of my understanding of enactments and their transformation. My point here is only that they are not the whole story. The mind is more than "the relationship between self-states and dissociation." The metaphor of dissociation may capture one important organizing principle of the psyche. But it does not, I will argue, describe the bedrock of the psyche; nor does it capture the processes through which that bedrock is formed or account for some of the psyche's primary motivations, including some which drive the analytic process.

The limitations of dissociation/multiple-self/enactment theory were presaged in this early, often-cited, passage from Mitchell (1988):

> Embeddedness is endemic to the human experience—I become the person I am in interaction with specific others. The way I feel it necessary to be with them is the person I take myself to be. That self-organization becomes my "nature"; those attachments become my sense of the possibilities within the community of others; those transactional patterns become the basis for my sense of interpersonal security and competence to function in the world. Adhesive devotion to the relational matrix reflects a terror of total loss of self and connection with others, as well as a deep loyalty and devotion to the interpersonal world which, no matter how skewed, allowed one to become one's own particular version of human.
>
> (p. 276)

As I have argued previously (S. Stern, 2002), this rendering of the self-organization, and sense of self, characterizes patients as entirely "captured" by, and captive to, the early (now internalized) relational milieu, with no dimension of self-experience posited to register the violation of trau-matizing early relationships to relational/developmental needs. Mitchell, an astute clinical observer, saw that patients did push back against the confines of their internalized relational matrices, but he theorized this, somewhat vaguely, as a reaction to extreme conditions and impingements and not as an aspect of self, motivated to proactively *seek and move toward* some kind of hoped-for developmental rectification and self-actualization. Mitchell believed that patients were seeking "something new" as well as "something old" in the analytic relationship, but that they could only imagine, and hence evoke, a new experience structured "along old lines." These ideas were in contrast, for example, to Bollas's (1987, 1989) ideas about personal idiom, true self-actualization, and a "destiny drive," or Stolorow's "developmental dimension of the transference" (Stolorow, Brandchaft, & Atwood, 1987). Mitchell was allergic to this kind of theorizing, as witnessed in his thoroughgoing critique of "develop-mental arrest" theories (Mitchell, 1988).[2]

One of the problems with this bias in Mitchell's early theorizing, and in subsequent "mainstream" relational theory, is that it implicitly leaves too much of the burden of therapeutic action, and the forward movement of therapy, in the hands of the therapist. Whereas in developmentally-oriented theories such as those of Balint, Winnicott, Bion, Kohut, Bollas, Tolpin, and myself, the patient is understood to be unconsciously pushing (albeit ambivalently) toward needed interaction, integration, and growth as a kind of engine of the analytic process; in Mitchell's relational theory the patient can mainly be counted on to recreate a version of the prob-lematic conditions of his past; it thus becomes the analyst's responsibility to imagine and provide the new relational experience which the patient needs to break out of old constraints.

While relational analysts, therapists, and theorists today probably do not think of themselves as adhering to Mitchell's early formulations, I think Mitchell's original "relational-conflict theory" left a conceptual, paradigmatic legacy, which, in a broad sense, still influences relational thought and practice. By organizing his theory around the internalization of problematic early object relations and the repetitive dimension of the analytic transference, and viewing those dimensions as reflecting the very nature of self, he left out the part of Sullivanian theory that posits a "drive toward mental health" (see below). If indeed such a drive exists, which I believe it does, it implies there are dimensions of self that orient toward and seek *needed relational experience,* which, in turn, implies that repetition, dissociation, and the existence of rigidly separated multiple self-states are not the whole story. And if they are not the whole story, what's missing?

I have come to believe, even more strongly than I did in my 1994 paper on "needed relationships," that the forward edge of the patient's motivations (conscious and unconscious) is a primary driver of the analytic process. To be somewhat reductive about it, if we think of patients' core struggles as stemming from some form or forms of early *negation* of their subjectivities and developmental needs by significant others, most are proactively motivated to *seek* experiences of *recognition*, and therapeutic responsiveness informed by that recognition, in an unconscious effort to secure needed developmental experiences, albeit in much more complex form than what occurs between an ordinary good-enough mother and her baby, given the adaptive and characterological vicissitudes of developmental trauma (S. Stern 2017, Chapter 1). On the analyst's side, there is a convergence among *many* theorists from diverse theoretical traditions implicating a fundamental principle of both healthy development and analytic transformation and growth—namely a principle of recurrent *matching* or *meeting* patients in state-specific ways that support the patient's self-consolidation, self-articulation, and forward movement toward their own developmental aims. Since these two trends are obviously related, many of the theorists who emphasize one also emphasize the other.

These are not new ideas to readers of these volumes. As I view our current situation, although much forward-edge theorizing is now viewed as residing inside a broadening relational "tent," it has not fully penetrated and transformed the core paradigm. In a sense, what we have now is a situation not unlike the situation of relational theories at the point Greenberg and Mitchell (1983) first recognized the implicit existence of an un-named relational paradigm. Although there were numerous brilliant theories and part-theories, it was not until Greenberg and Mitchell, and later Mitchell (1988), organized them into a new paradigm that they acquired the power to challenge the classical paradigm. Now, although there are numerous theories and part-theories that emphasize forward-edge relational thinking, and/or meeting patients in ways that are specific to their unique developmental and therapeutic needs, they are somewhat atomized—should I say, dissociated!—such that they have not fully penetrated and expanded the core theoretical and meta-theoretical assumptions of the contemporary relational paradigm. It would seem useful, therefore, to review some portion of this now-extensive literature, on the premise that, in aggregate, these theoretical lines will expand our core ideas about *theoretical bedrock*, enabling us to see more clearly the *bedrock of the psyche*.

The forward edge of the unconscious

The generative idea in this line of psychoanalytic theorizing is that in all but our most damaged and cynical patients there exists an inherent forward-tending, health-seeking, motivational push operating, in large part, at the level of unconscious communication. Thus, as early as 1954 **Sullivan** wrote:

> There is a great deal of fairly subtle data to support the notion that every human being, if he has not been tediously demoralized by a long series of disasters, comes fairly readily to manifest processes which tend to improve his efficiency as a human being, his satisfactions, and his success in living—a tendency which I somewhat loosely call *the drive toward mental health.*
>
> (1954/1970, p. 100)

This basic assumption was prominent in the thinking of other major late-mid-century psychoanalytic theorists, many of whom contributed in different ways to the general developmental-relational paradigm that emerged during that period. **Winnicott** posited "a tendency towards growth and development" as part of the infant's "inherited potential" (1960/1965, p. 43). In the same paper, he pictured "a child reaching toward independent existence" (p. 43). In general, Winnicott envisioned both young children and patients as leading the developmental process with spontaneous gestures and the communication (signaling) of needs; the job of the parent or therapist being to empathically *meet and "implement" such gestures and needs* in good-enough fashion.

Kohut (1984) viewed it as a pre-requisite for a self-psychologically informed analysis that "the analysand . . . be able to mobilize in the psychoanalytic situation the maturation-directed needs for structure building via transmuting internalization of the revived selfobjects of childhood" (p. 71). By likening a patient's need for selfobject responsiveness to the body's need for *oxygen,* Kohut posited the self's active, unconscious search for needed selfobjects throughout the lifespan as a virtual law of nature.

Ogden (2009) illuminates core aspects of **Bion's** "theory of thinking," which posits a number of forward-tending motivational elements. In contrast to the more explicitly relational theories of Fairbairn, Winnicott, and Kohut, all of which emphasized *object-seeking* in one form or another, Bion focused on *truth-seeking* as the fundamental human need. In his book, *Experiences in Groups* (Bion, 1961), while recognizing both the individual and group "hatred of learning by experience" (p. 86), Bion asserted that, more fundamentally, human beings are "hopelessly committed to a developmental procedure" (p. 89)—that is, in Ogden's words, "to thinking, learning from experience, and growing up" (Ogden, 2009, p. 94). In *Learning from Experience* (1962), Bion (using language similar to Kohut's regarding the life-long need for selfobjects) asserted that ". . . a sense of reality matters to the individual in the way that food, drink, air, and excretion of waste products matter" (Bion, 1962, p. 42, cited in Ogden, 2009, p. 94). For Bion, the capacity to think about and process experience, especially painful emotional experience, was central to human development and full, reality-based living. While Bion recognized human beings' ambivalence about facing their personal truths, he believed that, at the deepest levels— the levels at which suffering patients are drawn to psychoanalysis and its truth-seeking telos—we need and unconsciously seek our truths, though we also need (and seek) particular kinds of analytic help in doing so. Bion (1962) believed this help came in the form of a *container/contained* relationship understood as an unconscious enlistment of the mother/analyst in experiences of anxiety and emotional turbulence ("the contained") in need of "containment," where containment refers to the mother/analyst's capacity to experience, tolerate, process (through "reverie") and thereby moderate the infant's or patient's overwhelming, terrifying affect states, primitive proto-thoughts, and projective identifications, rendering them tolerable, integratable, and usable for psychological growth.

Moving forward in time to the relational/intersubjective turn beginning in the early 1980s, in contrast to Mitchell's (1988) emphasis on the repetitive dimension of enactments, **Bollas** argued that the "unthought known" was comprised not only of the sequelae of early pathogenic experiences—in his words, "the mother's logic of being and relating"—but also "the logic" of the patient's "true self" or "idiom" as it interacted, first with the early pathogenic environment, and now with the uniquely new intersubjective environment of analysis. Thus, he argued: enactments are "not merely a reliving of a relation to the mother or father, or a re-presentation of the child self, but a **fundamentally new experience** . . ." (p. 278). According to Bollas, this true self dimension implicitly seeks interaction with *needed* "transformational objects" so as to become intersubjectively articulated and thereby increasingly integrated—essential processes in the development of a healthy sense of self. Later, he fleshed out this unconscious, new-object-seeking dimension as part of a "destiny drive" (Bollas, 1989).

Writing during the same period, **Stolorow** posited something similar to Bollas in his concept of "the developmental dimension of the transference" (e.g., Stolorow & Atwood, 1992; Stolorow, Brandchaft, & Atwood, 1987). This was essentially an integration of Kohut's concept of selfobject transferences into Stolorow et al.'s intersubjective systems model wherein they "found that the central motivational configurations mobilized by the analytic process are not pathological drive derivatives but thwarted and arrested developmental strivings" (Stolorow et al., 1987, p. 10). "In this dimension of the transference, the patient hopes and searches for a new selfobject experience that will help him resume and complete an arrested developmental process" (p. 102).

A unique and interesting variation of the idea of a prospective dimension of the patient's unconscious can be found in **Gardner's** 1983 book, *Self Inquiry.* Gardner's ideas have continuities with Bion's, though I see no evidence of explicit influence. (In fact, this short, eloquent book has no bibliography!) Gardner characterized the analytic process as propelled forward by the *implicit questions* the patient is always contemplating, or close to contemplating, at the edge of awareness: one question leading into another. "I'd say an analyst helps people to wonder at center-of-awareness what they've been wondering at edge. An analyst helps—tries to help—people to find what they've been wondering and to pursue it more persistently and respectfully" (1983, p. 13). Gardner's is a more romantic view of the patient's drive to understand than Bion's. Bion argued that truth-seeking was in the service of reality orientation, learning from experience, and ultimately, survival. Gardner, on the other hand, wrote that:

> People are always inquiring [in their efforts to] try to unify the fragmentary, the divergent, and the conflicting within themselves and between themselves and others. At edge-of-awareness, people are always trying to find, to refine, and to make actual their hidden visions of harmony: truth, beauty, goodness, and fairness. They are always trying to make sense of and to make harmonious their feelings, their ideas, their aims, and their acts, one with the other and with those of others . . . This struggle for unity within self and with others, and the ever-present edge-of-awareness inquiry that seeks it, is what makes humankind most human, and occasionally kind.
>
> (1983, pp. 13–14)

Psychoanalytic theorist Joseph **Weiss** (1971), later joined by psychological researcher and theorist Harold **Sampson** (1986), built on and extended the thread in Freud's later, ego-psychological writings regarding patients' unconscious, forward-tending impulse toward "mastery" of earlier traumas through dreams and the repetition compulsion (e.g., Freud, 1920, 1926, 1933, 1940). Weiss (1986) argued that:

> . . . the psychoanalytic process is in essence a process by which the patient works with the analyst, both consciously and unconsciously, to disconfirm his pathogenic beliefs. He does this by unconsciously testing his beliefs in relation to the analyst and by assimilating insight into them conveyed by the analyst's interpretations.
>
> (p. 101)

In their "control-mastery theory," Weiss and Sampson envisioned the unconscious (within an analytic context) as active and operating with a forward-tending motivation to disconfirm, and thereby gradually free the patient from, old, implicit "pathogenic beliefs" and assumptions gleaned from early relationships (a concept similar to Stolorow's "pathological organizing principles"). The analyst succeeds in helping advance the patient's unconscious aims by "passing" these "transference tests," thereby "emboldening" the patient to take progressively greater emotional risks with the analyst, and to deepen both the positive connection and the power (vulnerability and risk) of successive tests.

In my paper, "Needed Relationships and Repeated Relationships: An Integrated Relational Perspective" (S. Stern, 1994), I reviewed the relevant contributions of **Racker, Sandler, A. and P. Ornstein, Bacal, Weiss and Sampson, Bollas**, and **Newman**, all in support of the idea that patients actively, unconsciously seek new, reparative and developmental relational experiences with the analyst in addition to evoking "old" retraumatizing enactments. Then, in my 2002 paper, "Identification, Repetition, and Psychological Growth: An Expansion of Relational Theory," building on earlier formulations by **Fairbairn** and **Loewald**, I posited a forward developmental impetus to seek new, needed identificatory experiences with the analyst ("identification with recognition") to combat and ultimately transform old, toxic "identifications with negation."

In her paper that inspired the title of this section, **Tolpin** (2002) built on Kohut's earlier use of the term "leading edge transference" to characterize the new selfobject transference configurations he had identified and was incorporating into his psychology of the self (Miller, 1985). Taking things in a somewhat different direction than either Kohut (with his distinct *types* of selfobject transference), or Stolorow et al. (1987) (with their "two dimensions of the transference"), Tolpin argued that there was always some implicit expression of a "forward edge transference," even if only a "tendril" of hope, and even when the dominant transference and/or relational configuration of the moment seemed to be mostly expressive of the pathological elements in the patient's psychological organization. She was focusing as much on *the analyst's interpretive lens or framework* as she was on the nature of patients' psychological organizations. She felt that all psychoanalytic theories erred in the direction of over-focusing on pathology rather than the healthy, "normal" developmental hopes and strivings that most patients still possess, and which are evident in some form at all times. She was seeking to reverse that theory-driven bias:

> At one and the same time, theory-induced blindspots restrict our clinical vision of the patient's (and our own) psychic reality because first, they lead us to expect transference repetitions of nuclear

childhood pathology and its later derivatives, and second, they obscure the subtle hints of *bona fide* transferences that derive their force and momentum from still-viable tendrils of healthy childhood motivations, strivings, expectations, and hopes of getting what is needed now from the forward edge transference to the analyst ... *Here it is crucial to stress that fragile tendrils of remaining healthy needs and expectations are not readily apparent on the surface. My clinical examples will show that we have to be primed to look for them in order to see them and tease them out from the trailing edge pathology in which they are usually entwined.*

(2002, p. 167)

Moving further ahead in time, relational thinking has increasingly embraced the idea of a "two-person" or "relational" unconscious (Aron & Atlas, 2015; Bromberg, 2011; Gerson, 2004; Lyons-Ruth, 1999), and some of the theorists in this area have focused, either explicitly or implicitly, on its forward-tending dimension.

The Boston Change Process Study Group (2013) finds a forward-tending movement toward increasing systemic complexity and competence to be a characteristic of implicit relational processes in analytic dyads, evidenced most dramatically during enactments. They argue that enactments, rather than being a manifestation of dissociated traumatic relational experience from the patient's past, as relationalists have theorized, represent the emergence ("eruption") of new, more complex and therapeutically potent modes of interaction that had already begun to occur implicitly as part of the dyad's natural movement toward greater complexity and fittedness.

Without naming it as such, **Grossmark** (2012a, b) has proposed a theory of enactments with an implied forward edge dimension of unconscious engagement. His theory begins with the intriguing proposal that, rather than seeking to detect and interpret the problematic or defensive meanings of enactments in an effort to transform or "get out of" them, analysts would do better to regard and treat them as the relational equivalent of free association. In a spirit akin to Bion's (1970) seeking "at-one-ment with O," Grossmark suggests that analysts "unobtrusively" seek to enter "the flow of enactive engagement," trusting that flow to carry both patient and analyst into the vortex of the patient's unmetabolized trauma and generate interactive processes which enable a reworking and transformation of the patient's underlying traumatized states and relational needs.

Aron and Atlas (2015) recently offered a rich synthesis and creative extension of various trends in psychoanalytic thought, beginning with **Jung** (1912), all focusing on a forward-looking dimension and function of the unconscious. Departing from Freud's predominant interest in the determining unconscious influence of the past on present experience, Jung found a "prospective function" contained in symbols and dreams—an active, teleological dimension of the unconscious that pulls us toward our destiny, and anticipates, rehearses, constructs, and shapes future possibilities. The authors join Grossmark (2012a), the BCPSG (2013), myself (S. Stern 1994), and other relational theorists (broadly defined) by extending Jung's ideas to the area of analytic interaction and enactments. Unlike Grossmark and the BCPSG, and more similar to my (1994) thinking, they view enactments as having both a prospective and a repetitive dimension; or, to use Tolpin's (2002) terms, both a forward edge and a trailing edge. This is different from Grossmark's and the BCPSG's formulations in that the latter authors, as I have just reviewed, propose reframing enactments as *fully* prospective when interpreted and/or managed in light of the theoretical schemes they are advocating.

Finally, in my recent book (S. Stern, 2017), I posit a systemic tendency in analytic dyads that moves toward progressively inclusive forms of relational fittedness, implying a "forward edge of the relational unconscious".

The foregoing literature review attests to the fact that a very large number of the most prominent analytic theorists of the past 75 years have assigned a central role to the unconscious forward-edge strivings of both the individual patient and, more recently, the patient-analyst system. Some of these theorists fall within the "developmental arrest" category targeted by Mitchell (1988), but many do not; and in any case, even if such forward edge strivings are seen to imply some form of developmental arrest, such an arrest does not have to take the totalizing, literal form Mitchell found so problematic. In my own experience, analytic treatment invites and requires the co-participation of both the "child" and "adult" dimensions of each patient's unconscious subjectivity, and it is our ability to meet each patient in ways that recognize both of these dimensions as expressed in the complexity of the present analytic moment that is one of the ongoing conditions needed for analytic transformation and growth.

Meeting patients at points of therapeutic and developmental urgency

Just as there have been many characterizations of our patients' forward edge strivings and needs, there have been many renderings of what is involved in *meeting* each patient within the analytic space in ways that advance both the patient's implicit developmental/therapeutic aims and the analytic process more generally (e.g., Aron, 1996, 2006; Benjamin, 2004; Bollas, 1987; Boston Change Process Study Group, 2010; Bromberg, 1991, 2011; Cooper, 2000, 2014; Davies, 2004; Fonagy et al., 2002; Galatzer-Levy, 2009; Geist, 2009; Gedo, 1979; Ghent, 1992; Grand, 2013; Grossmark, 2012a, b; Havens, 1989; Hoffman, 1994; Modell, 1993; Newman, 1988; Poland, 2000; Reis, 2009; Sander, 1995, 2008; Schwaber, 1983; Shane, Shane & Gales, 1997; Slavin, 2010; Slavin & Kriegman, 1998; Slochower, 1996a, b; D.N. Stern et al., 1998; S. Stern, 2017; Stolorow, 2014).

As far as I am aware, Louis Sander (1962, 1987) was the first to introduce the word meeting into the psychoanalytic lexicon with his concept of "moments of meeting," though he repeatedly acknowledged his debt to Winnicott. The concept grew out of his studies of adaptive processes in infant development, but later was applied by the Boston Change Process Study Group (D.N. Stern et al., 1998), of which he was a member, to analogous processes in the adult analytic therapy relationship. Sander's original use of the phrase "moments of meeting," unlike the BCPSG's later use of the term to refer to infrequent, charged, dramatic analytic moments of attuned, authentic therapist responsiveness, is essentially synonymous with his concept of relational "fittedness" (Sander, 1995, 2008). It refers to the interaction between a baby and a good-enough mother in which the mother, *on an ongoing basis*, intuitively recognizes the infant's need or state of the moment and, in concert with the infant's implicit signaling, responds in ways that are specifically fitted to the infant's need or state, or its movement toward a coordinated task such as breast-feeding or wake-sleep. Sander underlines the fact that such moments of recognition and fittedness are "needed events," and that the reliable recurrence of such moments over time provides a *needed foundation* for the infant's development of basic trust, and ultimately a child's sense of agency and identity.[3]

In other words, *it is recurrent experiences of having one's states, needs, and gestures met or "matched"* (P. Weiss, 1970)—*repeated experiences of "knowing oneself as one is known"* (Sander, 2008)—*which cumulatively, incrementally, establishes the bedrock of the psyche.* Each of the forward-edge theorists reviewed above proposes, explicitly or implicitly, some variation of this basic idea applied to the dimensions of psychic experience each is focusing on, whether it be a spontaneous gesture (Winnicott), a projective identification (Bion), a selfobject need (Kohut), an implicit urgent question at the edge of awareness (Gardner), a pathogenic belief (Weiss & Sampson), a forward edge tendril of hope or need (Tolpin), or an unconscious hoped-for future outcome (Aron & Atlas).

Relational theorists beginning with Mitchell expanded this idea to include the problem of meeting patients from within the turbulence (or dissociative "blindness") of intersubjectively co-created enactments and impasses. In contrast to early versions of developmental-arrest thinking, which framed this meeting or matching process as analogous to a parent's (usually the mother's) good-enough (really, idealized) meeting of normal developmental states and needs, the early relational theorists, influenced by the interpersonal tradition, reframed the meeting process as a fully "two-person" encounter between two distinct, adult subjects (e.g., Ehrenberg, 1992; Mitchell, 1988). Within this frame, the analyst's fully human, less idealized subjectivity came into play in two principle ways: (1) The analyst's countertransference became the new privileged vehicle or "instrument" for accessing and grasping the relational dynamics of the moment, and thus ultimately, the patient's subjectivity (internalized relational world); (2) The analyst's authentic, expressed subjectivity (voice; shared self-state) came to be seen as the privileged form of "meeting"— the necessary and best way to "speak from within," and ultimately transform, enactments. Thus Bromberg (2011) writes:

> If there can be said to be an interpersonal or relational technique, it is mainly in the ability of the analyst throughout the course of each analysis to negotiate and renegotiate the meaning of what constitutes self-state sharing.
>
> (p. 136)

I am focusing here on a certain, influential line of theorizing (and theorists) within the contemporary relational tradition. There is now an expanding and increasingly nuanced literature on working with enactments, and many authors have diverged from this mainstream relational paradigm (e.g., Aron & Atlas, 2014; Boston Change Process Study Group, 2013; Grossmark, 2012a; Slochower, 1996a, b). Just as one example, Slochower (1996a, b) offered an integrated model in which, even during enactments, therapists may choose to "bracket" their reactive subjective states in recognition of what they sense the patient will be able to "hear" and use, given the current state of the patient's self—that is, a complex, fluid form of meeting or matching. Nevertheless, I believe my distillation in the preceding paragraph highlights a real form of slippage from the core understanding of "meeting" embodied in the forward-edge theories reviewed earlier, and captured in Sander's concepts of moments of meeting, fittedness, and specificity of recognition. The slippage is in the creeping assumption that the central developmental problems for which analytic patients are seeking help will manifest primarily in the context of repetitive or problematic enactments. This is a theoretically driven assumption that grows out of Mitchell's (1988) "relational-conflict theory" and a dissociation-based model of the mind, and constitutes a form of slippage from the idea of *meeting patients in their unique "areas" of difficulty and developmental breakdown, however these manifest in the clinical interaction.* A related assumption or assertion in mainstream relational theory is that all enactments reflect a similar underlying dynamic: a "mutual dissociation" of "not-me" self-states, being activated by current interactive tensions (Bromberg, 2011; D.B. Stern, 2010). From the standpoint of the theory of mind that underpins my arguments in this chapter, *no two enactments are alike; rather each reflects the infinitely complex intersubjective elements in play between two unique individuals during a particular moment or period of work* (see also S. Stern, 2017). Thus the intersubjective processes through which each enactment is grasped and worked through will be specific to that enactment and that analytic pair. Moreover, as I argued in the introduction to this chapter, and as Tolpin argued in the earlier quote from her 2002 paper, how a given enactment is experienced, interpreted, and clinically managed is inextricable from the analyst's conceptual/interpretive framework.

Personal synthesis

I believe it is possible to integrate the important advances in relational theory within a framework that retains both a forward-edge orientation and the core therapeutic idea of meeting patients in their (ever-evolving) areas of therapeutic and developmental need. The following quote from S. Stern (2017) represents my current attempt at such a narrative:

Contemporary analytic theorists beginning with Winnicott (1965) have alerted us to the degree to which patient and analyst, like mother and baby, form an intersubjective system (e.g., Beebe & Lachmann, 2002, 2014; Boston Change Process Study Group, 2010, 2013; Coburn, 2002, 2014; Galatzer-Levy, 1978, 2002; Ghent, 2002; Marks-Tarlow, 2008, 2011; Ogden, 1994; Sander, 2008; Seligman, 2005; Stolorow, 1997a, b). The analytic process is in some ways analogous to successful problem-solving and interactive regulation between a caregiver and baby. Yet it is also far more complex because it is a system competence (Sander, 1995) that must be responsive to the patient's history of relational trauma and system-*incompetence*, and the patient's complex psychological organization growing out of that history, as these now constitute and drive the patient's struggles. Because developmentally traumatized patients have grown up in situations that were decidedly *unfitted* to their early needs, their relational expectancies (transferences) and character adaptations incline them to be suspicious of, unpracticed in, resistant to, and even destructive of, the natural collaborative tendency observed between good-enough parents and their young children. *Thus analytic collaboration and fittedness must begin by meeting patients in spaces where being met is an alien, distrusted experience, which patients may misread, avoid, negate, or attack even as they unconsciously long for and seek it.* Analytic patients' distrustful, terrified, fragmented, deadened, overwhelmed, dysregulated, somaticized, disorganized, dissociated, colonized, and otherwise turbulent mental states (which are always embedded in, reactive to, and emergent from the ongoing analytic interaction) can only be transformed through systemic processes wherein the analyst learns through complex ongoing feedback at all levels of processing how to understand and respond to (meet) these states in increasingly individualized and nuanced ways. Moreover, leaps in analytic system-competence often emerge from some form of enacted "incompetence" (Russell, 1998, 2006). Inevitably, there is trial and error, disruption and repair, negation and recognition, enactment and emergence from enactment, confusion or uncertainty and illumination, as the system gropes toward greater fittedness, specificity of recognition, mutual recognition, and hence greater system-competence.

(pp. 27–28)

Within this general frame, enactments are fully integrated but not viewed as always, necessarily, central to the meeting process. And within this frame, dissociation is recognized as one core "principle of mental functioning," but is secondary to, and in pathology an aberration of, the more fundamental principle of healthy self-organization that evolves through recurrent experiences of being met and of coming to "know oneself as one is known." The therapeutic aim is to meet the patient in the complexity of his current state, using "the tools at hand"—that is, all the wisdom we have managed to accrue from psychoanalytic theories, clinical experience, and life experience. I offer the following clinical example to illustrate the sensibility I'm trying to describe.

Tom[4]

Tom, a man in his mid-30s, came for therapy and ultimately analysis, because he was significantly depressed with frequent suicidal ideation. There were also serious sexual concerns. He felt he had a small penis and thus felt inadequate to satisfy women sexually, despite considerable evidence to the contrary. For example, his girlfriend of five years was very affirming in this regard.

The family scenario for Tom, growing up, was that he had been enlisted by his mother as an ally in her relentlessly hostile relationship with his father. He regarded his mother as an embattled saint, devoted to her children but victimized by her angry, emotionally immature, intellectually limited father. Thus he devoted himself to making his mother happy by trying to be the kind of person he sensed she wanted him to be—responsible and high-achieving—and by defending her against the father's verbal attacks by getting in the middle and verbally attacking him himself.

In treatment, Tom's initial ways of engaging with me were complex and contradictory. He was skeptical that therapy could have much to offer that he, an intelligent, Ivy League-educated, introspective person, could not figure out for himself. Yet, at the same time, he seemed genuinely grateful for, and excited by, the insights into his current paralysis that I offered during the first few months of treatment. There were sessions in which he seemed in touch with his depression, the problems in his life and his increasing reliance on our relationship as a source of insight and hope. Just as often, however, he would come in in a more ironically detached mood and regale me with reports of his many cultural activities and the insights *they* had inspired. I noticed that in his reports of these activities he focused on the author as much as the work, emphasizing the author's brilliance or wisdom or originality, and how the author's ideas had given him new and meaningful insight into some aspect of himself or the world.

During this early period I began to be aware of a subtle sense of evaluative detachment in Tom's attitude toward me. It was clear he was scrutinizing me in terms of the intellectual value I added to his life, and the jury was still out. I found myself trying to be particularly sharp and incisive, preconsciously working to engage him. When I said something that obviously struck him I felt relieved and gratified. But when whole sessions or strings of sessions went by without any new insights from me, I could sense his disappointment and withdrawal. This was the uncomfortable atmosphere I was "living in" with Tom for some months, feeling anxiously uncertain of how to navigate.

As the tension built around this I felt I needed to say something. Finally, during a session in which Tom could barely contain his disgust that I had liked the movie *Good Will Hunting*, which he had hated, I expressed my awareness of how disappointed he obviously was in me. He admitted that, although he thought I was probably doing the right thing by not giving too many interpretations, he was having questions about how smart I was. Having said this, he immediately wondered if I felt like strangling him! I reflected for a moment and said, "No, but I'm aware of feeling alone in our relationship." He paused, and said: "That makes me feel sad. I know I keep a critical distance from everyone, and the more intense a relationship, the more dissatisfied I am." With this opening, I went on to interpret that I thought there was an addictive quality to his pursuit of what I called "intellectual orgasms," and that when he did not get these from me he felt intensely frustrated and disappointed. Obviously struck by this, he admitted that at times he wished he could be in analysis with Sigmund Freud, imagining that with Freud there would be one brilliant insight after another.

In the sessions following this interaction there was a sense of Tom's being less critically detached. He revealed that he was having homosexual anxieties triggered by several homosexual dreams. In one he was sucking on a big penis. His own association was that it related to his father in some way. He said that he resonated to the idea that his intellectual strivings were connected to his sexuality and admitted that my interpretation had confirmed his own suspicion that there was something about his intellectual life that was not all healthy. He had always been afraid that he was not capable of his own original thoughts and that he secretly relied upon the thoughts of others whose intellects he respected in order to appear intelligent. I interpreted that his compliance and identification with his mother's expectation that he devote himself to her over his own development had left him out of touch with himself—his own feelings, needs, desires, perceptions, and beliefs. He did not know who he was, thus had no sound basis for guiding his own life. At the same time, her expectations that he be intellectually high-achieving, and that he protect her from his father, placed him in a position of having to act more mature, intelligent, and man-like than he felt, with no hope of receiving the positive experiences with his father that might have helped him in this regard.

This sequence of interpretations seemed to reach Tom in a new way. He said "I've always felt embattled, always had to show my big ideas, my big thought. It's exhausting. I always had to have an intellectual erection, yet I felt so inadequate sexually." In the following session he reported having had better sex with his girlfriend, during which he had not felt small. Several sessions later he reported having cried the night before "because I realized that ideas are less important than feelings." He also reported having told his girlfriend about a fantasy he had of crawling into my lap like a child (2002b, pp. 732–734).

Discussion

Stepping back from the interaction, I would say that the theory of the nature of mind and the theory of analytic "technique" I am working from in this vignette represent an amalgam of ideas from multiple theoretical traditions: Winnicottian, Kohutian, Sullivanian/Interpersonal, Bionian, Relational, and non-linear dynamic systems. My dawning awareness of the enactment going on in the early months reflects my immersion in relational approaches to enactment. In hindsight, I can see clearly how Tom's initial stance of evaluating my therapeutic value against impossibly high standards was unconsciously evoking my own early experience with my similarly critical-evaluative mother, undoubtedly contributing to my anxiety and pre-conscious efforts to prove myself to him, and impairing my capacity to think freely about how to be his analyst during this period.

At the same time, even as the enactment was going on, I could see that Tom was desperately, almost addictively, searching for something that he felt he was missing, and my basic assumption about this was that it reflected some problem or deficit in the "bedrock of the psyche"—some essential way that Tom was not "met" in his relational development, and/or *was* "met" in destructive ways, causing pervasive feelings of impotence and inadequacy side by side with a compensatory grandiosity and critical-ness, and a subtle paranoid distrust. (See my discussion of this case in S. Stern, 2002 for a more in-depth conceptualization of Tom's core struggles.) So, given my forward-edge "lens," even as the enactment was developing, I was gathering data that was slowly illuminating the specifics of Tom's developmental traumas.

As the enactment reaches a crescendo I am pulled into "the eye of the storm"—the here-and-now urgency and tension that I sense is an uncon-scious test of the viability of Tom's and my analytic potential. That is, I'm not only focused on the question, "What's going on around here?" Rather, I am seeking to use that data in service to the larger question of "what Tom needs from me." I don't know "where" exactly my spontaneous admission that I felt alone in our relationship "came from." It seems closest to the kinds of things Bollas (1987) might say as an "expressive use of the countertransference." Unlike later relational theories of enact-ment, beginning with Mitchell's (1988), Bollas viewed these kinds of expressive interventions as forms of meeting or recognition—a giving voice to central aspects of a patient's early traumatic experience, which, though difficult to hear, named some feature of the patient's "unthought known" experience of self-with-other, thereby precipitating a "transfor-mational," integrating, and strengthening experience at the level of the bedrock of the psyche (true-self consolidation). In addition to Bollas' influence, I think my giving voice to my feelings of aloneness with Tom came out of a process of the kind Ogden (2005, 2009), following Bion (1962), calls "waking dreaming". It had probably been "gathering" in me unconsciously for some time, only emerging into consciousness at the point of urgency when it "needed" to.

Significantly, it was not a retaliatory or complementary response to Tom's disgust, disdain, and doubt, as I imagine his father might have reacted. It was simply a direct, firm, but non-defensive disclosure of how working with him had been making me feel. Moreover, it stepped outside the realm of Tom's preoccupation with intellectual superiority into the realm of affect. Thus, in an unpremeditated way, I was able to survive the potential destructiveness of the enactment that had been building (Winnicott, 1969), meet Tom at multiple levels of engagement, and implicitly open our system in a way that invited and emboldened him to reciprocate with his own deeper, truer affects and anxieties. This "meeting of minds" (Aron, 1996; Loewald, 1980) had not been consciously intentional on my part—we were both part of a system that was moving toward greater inclusiveness and fittedness (Boston Change Process Study Group, 2013; S. Stern 2017).

This opening allowed me to make a major interpretation, which *had* been pre-consciously forming itself for some time prior to this heightened clinical moment. As significant as its content was the explicit language I used to capture the quality of Tom's compulsive quest for infusions of intellectual potency from idealized others, primarily men. The live, edgy language seems, in retrospect, to have emerged from some link between Tom's unconscious and mine, and generated a different form of meeting than my earlier affective disclosure. I was trying to capture a prominent dimension of Tom's self-organization—a form of understanding and intervention I associate with Wilhelm Reich's (1933) "character analysis". By making his self-organization an "object of analysis" (Ogden, 1994), using language he could viscerally, instantly connect with, we were able to open up his previously-closed system, rendering it accessible to reflective awareness, unconscious processing, and a "Squiggle"-like form of serious play (between Tom and me and between Tom and his own unconscious) as Tom allowed the implications of its meanings to expand into new insights of his own.

Finally, in yet a different register, my more discursive illumination of the developmental reasons for his particular deficits and vulnerabilities—his life-long accommodations to, and identifications with, his mother's needs and expectations at the expense of his own developing senses of self and agency (Brandchaft et al., 2010; S. Stern, 2002, 2015)—also resonated with Tom, leading to his further recognition and elaboration of the actual self-states he had been living with much of his life.

Although my extended moment of meeting with Tom took place long before my full integration and formulation of the ideas in this chapter, it seems a good illustration of my main thesis. My handling of the enactment (at least the one I was aware of!) played a critical, transformational role in this interaction. But, as critical as it was, it was not the "main course" of the total interaction. Rather, the various ways in which I was able to *meet* Tom at different levels of experience, resulted in the co-creation of a developmentally and therapeutically needed experience of "knowing oneself as one is known," a cascade of "openings" in our process and Tom's psychic rigidities, and the beginning of the fundamental work at "the bedrock of Tom's psyche" that oriented our analysis as it unfolded from here.

Notes

1   Sections of this chapter are excerpted from my recently published book, *Needed Relationships and Psychoanalytic Healing: A Holistic Relational Perspective on the Therapeutic Process* (S. Stern, 2017). While the central focus of the present essay is on issues not as fully or directly addressed in my book, readers are referred to the book for a more comprehensive narrative of the theoretical and meta-theoretical positions and assumptions which underlie this essay. All excerpts are marked by indentation and/or endnotes.

2   Mitchell (2000) later incorporated a number of complex developmental perspectives into his thinking—especially those of Loewald, Fairbairn, attachment theorists, and the systems models emerging from psychoanalytic mother-infant observation studies—as he attempted to delineate different modes of interaction organized as a developmental hierarchy. However, even in this later, expanded integration, he did not seem to embrace the *forward-edge motivations* implicit in the developmental-arrest theories he had earlier repudiated. And, in any case, there was a way that his earlier thinking had taken on a life of its own as a foundational paradigm for relational theorizing.

3   Much of this paragraph is excerpted from S. Stern (2017, p. 45, footnote 4).

4   I have used this clinical example in two previous publications (S. Stern, 2002, 2017), each focusing on a different set of theoretical ideas. In the present context I'm using it to illustrate yet a different set of ideas—those developed in this chapter.

References

Aron, L. (1996). *A meeting of minds: Mutuality in psychoanalysis*. Hillsdale, NJ: The Analytic Press.

Aron, L. & Atlas, G. (2015). Generative enactment: Memories from the future. *Psychoanalytic Dialogues, 25*: 309–324.

Baranger, M. & Baranger, W. (1961–1962/2009). The analytic situation as a dynamic field. *International Journal of Psychoanalysis, 89*: 795–826.

Beebe, B. & Lachmann, F.M. (2002). *Infant research and adult treatment: Co-constructing interactions*. Hillsdale, NJ: The Analytic Press.

Beebe, B. & Lachmann, F.M. (2014). *The origins of attachment: Infant research and adult treatment*. London: Routledge.

Benjamin, J. (2004). Beyond doer and done to: An intersubjective view of thirdness. *Psychoanalytic Quarterly, 73*: 5–46.

Bion, W.R. (1959). *Experiences in groups and other papers*. New York: Basic Books.

Bion, W.R. (1962). Learning from experience. In: *Seven Servants*. New York: Aronson, 1977.

Bion, W.R. (1970). *Attention and interpretation*. London: Karnac.

Bollas, C. (1987). *Shadow of the object: Psychoanalysis of the unthought known*. New York: Columbia University Press.

Bollas, C. (1989). *Forces of destiny: Psychoanalysis and human idiom*. Northvale, NJ: Jason Aronson.

Boston Change Process Study Group (2010). *Change in psychotherapy: A unifying paradigm*. New York: W.W. Norton.

Boston Change Process Study Group (2013). Enactment and the emergence of new relational organization. *Journal of the American Psychoanalytic Association, 61*: 727–749.

Bromberg, P.M. (1991). On knowing one's patient inside out. *Psychoanalytic Dialogues, 1*: 399–422.

Bromberg, P.M. (1993). Shadow and substance: A relational perspective on clinical process. In: *Standing in the spaces: Essays on clinical process, trauma, and dissociation*. Hillsdale, NJ: The Analytic Press.

Bromberg, P.M. (1998). *Standing in the spaces: Essays on clinical process, trauma, and dissociation*. Hillsdale, NJ: The Analytic Press.

Bromberg, P.M. (2006). *Awakening the dreamer: Clinical journeys*. Mahwah, NJ: The Analytic Press.

Bromberg, P.M. (2011). *The shadow of the tsunami and the growth of the relational mind*. New York and London: Routledge.

Coburn, W.J. (2002). A world of systems: The role of systemic patterns of experience in the therapeutic process. *Psychoanalytic Inquiry, 22*: 655–677.

Coburn, W.J. (2014). *Psychoanalytic complexity: Clinical attitudes for therapeutic change*. New York and London: Routledge.

Cooper, S. (2000). *Objects of hope: Exploring possibility and limit in psycho-analysis*. Hillsdale, NJ: Analytic Press.

Cooper, S. (2014). The things we carry: Finding/creating the object and the analyst's self-reflective participation. *Psychoanalytic Dialogues, 24*: 621–636.

Davies, J.M. (1996). Linking the "pre-analytic" with the post-classical: Integration, dissociation, and the multiplicity of unconscious process. *Contemporary Psychoanalysis, 32*: 553–576.

Davies, J.M. (2004). Whose bad object are we anyway? Repetition and our elusive love affair with evil. *Psychoanalytic Dialogues, 14*: 711–732.

Ehrenberg, D.B. (1992). *The intimate edge: Extending the reach of psycho-analytic interaction*. New York: W.W. Norton.

Fonagy, P., Gergely, G., Jurist, E.L. & Target, M. (2002). *Affect regulation, mentalization, and the development of the self*. New York: Other Press.

Freud, S. (1920). Beyond the pleasure principle. In: J. Strachey (Ed. & Trans.) *The standard edition of the complete psychological works of Sigmund Freud* (Vol. 18, pp. 3–64). London: Hogarth Press, 1955.

Freud, S. (1926). Inhibitions, symptoms and anxiety. In J. Strachey (Ed. & Trans.), *The standard edition of the complete psychological works of Sigmund Freud* (Vol. 20, pp. 77–175). London: Hogarth Press, 1959.

Freud, S. (1933). New introductory lectures on psychoanalysis. In J. Strachey (Ed. & Trans.), *The standard edition of the complete psychological works of Sigmund Freud* (Vol. 22, pp. 3–182). London: Hogarth Press, 1964.

Freud, S. (1940). An outline of psychoanalysis. In J. Strachey (Ed. & Trans.), *The standard edition of the complete psychological works of Sigmund Freud* (Vol. 23, pp. 141–207). London: Hogarth Press, 1964.

Galatzer-Levy, R. (1978). Qualitative change from quantitative change: Mathematical catastrophe theory in relation to psychoanalysis. *Journal of the American Psychoanalytic Association, 26*: 921–935.

Galatzer-Levy, R. (2002). Emergence. *Psychoanalytic Inquiry, 22*: 708–727.

Galatzer-Levy, R. (2009), Good vibrations: Analytic process as coupled oscillations. *International Journal of Psychoanalysis, 90*: 983–1007.

Gardner, R.M. (1983). *Self-Inquiry*. Boston, MA and Toronto, ON: Little, Brown and Company.

Gedo, J.E. (1979). *Beyond interpretation: Toward a revised theory for psychoanalysis*. New York: International Universities Press.

Geist, R.A. (2009). Empathy, connectedness, and the evolution of boundaries in self psychological treatment. *International Journal of Psychoanalytic Self Psychology, 4*: 165–180.

Gerson, S. (2004). The relational unconscious: A core element of intersubjectiv-ity, thirdness, and clinical process. *Psychoanalytic Quarterly, 73*: 63–98.

Ghent, E. (1992). Paradox and process. *Psychoanalytic Dialogues, 2*: 135–159.

Grand, S. (2013). God at an impasse: Devotion, social justice and the psycho-analytic subject. *Psychoanalytic Dialogues, 23*: 449–463.

Greenberg, J. & Mitchell, S. (1983). *Object relations in psychoanalytic theory*. Cambridge, MA: Harvard University Press.

Grossmark, R. (2012a). The flow of enactive engagement. *Contemporary Psychoanalysis*, *48*: 287–300.

Grossmark, R. (2012b). The unobtrusive relational analyst. *Psychoanalytic Dialogues*, *22*: 629–646.

Havens, L. (1989). *A safe place: Laying the groundwork of psychotherapy*. Cambridge, MA: Harvard University Press.

Hoffman, I.Z. (1994). Dialectical thinking and therapeutic action. *Psychoanalytic Quarterly*, *63*: 187–218.

Jung, C.G. (1912). *Psychology of the unconscious: A study of the transformations and symbolisms of the libido, a contribution to the history of the evolution of thought* (B.M. Hinkle, trans., 1916; rev. 1952 as Symbols of transformation, selected works, Vol. 5), London, UK: Kegan, Paul, Trench, Trubner.

Kohut, H. (1984). *How does analysis cure?* (A. Goldberg & P. Stepansky, Eds.). Chicago, IL: University of Chicago Press.

Levenson, E.A. (1972). *The fallacy of understanding*. New York: Basic Books.

Levenson, E.A. (1983). *The ambiguity of change: An inquiry into the nature of psychoanalytic reality*. New York: Basic Books.

Lyons-Ruth, K. (1999). The two-person unconscious: Intersubjective dialogue, enactive relational representation, and the emergence of new forms of relational organization. *Psychoanalytic Inquiry*, *19*: 576–617.

Marks-Tarlow, T. (2008). *Psyche's veil: Psychotherapy, fractals and complexity*. London and New York: Routledge.

Marks-Tarlow, T. (2011). Merging and emerging: A non-linear portrait of intersubjectivity during psychotherapy. *Psychoanalytic Dialogues*, *21*: 110–127.

Mitchell, S.A. (1988). *Relational concepts in psychoanalysis: An integration*. Cambridge, MA: Harvard University Press.

Mitchell, S.A. (1993). *Hope and dread in psychoanalysis*. New York: Basic Books.

Mitchell, S.A. (1997). *Influence and autonomy in psychoanalysis*. Hillsdale, NJ: The Analytic Press.

Mitchell, S.A. (2000). *Relationality*. Hillsdale, NJ: The Analytic Press.

Modell, A.H. (1993). *The private self*. Cambridge, MA: Harvard University Press.

Newman, K.M. (1988). Countertransference: Its role in facilitating the use of the object. *The Annual of Psychoanalysis*, *16*: 251–275. Madison, CT: International Universities Press.

Ogden, T.H. (2005). *The art of psychoanalysis*. London and New York: Routledge.

Ogden, T.H. (2009a). Bion's four principles of mental functioning. In: *Rediscovering psychoanalysis*. London and New York: Routledge.

Ogden, T.H. (2009b). *Rediscovering psychoanalysis*. London and New York: Routledge.

Orange, D.M. (2011). *The suffering stranger*. New York and London: Routledge.

Orange, D.M. (2012). Development and response to the other: Engagement and enactment as bridging concepts among contemporary psychoanalytic groups. Paper given at St. Paul University, Ottawa, April 20, 2012.

Pizer, S.A., (1998). *Building bridges: The negotiation of paradox in psychoanalysis*. Hillsdale, NJ: The Analytic Press.

Poland, W.S. (2000). The analyst's witnessing and otherness. *Journal of the American Psychoanalytic Association, 48*: 17–34.

Racker, H. (1968). *Transference and countertransference*. New York: International Universities Press.

Reich, W. (1933). *Character analysis*. New York: Farrar, Straus and Giroux, 1949.

Reis, B. (2009), Performative and enactive features of psychoanalytic witnessing: The transference as the scene of address. *International Journal of Psychoanalysis, 90*: 1359–1372.

Russell, P.L. (1998). Trauma and the cognitive function of affects. In: J.G. Teicholz & D. Kriegman (Eds.), *Trauma, repetition, and affect regulation: The work of Paul Russel* (pp. 23–47). New York: The Other Press.

Russell, P.L. (2006). The theory of the crunch, In: *Smith College Studies in Social Work, Volume 26* (pp. 9–21). Haworth Press.

Sander, L. (1962). Issues in early mother-child interaction. *Journal of the American Academy of Child Psychiatry, 1*: 144–166.

Sander, L. (1987). Awareness of inner experience. *Child Abuse and Neglect, 2*: 339–346.

Sander, L. (1995). Identity and the experience of specificity in a process of recognition: Commentary on Seligman and Shanok. *Psychoanalytic Dialogues, 5*: 579–592.

Sander, L. (2008). *Living systems, evolving consciousness, and the emerging person: A selection of papers from the life work of Louis Sander*. (G. Amadei & I. Bianchi, Eds.). New York and London: Routledge.

Schwaber, E. (1983). Psychoanalytic listening and psychic reality. *International Review of Psychoanalysis, 10*: 379–392.

Seligman, S. (2005). Dynamic systems theories as a metaframework for psychoanalysis. *Psychoanalytic Dialogues, 15*: 285–319.

Shane, M., Shane, E. & Gales, M. (1997). *Intimate attachments: Toward a new self-psychology*. New York: Guilford Press.

Slavin, M.O. (2010). On recognizing the psychoanalytic perspective of the other: A discussion of "Recognition as: Intersubjective vulnerability in the psychoanalytic dialogue" by Donna Orange. *International Journal of Psychoanalytic Self Psychology, 5*: 274–292.

Slavin, M.O. & Kriegman, D. (1998). Why the analyst needs to change: Toward a theory of conflict, negotiation, and mutual influence in the therapeutic process. *Psychoanalytic Dialogues*, *8*: 247–284.

Slochower, J. (1996a). The holding environment and the fate of the analyst's subjectivity. *Psychoanalytic Dialogues*, *6*: 323–353.

Slochower, J. (1996b). *Holding and psychoanalysis: A relational perspective.* Hillsdale, NJ: The Analytic Press.

Stern, D.B. (1997). *Unformulated experience: From dissociation to imagination in psychoanalysis.* Hillsdale, NJ: The Analytic Press.

Stern, D.B. (2010). *Partners in thought: Working with unformulated experience, dissociation, and enactment.* New York and London: Routledge.

Stern, D.N., Sander, L.W., Nahum, J.P., Harrison, A.M., Lyons-Ruth, K., Morgan, A.C., Bruschweiler-Stern, N. & Tronick, E.Z. (1998). Non-interpretive mechanisms in psychoanalytic therapy: the "something more" than interpretation. *International Journal of Psychoanalysis*, *79*: 903–921.

Stern, S. (1994). Needed relationships and repeated relationships: An integrated relational perspective. *Psychoanalytic Dialogues*, *4*: 317–346

Stern, S. (2002). Identification, repetition, and psychological growth: An expansion of relational theory. *Psychoanalytic Psychology*, *19*: 722–738.

Stern, S. (2017). *Needed relationships and psychoanalytic healing: A holistic relational perspective on the therapeutic process.* London and New York: Routledge.

Stolorow, R.D. (2014). Undergoing the situation: Emotional dwelling is more that empathic understanding. *International Journal of Psychoanalytic Self Psychology*, *9*: 80–83.

Stolorow, R.D. & Atwood, G.E. (1992). *Contexts of being.* Hillsdale, NJ: The Analytic Press.

Stolorow, R.D., Brandchaft, B. & Atwood, G.E. (1987). *Psychoanalytic treatment: An intersubjective approach.* Hillsdale, NJ: The Analytic Press.

Sullivan, H.S. (1954). *The psychiatric interview.* New York: Norton.

Tolpin, M. (2002). Doing psychoanalysis of normal development: Forward edge transferences. *Progress in Self Psychology*, *18*: 167–190.

Weiss, J. (1971). The emergence of new themes: A contribution to the psychoanalytic theory of therapy. *International Journal of Psycho-Analysis*, *52*: 459–467.

Weiss, J., Sampson, H. & the Mount Zion Psychotherapy Research Group (1986). *The psychoanalytic process: Theory, clinical observations and empirical research.* New York: Guildford Press.

Weiss, P. (1970). Whither life science? *American Scientist*, *58*: 156–163.

Winnicott, D.W. (1960). The theory of the parent-infant relationship. In: *The Maturational Processes and the Facilitating Environment* (pp. 37–55). New York: International Universities Press, 1965.

Chapter 6

Inaction and puzzlement as interaction

Keeping attention in mind

Stephen Seligman

Relational theorists have defined the contemporary view that the analyst's behavior, sensitivity and sensibility vary in each analytic dyad, and thus helped to liberate contemporary analysis from an array of unfortunate constraints and misconceptions. The relational turn opened up the virtues of enlivening interpersonal contact, openness to the powerful back-and-forth of mutual influence, and the immediacy of intense emotional engagement. We breathe more freely now that we have acknowledged that the analyst is affecting the course of the evolving relationship in multiple ways, conscious and unconscious, such that each analysis is distinctive and dependent on both partners in the effort.

Here, however, I wonder whether Relationalists are not sufficiently valuing the analyst's special aptitude for an open, quiet, focused mind in the midst of deep emotional and interpersonal activity. There may well be an emerging overvaluation of interaction, especially under conditions of high affective arousal, that divert us from the opportunities offered by reflective, steady attention—one which may be, paradoxically, supported by a thoughtful suppression of the usual impulses to interaction. This is not to call for a return to the traditional privileging of some kind of misconceived, idealized inaction, but rather to ask whether there are times that we jump toward more vocal or visible interventions at times when watching and waiting, maintaining a thoughtful inwardness, might open things up even further.

Each analytic school has its own suppositions about what is helpful to patients. These lead to a kind of technical hierarchy, a set of preferences influencing the specific practical choices that analysts make in each session: These shape the "reflexes" that steer our moment-to-moment "decision-making," unconscious and implicit as it often is. Listening to the "same material," the self psychologist, for example, may be more likely to seek an empathic link, while the ego psychologist might tend to interpret conflict. Analytic orientations, then, are just that: principles for thinking and acting that help make our difficult work a bit easier, a kind of "analytic preconscious," as Victoria Hamilton (1996) proposed. It is difficult to imagine an analyst who could proceed without such preconceptions: Everyday analytic practice is very complex, presents extraordinary emotional strains and pressures, and encounters a very large array of highly ambiguous and idiosyncratically-organized information that resists ordinary classification. Such principles are embedded in a set of theories and clinical aesthetics and transmitted through varied formal and informal pathways, including courses, supervisions, choices and fashions from the analytic literature, informal discussions and other cultural events, status hierarchies within institutes and the broader communities, and of course, personal analyses (Seligman, 2006).

The classical analytic schools have typically been most rigid in this regard, regarding interpretation as the preferred interventions. Psychiatric residents at one major psychoanalytically-oriented hospital in the 1950's, for example, would compete over who spoke the least in their clinical hours (Robert Wallerstein, personal communication). Career progress often depended on one's choice of "the right" analyst and supervisors, and practices and practitioners who deviated, even marginally, were stigmatized as "not analytic." Relational theory and practice have been in the vanguard of opening these orthodoxies, even in the more conservative centers. Our approach to "technique" is inclusive, backed up by our tolerant analytic culture and our theoretical view that each analytic dyad develops its own specific personal way of being helpful (Bass, 2014).

But this does not mean that we are immune to the risks of over-valuing certain kinds of interventions at the expense of others (See Stern, 2014, for an elaboration of this view). Relational case reports frequently highlight a crucial moment of impasse and its resolution, perhaps at the expense of all the everyday incremental, messy routine of working through indeterminacy that precedes and follows such moments. Certain therapeutic processes are frequently featured, including analysts' self-analysis of problematic countertransferences, therapeutic relationships disrupted by more or less out-of-control emotional interactions that end in transformative repair, and self-disclosures of various types.

I am aware that I may be caricaturing here, and in any case, know that such scenarios are in fact quite common and regularly therapeutic. Relational psychoanalysis' creating the theory to understand them and the spaces to talk about them may be the single most important development in the overall analytic scene in the last several decades. For example, Slochower (1996) has elaborated the Winnicottian ideas about "holding" in the relational context, and Bass (2007) has preserved some of the established ideas about the analytic frame, even as he has seen it as an interactive context. Like many others, Mitchell (1988, 1993) cast the relational analytic perspective as both additive as well as critical of the established analytic approaches.

Still, and especially in writing for this volume, I want to raise my concern that our enthusiasm for the different modes of interaction that we have "liberated" from the shadow of the classical orthodoxies may be leaving us less aware of the importance of some of the more quotidian aspects of everyday analytic work. Much of each analysis is spent uneventfully, or at least routinely, with the patient speaking and the analyst listening. Indeed, this seems to be what keeps many patients returning to analysis when there isn't something more compelling going on, especially in the early stages. From the point of view of naïve observation, it seems fair to say that one of the most fundamental characteristics of clinical psychoanalysis, as it is actually lived every day, is that the analyst is usually paying careful attention to the patient. However, this fundamental fact is often overlooked, despite wide agreement about how important it is— perhaps because it is so fundamental that it is "hidden in plain sight."

It may be that the relational innovation featuring the analyst's interactive participation may be a factor leading us to "inattention to attention." This is hardly a uniquely relational problem: Psychoanalytic metapsychologies and clinical presentations often operate at some distance from a comprehensive account of the concrete, specific activities that constitute everyday practice. The intense pressures of clinical work along with trends in analytic institutional cultures tend to distract us from the less dramatic parts of our routines; the more sensational moments tend to get the emotional and intellectual juices flowing.

But there is something quite generative and even transformative in disciplined observation and quiet concentration, even when this may involve a kind of reserve and even self-withholding that would not seem to be most encouraged by the relational orientation, at least on its face. This can lead to great depth and a powerful sense of safety and recognition that can lead to both insight and growth-promoting interactions.

This is not to call for a return to the tired conventions of "neutrality" and "abstinence." The analytic rituals can render us lifeless and become instruments of a kind of knowledge-power that can be especially destructive especially when patients can be so vulnerable. Rituals and other similar practices often have substantial, special effects. As has been well-described, the ritualized dimensions of the analytic situation are a key part of its evocative power.

From the relational perspective, whatever analyst and patient are doing together is a form of relating in its own way, and should be considered in terms of its meanings and effects. The prescribed asymmetrical role structures of each analytic couple potentiate the analyst's thoughtful, considerate and inward absorption in both the patient's internal world and in what is going on in the room; this in turn can be a source of creativity and vitality that might not otherwise develop. As Cooper, Corbett and I wrote in summarizing these views: "When thoughtfully approached, the analyst's disciplined concentration can expand the analytic field, disrupt the patient's (and sometimes the analyst's) overly rigid personality styles, beliefs, defensive operations, and internal object relations" (Cooper, Corbett & Seligman, 2014).

Other analytic groups, such as classical Freudians and Bionians, have featured this mindset more centrally in their clinical thinking, describing "freely-floating attention," "reverie," and other special forms of listening. Relational psychoanalysis has established its own foundations strongly enough that we can revisit such thinking without sacrificing our own vital foundations. As we come to think of ourselves as a "Big Tent" (Bass, 2014), we may have more room to highlight and indeed, re-interpret some of the traditional conceptualizations without losing the value of our overall intersubjective, phenomenological viewpoint.

The creative element of the analyst's chronic puzzlement: the central role of chaos in the analyst's experience

As background to a more specific discussion of the analyst's concentrated attention, I want to consider the role of uncertainty in the analytic process, especially in relation to the analysts' anxieties. A puzzled and uncertain mood and mindset characterizes most of our everyday work, whether in the foreground or background. Although they are sometimes viewed as impediments, these feelings are actually at the core of analytic progress.

Several factors may be involved in the frequency with which these perplexing states occur, varying within and across cases. Psychoanalysis in general calls attention to the elusive and enigmatic nature of the mind, especially when viewed through the analytic prism. Generally, unprocessed, intense, painful emotions are central and disorganizing. In addition, as such feelings are generally not explicit and thus often present in the analytic field in a barely perceptible form, they remain unacknowledged while nonetheless driving the situation. Relational psychoanalysis has been indispensable in acknowledging how much analysts' minds are also elusive and subject to similar pressures. The analyst may find herself struggling with ideas and emotional states that seem sudden, unbidden, inarticulable, forbidden, out-of-synch, all while the patient may seem to be more or less somewhere else. In addition, the ubiquity of projection, identification and empathy make it difficult to sort out who is leading whom to feel what. Furthermore, that transference and countertransference do not always unfold synchronously makes all of this more puzzling, even when the analyst and patient are in communicative contact.

Another factor for the chronicity of the unsteady mood is that change in psychoanalysis is frequently incremental and uneven, becoming apparent only over extended periods of time. One sign of the importance of the ongoing immersion in uncertainty comes when colleagues in consultation groups who hear one another's cases periodically are more aware of shifts than the therapists themselves. The presenters are just going along, but their colleagues see the emergence of something new. There is a tendency to get used to what is going on, to habituate, that may subtly occlude the analyst's vision.

Dynamic systems theories inform both the more destabilizing and routine aspects of analytic progress. In systems terms, routine analytic work involves building more complex, inclusive structures over time, with all the ebbs and flows, fluxes and shifts that are involved in such changes. The systems theories also show that uncertainty is a reflection of the transformational, chaotic nature of the analytic process: *the analyst may well be puzzled when in touch with potential change* (see, for example, Coburn, 2014; Seligman, 2005; Thelen, 2005). In addition, the analyst's commitment to attention and to the creative possibilities of inaction can itself be a source of change.

Each psychoanalysis can be observed as a series of interactions at a variety of time scales—years, months, hours, seconds and even microseconds. Analysts often think that we are proceeding with some sense of where we are going, and indeed that may sometimes be true. There is thus value to explicit discussions of "technique." At the same time, as relational analysts are acutely aware, we are responding to a multi-dimensional array of factors, many of which are on the margins of our awareness. Much of what we think of as clinical acumen emerges from an implicit sense of what is going on, emerging without conscious preparation or anticipation. This is why we are often tempted to use terms such as "intuition," "tact," "timing," "natural talent," and the like. Analysts' abilities to maintain a generally reflective, attentive state of mind provide a working backdrop for this kind of less than conscious, subtle judgment under uncertain, anxious and often emotionally turbulent conditions.

From a convergent literary-philosophical perspective, Bachelard (1969/ 1984) affirmed the emotional impact emerging from spontaneous creative imagination in the midst of apparently disordered processes:

> Very often, then, it is in the opposite of causality, that is, in reverberation . . . that we find the real measure of a poetic image . . . To say that the poetic image is independent of causality is to make a rather serious statement. But the causes cited by psychologists and psychoanalysts can never really explain the unexpected nature of the new image, any more than they can explain the attraction it holds for a mind that is foreign to the process of its creation . . . The poet does not confer the past of his image upon me, and yet his image immediately takes root in me.
>
> (pp. xvi–xvii)

Affirming uncertainty as a source of dynamic change

Life along these fault lines is therefore basic to the everyday worklife of the practicing analyst. When we are on our game, we react differently from most people going about their business. In ordinary situations, most of us may well be motivated to reduce uncertainty, to resolve matters, to habituate to others and to our own experience both with others and also intrapsychically. There may be some costs to this, but it is often valuable in getting things done and providing a sense of ongoing security.

But one of the distinctive properties of the analytic situation, oriented to change as it is, is that such resolutions are not sought in the short run, and probably not in the middle run, either. Psychoanalysis has a different "set point" with regard to anxiety and uncertainty. The interest in the internal world moves the focus away from the effect on actual objects and toward empty, open space and time. "Good analysts" may well be biased toward postponing resolution until the potentials for effective change have emerged: This is supported by openness and optimism that things can work out for the best, even in the face of suffering. This hopefulness is paradoxical, since it rests on an interest in that same suffering (Mitchell, 1993).

Technical decisions will often turn on questions about the resolution of uncertainty and related anxieties: What level of uncertainty and anxiety works for analytic progress in a specific case and in general? Analysts are generally making decisions, usually implicit ones, about how much anxiety to tolerate. For example, the common dilemma of whether to answer a patient's questions often turns on such issues, although more elaborate accounts are sometimes offered: A patient began a recent hour after a long weekend by asking whether I would charge him for the appointments that he recently missed due to his daughter's illness. I asked a question or two about his feelings, but as I felt anxious and uncertain about what to do, along with pressure to catch up on a number of important themes that had been in the air before the missed appointments, I offered a quick, practical answer. As time went on, however, I saw that this original question was laden with emotion and meaning, and that my answer had struck a quite dissonant note with the patient, leaving a residue that has been difficult to repair. My point here is not that I made the "wrong" decision or that one should not answer questions or reach practical solutions (these are complex and situation-specific matters), but that my reaction emerged out of my urgency to reduce anxiety.

In the face of such strains, identifications with one or another analytic grouping and its ideas may buffer the analyst against her own anxiety in the face of the ubiquitous indeterminacy and seclusion of analytic work. These identifications may be useful, and perhaps even necessary to some extent. But they run the risk of distracting us from the more immediate personal, private and dyad-specific dimensions of what is going on. There may be a tradeoff between staying in touch with all of what is happening, on the one hand, and feeling competent and admirable in the isolation of practicing analysis, on the other. In service of these motivations (among many others), clinical theoretical positions are invoked; but this kind of thing often relies on idealization of theories and groups, along with the precocity that can go along with it. The analyst's specific concerns about professional identity are often in play: For example, some of us will do what we think is expected of us by certain colleagues, real and imagined, so that we feel a comforting sense of belonging to or approval from a group or set of ideas that we value, and thus less beleaguered by loneliness and fears of inferiority. Sometimes, a fantasized competitive edge is sought. In addition to all this, of course, all the usual pressures, such as responsive countertransference, are very substantial.

The relational critique of the classical orthodoxies contributed to exposing these difficulties (Mitchell, 1989, for example). But we should be sure not to get lost in the all-too-human tendency to imagine that we have avoided problems just because we have identified them in someone else, or even worse, to indulge in excessive self-congratulation. Psychoanalysts, including Relationalists, tend to emphasize those moments, experiences and observations that confirm or at least illustrate our own preferred concepts. There is something to be said for this approach: We follow our own theories in conducting treatments and will therefore be likely to create interactions that enact those theories and/or, to read our interactions along such lines (Seligman, 2006). But this may also lead us to overlook other important clinical configurations and opportunities.

Beginning analysts may be especially prone to such pitfalls. I have recently been consulted by a quite sensitive therapist, Tim, who was beginning analytic training. The talk at the Institute emphasizes the effect of the patient's transference on the analyst. This is useful, of course, but my own impression is that this is applied overzealously, diverting attention from other dimensions of the situation at hand. In any case, Tim seemed especially interested in talking to his patient about how the patient is making him feel, quite early in the treatment and early in hours, before anything real got going with this quite detached man. For example, when the analysand began an hour talking about his girlfriend wanting expensive gifts, Tim immediately said something about how this made him feel concerned about the fee. It seemed like Tim was talking to a virtual patient, not the one in the room. (Berman [2014] has noted the extent to which analysts in training take on their supervisors' biases unconsciously and may apply them indiscriminately, for a variety of motives other than their nonetheless earnest wishes to help their patients.)

Our work in the supervision has been to get Tim to *feel better about "doing nothing,"* to focus on patient attention and being hopeful about that activity *in itself*, rather than letting his need for certainty or his ambition to satisfy his internalized teachers and colleagues drive him. As we have developed our own rapport around this, things have gotten freer and easier; the patient has come forward in new and very touching ways.

At the same time, Tim has become more able to tolerate his own discomfort. In addition to the usual experiences of anxiety and uncertainty, his particular unease includes his worries about being a beginning analyst—feeling inferior, idealizing a new professional identity which he has not yet inhabited, fears of doing something wrong, and the like. My effort was to help create a framework in which Tim's anxieties could have some space for his own attention, rather than being acted upon and thus suppressed. The growing capacity for attention is itself a key factor in how he works differently with his patients, since his way of working against them had rendered him inattentive, even as he thought that he was understanding "the right things."

In offering this vignette, I do understand that Tim was a beginner and that this kind of "bias" may not be typical. I offer it to illustrate a potential pitfall in the relational enthusiasm for such (regularly valuable) innovations as the analyst's acknowledging his own subjective experience. I also want to be very clear that it would be quite easy to find similar examples involving other orientations.

It may be that Tim's development (and my response to it) illustrates a certain kind of intergenerational process in innovative movements, of which relational psychoanalysis is but one. Many in the first generation of relational innovators began their careers immersed in approaches to which they reacted ambivalently or even negatively. However, they nonetheless internalized and often valued them, even as they also critiqued and even attacked them. But their enthusiasm for the exciting innovation is what is most communicated to the subsequent generations. This can be quite inspiring, and builds the strength of the new movement. But at the same time, the members of the younger generations may not have absorbed those aspects of the earlier traditions that the older ones have taken for granted, having them "in their bones." I started my career saturated in Freudian and object relational thinking, and I still regard those as essential perspectives, despite my strong sense of their problems. (See Harold Bloom [1997] on the Oedipal dimensions of "the anxiety of influence," and Thomas Kuhn [1970] on "the structure of scientific revolutions," for a broader and enlightening treatment of these intergenerational themes.)

Attention and engagement as pillars of the analytic approach

Overall, then, we should welcome confusion as a desirable state of mind rather than something to be obviated. The indeterminacy in the world is all around us. Tolerating, describing, engaging and even embracing it is at the core of the psychoanalytic aesthetic and therapeutic model; we know a great deal about dialectics of ambiguity and of concealment and unconcealment. Although this is widely acknowledged, a re-orientation of our own analytic outlook may be in order—for many of us some of the time, and some of us most of the time. We cannot avoid being motivated by the same affinity for predictability and order that captures us and our analysands elsewhere. But it is actually quite liberating to be oriented such that *it is our business to be puzzled about what is going on,* to be ready to get lost. To the extent that I'm able to do this, I find my own work more enjoyable. Days in the office are a little like traveling, going from town to town with a rough map, knowing that I'll find somewhere to stay most all the time, but not knowing exactly where it will be, or whom you will meet or see along the way. The point is to stay interested, to stay aware, to pay attention, and not to get unbearably uncomfortable. When I leave the office on such days, I might feel a bit exhausted, but, oddly, psychologically refreshed, since I've gone to some new places without worrying that I wouldn't get home at night. It might be hard to develop confidence in this kind of position without having had some considerable experience with analyses, but we might see our careers as works in progress toward this. We would do well to support and encourage our colleagues and students in developing and sustaining this pleasure, which is often an acquired one.

Analytic attention as presence and absence

With this in mind, we can turn more directly to the central role of attention as a core analytic virtue. My working assumption these days is that if I pay attention and try to stay involved, my patients and I are likely to find ourselves doing something helpful. From this vantage point, paying attention while staying really involved is the immediate goal—an orienting set point from which we are constantly derailed but to which we try to return; few of us focus on the longer run outcome in the midst of any particular analytic hour. Freud (1912) refers to something like this in his call for the analyst to suspend everyday preoccupation and the effort to abstract from the analytic situation mindset to maintain "freely floating attention." Bion (1970) specifies this in his advice to the analyst that s/he listen "without memory or desire."

The most striking exemplars of this come from several analytic schools, which suggests that this virtue is mostly atheoretical. There are some analysts who just seem like they have emptied their minds of ordinary preoccupation when they listen, able to get in vibration with a new space of attention and possibility. Erik Erikson, Joseph Sandler (a Contemporary Freudian), and Betty Joseph (a Contemporary Kleinian) all come to mind.

Relational analysis may be depriving itself of the widest array of possible resources, to the extent that we don't reach beyond our own circles, when there are so many profound figures and ideas available. In a sense, this paper is my effort to highlight these ideas about the analytic attention, which are more prominently featured in the Freudian tradition, so as to more fully import them onto the relational scene. That said, I must make special mention here of Emmanuel Ghent's presence and more broadly, his aesthetic and spiritual orientations. (Jessica Benjamin's [2005] homage to Mannie was all about attention.) Like the other analytic masters to whom I referred, Ghent, who was a practicing Buddhist, reminded me of the Zen practitioners that I have seen in my occasional and casual encounters with those domains (Baba Ram Dass, Allen Ginsburg, and most notably, a monk from Japan who seemed to remove the weight from the room at the San Francisco Zen Center that I just happened to be in when he walked in. I really could imagine that this guy might be one of those that needed to be held down by chains when he meditated.)

One might be tempted to think of this kind of attention as exquisitely passive. This might capture something, but it would be very much incomplete. The analyst's open attention is a corollary of how the analytic situation cultivates the analysand's engagement with absence, as a stimulus for projection, for transference, for contact with the past, for loss and all the essential gaps between what can be said, what can be grasped, what can be known, what can be felt, what can be communicated, and so on. All of this is vital, creative and energetic, if paradoxically so. An analyst working this way usually feels like s/he is doing something, even as it looks like nothing is happening. (I imagine that the analyst's brain would look very active on an fMRI.)

Muriel Dimen (personal communication), drawing on comments from Ken Corbett and Gayle Salamon wrote:

> In this reflective state, one "is capable of being in uncertainties, Mysteries, doubts without any irritable reaching after fact & reason," making it possible, desirable, and expectable to bear irresolution, or what you might call "unknowing." Queer theorist Gayle Salamon, commenting on Corbett, expands: unknowing is not not-knowing, but an active state: "to unknow is to revise or undo knowledge" one already has. . . . It is not just to withhold judgment, to "mark [. . .] the limits of knowledge," but to "engage [. . .] something beyond that marking of limits." A path to the doing and undoing of the clinical hierarchy between analyst and patient, unknowing affirms that one is "no longer within the regime of knowledge, but [. . .] engaged in something else too."

From a rather different point of view, the psychophysiologically-oriented psychologists Geller and Porges (2014) have written convergently:

Therapeutic presence involves therapists being fully in the moment on several concurrently occurring dimensions, including physical, emotional, cognitive, and relational. . . . Expert therapists have reported that the experience of therapeutic presence involves concurrently (a) being *grounded* and in contact with one's integrated and healthy self; (b) being open, receptive to, and *immersed* in what is poignant in the moment; and (c) having a larger sense of spaciousness and *expansion* of awareness and perception. . . . By being grounded, immersed and spacious, with the intention of being with and for the other, the therapist invites the client into a deeper and shared state of relational therapeutic presence.

(Geller and Porges, p. 179, italics theirs)

The analyst's attention to her own attention

But analysis differs from meditative spiritual practice, of course. Finally, it is not oriented toward peace or even clarity, but to the freedom to find and be found, with all its variations, frustrations and anxieties. This includes awareness of all the ways that the analytic relationship falls short, including leaving the patient alone with his often quite painful feelings. Along similar lines, the analyst cannot be expected to maintain clear attention, and certainly not to be without memory or desire; that would be to deny that she is a person. To the extent that Freud's (1912) and Bion's (1970) prescriptions for freely floating attention and listening without memory or desire are useful, they must be understood as ideals, touchpoints to be sought, with the expectation that these pure positions can never be maintained. Disruptions and distractions from this pure clarity are to be expected; indeed these are the key touch points for the analyst's introspective attention to what is throwing her off, what is coming up, and how her own states of mind may be linked or unlinked to the patient's. Thus, the interest in the analyst's attention is not only a guide to a way of thinking that is valuable in itself, but also a key way of organizing and selecting all the varied, baffling and often all too numerous array of feelings, images, impressions, perceptions, and the like that occur in the course of a session.

For example, when I find myself distracted with patients, I try to recall (as best as I can) when I became distracted, what was going on at that moment, and what has occupied my attention since then. To a greater extent than I had anticipated, doing this routinely has yielded both productive understandings and a return to relative equanimity and attention. For example, I have sometimes noticed that I have a "song in my head," which turns out to be quite related (apparently uncannily) to the patient's material, as when I heard the song "Won't Get Fooled Again," and realized I felt that my patient wasn't being entirely forthcoming about his drug abuse.

One patient recently told me how he was, uncharacteristically, starting to feel confused. Since we had been talking about his father's constant and harsh admonitions, he said that it seemed that his memories were under the floor that he was standing on, leaving him uncertain and empty. Meanwhile, I found myself thinking about a scene from the film, "Inglourious Basterds," (Tarantino, 2009), in which a Paris theater explodes into flames, immolating both the top Nazi leaders and many of the American infiltration team and French resistors who arranged the fire. Apparently distracted, I realized that I had begun my "reverie" with an earlier scene in the film, one in which a Gestapo officer exposes and kills a Jewish family hiding under the floorboards of the home of a French farmer who is protecting them. The image of that horrible inferno consuming everyone within the confined theater allowed me to imagine something more about how utterly unmanageable the patient's childhood had been. I could then tell the patient I wondered whether his memories were even more disturbing and chaotic than he imagined.

In addition, this approach also offers a basis for confidence in what might otherwise seem like *apparent impracticalities* of psychoanalytic method. It also can help shape an explanation of how analysis works that can be helpful to both patients and therapists in training. I have found it useful to reply to patients who urgently (and sometimes skeptically) ask for specific, practical solutions by explaining that I believe that attending to the feelings and other aspects of what is going on in the midst of a difficult situation is likely to lead to a new and better outcome. I regard this response as "relational" (such as that matters), since I am describing how our relationship might work and also declaring my authentic conviction about what I am doing.[1] Similarly, when supervisees ask, often forlornly, "But what should I do?" after we have come to some understanding about a case, I will often advise that they "just pay attention" to what we have been talking about. It's like batting in baseball: When you are at the plate, you don't actually plan how you will swing the bat and you definitely shouldn't think about the score: You just try to see the pitch, and if you see the ball well, you will be much more likely to hit it well, and change that very score (see Seligman, 2010, for a more extended discussion.)

Therapeutic action and the aesthetics of psychoanalysis

Along with the emerging complexity in our views of therapeutic action, the emphasis on the analyst's reflectiveness supports a complex, multi-modal model of analysis. In addition to the direct effects of recognition processes, personal change can occur through a variety of pathways that can emerge under the special conditions of the reflectively-oriented relationship system, including insight, disconfirmation of expectations, new developmental opportunities and empathic responsiveness, among others. Emphasizing reflection does not imply that insight is the only form of analytic change. Understanding is not only *about* experience, it is itself an experience.

Relationalists will do well to feature a basic psychoanalytic aesthetic of absorption in the patient's psyche, along with our firm conviction that we are always affected by and affecting the analytic process, such that "technique" is a matter of improvisation and experimentation (if it "exists" at all). This kind of active engagement may well span the theoretical persuasions, although different schools may frame it differently: What analysts do is to provide constant availability of our minds (and hearts), often with great effort and amidst substantial pressure. Again, this is not to renovate the caricature of the "neutral" analyst. The emphasis on contained reflectiveness does not contradict our radical understanding of the inevitability of analysts' acting with patients: From the relational perspective, the analyst's understanding, in whatever analytic model, is the defining characteristic of an actively constructed, and evolving, social relationship, rather than a matter of just apprehending something pre-existing in the patient's mind.

The analyst's commitment to reflection supports a certain kind of rela-tionship that then enables therapeutic action along the multiple lines of which we are increasingly aware: Understanding is also a kind of relationship, and indeed, understanding and being understood within relationships–thinking together with someone—is a relationship form with especially transformative potentials. As one of my senior, classical Freudian supervisors put it, when "two people get together to think about one of them something good is likely to happen" (Herbert Lehmann, personal communication).

Attention and relational-analytic practice

Psychoanalysis involves two people, at least one of whom usually is in emotional need and pain, is pretty worried, and explicitly wants to be helped, and another who has agreed to try to be helpful: the requirements for us are quite different from those of the corollary spiritual practices. The relational stance today must preserve the simultaneity of engagement, absorption and attention, all organized in our knowledge of what is really involved in being needed and trying to help. This is of course very demanding. While this may appear obvious, there has been a misconception among our critics that the analyst's taking action or otherwise being affected by the analytic field is necessarily antagonistic to these commitments.

The conservative critics of relational analysis are mistaken when they roll out a concern that analysts who feel free to express themselves in the transference-countertransference lose track of deeper dimensions: That we affirmatively admit that we are affected doesn't imply that we don't know what it means to be open, mindful and observant. The emerging relational approach is well served to stay rooted in the same commitment to attention and understanding that has appeared in some other analytic orientations, but with the more realistic idea that we have no choice but to be caught up in the analysand's influence when we allow ourselves to be so permeable to it. In one sense, the analytic project always settles and unsettles around tensions between a basic awareness of unpredictability, incoherence and even chaos, on the one hand, and the need for something more organized and steady, which is shared by the analyst and patient and also experienced and managed by them in different and separate ways. The elaboration of these differences occurs in a variety of ways, including talk, enactments, private thoughts and other individual and joint experiences of all sorts, mutual regulation and recognition, frustration and confusion, and on and on. Altogether, if things are going well, these lead toward a growing shared capacity to tolerate uncertainty and anxiety together, with more spaciousness and freedom.

Relational analysts have correctly argued that we understand best by getting involved, and that we imagine otherwise at our patients' perils. The relational revolution offers the liberating destruction of the idealization of the analyst's mind as disembodied. Although this may seem tragic or even heretical for some of our more nostalgic colleagues, we have led the way in bringing reality to bear on the analytic myth. We should stay involved with what we know about the virtues of doing nothing when it supports our paying attention, since paying attention is not doing nothing, at all. Our paradoxical interest in getting involved while valuing attention and inaction can be a steady, but disequilibriating factor which can facilitate change if things are working out right.

Notes

1   This is not to rule out other options, of course, including offering a practical solution, inquiring about the urgency, explaining that the therapeutic process might take some time, describing other parts of my response (such as feeling pressured, for example), offering a specific interpretation, and so on.

References

Bachelard, G. (1969/1984). *The Poetics of Space*. Boston, MA: Beacon Press.

Bass, A. (2007). When the frame doesn't fit the picture. *Psychoanalytic Dialogues*, 17:1–27.

Bass. A. (2014). Three pleas for a measure of uncertainty, reverie, and private contemplation in the chaotic, interactive, nonlinear dynamic field of interpersonal/intersubjective relational psychoanalysis. *Psychoanalytic Dialogues*, 24:6, 663–675.

Benjamin, J. (2005). From many into one: Attention, energy, and the containing of multitudes. *Psychoanalytic Dialogues*, 15:2, 185–202.

Berman, E. (2004). *Impossible Training: A Relational View of Psychoanalytic Education*. Hillsdale, NJ: Analytic Press.

Bion, W.R. (1970). *Attention and Interpretation: A Scientific Approach to Insight in Psycho-Analysis and Groups*. London: Tavistock.

Bloom, H. (1997). *The Anxiety of Influence: A Theory of Poetry*. (2nd ed.) New York: Oxford University Press.

Coburn, W.J. (2014). *Psychoanalytic Complexity: Clinical Attitudes for Therapeutic Change*. New York: Routledge.

Cooper, S.H., Corbett, K. and Seligman, S. (2014). Clinical reflection and ritual as forms of participation and interaction: Reply to Bass and Stern. *Psychoanalytic Dialogues*, 24:6, 684–690.

Freud, S. (1912). Recommendations to physicians practicing psycho-analysis. Standard Edition, 12:111–112. London: Hogarth Press, 1958.

Geller, S.M. and Porges, S.W. (2014). Therapeutic Presence: Neurophysiological mechanisms mediating feeling safe in therapeutic relationships. *Journal of Psychotherapy Integration*, 24:3, 178–192.

Hamilton, V. (1996). *The Analyst's Preconscious*. New York: The Analytic Press.

Kuhn, T.S. (1970). *The Structure of Scientific Revolutions*. (2nd ed.). Chicago, IL: University of Chicago Press.

Mitchell, S. (1993). *Hope and Dread in Psychoanalysis*. New York: Basic Books.

Seligman, S. (2005). Dynamic systems theories as a metaframework for psychoanalysis. *Psychoanalytic Dialogues: A Journal of Relational Perspectives*. 15:2, 285–319.

Seligman, S. (2006). The analyst's theoretical persuasion and the construction of a conscientious analysis: Commentary on a paper by Meira Likierman. *Psychoanalytic Dialogues: A Journal of Relational Perspectives*, 16:397–405.

Seligman, S. (2010). The sensibility of baseball: Structure, imagination and the resolution of paradox. *Contemporary Psychoanalysis*. 46:4, 562–577.

Slochower, J. (1996). *Holding and Psychoanalysis: A Relational Perspective*. Hillsdale, NJ: The Analytic Press.

Tarantino, Q. (2009). *Inglourious Basterds*. (film).

Thelen, E. (2005). Dynamic systems theory and the complexity of change. *Psychoanalytic Dialogues: A Journal of Relational Perspectives*. 15:2, 255–284.

Chapter 7

The analyst's private space
Spontaneity, ritual, psychotherapeutic action, and self-care

Ken Corbett

That which is private, that which belongs to one person, or the act of choosing not to share what is on one's mind has been paid relatively little heed in our modern discourse on the psychoanalytic situation. This limited attention follows on the ways in which privacy has been soundly deconstructed. There is no private space outside the ever-present and pressing social order. There is no private body that is not exposed to social crafting and anxious normative regulation. There is no private mind that thinks alone, separate, or alongside the busy buzzing congress of human interchange. We are not even dreaming when we are dreaming; the ego and the social push their way into that permeable fantastic.

The proposition that there is never one person, never one mind, is in fact the leading edge of relational psychoanalytic theory. Experience-near collaboration is the ideal, not perpendicular symbolic abstraction that hails from a mind that is containing and considering another mind. Lives and lively minds are co-created and brought to life by the patient and analyst. Key to this life that affords more life is spontaneity, the inevitable tumble into enactments and relational knots that are then patiently unknotted so as to afford access to unformulated or unsymbolized aspects of experience that would otherwise be impossible to reach.

We are, none of us, ever one. Still, I believe there is room—room that has been neglected in recent discourse on psychotherapeutic action—to consider the analyst's private space. This space is to be distinguished from the impossibility of the analyst's private mind.

Our modern turn toward interaction and the intersubjective weave of the analytic situation has drawn focus from the consideration of what

I broadly speak of as listening and contemplative practices. We have attended principally to the relational configuration of countertransference and how it ushers the analyst's capacities for receptivity and listening. The divining rod of countertransference culls affects that serve to select what James Strachey as early as 1934, following on Melanie Klein, referenced as the "point of urgency" (p. 141), which in turn stimulates the work of interpretation (p. 150).

But what about other analytic modes of being, as the analyst reflects on her countertransference or listens to the side of urgency's grip in the progressive construction of the analysis? Even if we were to grant that analysts are irrevocably taken up into their own subjectivities and affect states and in so doing grant that we cannot and should not split reason and emotion, we might also grant that there are contemplative and containing modes of listening, reflecting, and speaking. These contemplative and containing processes do not necessarily dampen affect or result in withholding. For example, we might think of the role of containment as it holds and builds toward collaborative contemplation (Cooper, 2010; Grossmark, 2012; Slochower, 2004, 2006).

We now have abundant literature to support the ways in which collaboration and negotiation happen in active relation. To wit, our modern discourse on enactment. As well, this relational discourse almost always includes the analyst's reflections on her listening and contemplative practices through the combustion of relationship. But what, I ask, about the collaboration that may happen in rest, or what I once termed "relational rest" (Corbett, 2001), or that toward which Donnel Stern (2013a) turns when he speaks about relaxing constrictions in the interpersonal field? Or what of the reverie that may follow on the combustion of enactments, as analysts push into the unknowing that so often characterizes analytic work?

Following on the ideas Winnicott (1958) set forth in his seminal essay, "The Capacity to be Alone," I suggest that subjects and analyses come alive as much in the combustion of interaction, recognition, and negotiation as they do in the rest of reverie, reflection, and rambling. Granting the necessary structural and negotiated conditions of living-feeling-talking-relating that are vital to the analytic enterprise, I suggest that there is valuable psychic life to be found in more quiet and less active modes of being-contemplating-unknowing-reflecting. Private space, I argue, is requisite for this necessary quiet.

Steven Cooper (2010) aimed at the same territory when he asked about the one-person practices that are required to keep two-person analyses going. Alongside Cooper, I ask: What of our efforts to carve out the psychic space and time needed for listening? What of the analyst's quest for the breather of mental freedom? What of the value of unknowing? What of the analyst's need for and experience of being alone in the presence of another? As Cooper pointed out, "It is interesting and a bit paradoxical that in many ways most psychoanalytic models have more procedural transparency regarding maintaining the analyst's privacy than is so for the relational model" (p. 40).

I suggest that the modes of being that populate the analyst's private space afford the work of conscious contemplation and the work of unknowing, both of which are necessary for analytic work and fantastic spontaneity. I argue as well that these modes of private practice can be thought of as rituals that promote the analyst's self-care.

I do not set out on this course to critique the utility and life of enactment, the rogue moment, intersubjective entanglements, or interpersonal influence. Enactment is constant. We are recruited and recruiting. And if we are not, we are missing something. I do mean, however, to question our tunneled focus on enacted spontaneity and how this focus risks distortion as well as the creation of yet another sacred cow. One used to put one's analytic identity at peril by questioning free association. Today, one treads cautiously in criticizing the elasticity of enactment and the authenticity of interpersonal influence.

Spontaneity and ritual

Let us begin then with spontaneity and ritual. In 1998, Irwin Hoffman set forth what was to become a shibboleth of relational theory: the dialectic of ritual and spontaneity. Yet in the 15 years that have followed on Hoffman's influential contribution, and in fact for many years prior to Hoffman's publication, psychoanalytic theorists in a variety of quarters have almost exclusively focused on spontaneity. Ritual has become less of an equal and opposing force, leaving us to question whether the dialectic is still in place, or if indeed it ever was.

Spontaneity is more visible, while ritual by habit fades into the background. Perhaps this fading helps us to understand how ritual has been overlooked and/or presumed. Consider, for example, how Hoffman (1998) interchanged "routine" for ritual in speaking about the relationship of enacted spontaneity to ritual: "It's routine analytic work before that [enacted spontaneous] moment and routine analytic work afterward" (p. 914). Routines are by definition regular courses or procedures upon which presumption can easily rest. One might say they allow us not to think.

It is intriguing to note that psychoanalysts have in fact long been pre-occupied with spontaneity as vital to psychotherapeutic action. As early as 1914, Freud, in discussing matters of technique, spoke of "the element of spontaneity which *is* so convincing" (p. 162). Note the way that Freud italicizes/emphasizes the link between spontaneity and impact. The spontaneity to which Freud referred was to be found in the unconscious communication between patient and analyst, and through the heft of transference interpretations that he argued could follow there upon.

The mode of spontaneity to which relational theorists refer encompasses the uncanny force of unconscious transfer but departs from the centrality of transference interpretations. Turning from the ultimate pivot of transference, relational clinicians have moved psychotherapeutic action to the more immediate realm of interpersonal influence and onto an expansive intersubjective field. Working in this relational field, the analyst seeks to examine and regulate affect states, to negotiate mutual recognition, to expand mental freedom, and to transform meaning through narrative transformations, which in turn help to build and traverse a relational matrix, up to and including the examination of transference and countertransference reclamations.

Moreover, spontaneity follows as the necessary and necessarily therapeutic response to the ways in which relational theorists are now reimagining the mind. Dissociation (as opposed to repression) is configured as the principal process by which unformulated minds are (un)made (Bromberg, 1998, 2006, 2011; Stern, 1997, 2010). The psychoanalytic endeavor is then critically linked with the emergence of the unformulated—the new—which is yet to be found. Key to such discovery is spontaneity.

Spontaneous open expression and interpersonal influence, humming through the life of elastic enactments and rouge interpretive moments, are routinely linked with that which is called authentic, specifically, "the analyst's authentic personal availability" (Hoffman, 1998, p. 912). This spontaneous authenticity is depicted as necessary not only for the action in psychotherapeutic action but for growth as well (see, e.g., Bass, 1996, 2007; Bromberg, 2006, 2011; Ehrenberg, 1992; Hoffman, 2006, 2009). I venture we can agree, and have agreed from the very beginning of our contemplation of psychotherapeutic technique, that spontaneity, in one way or another, is an imperative lynchpin. I think we might agree as well that spontaneity is authentic, when authenticity is understood as that which is indicative of emotional significance and/or mental freedom.

I am troubled, however, by the assumption that spontaneity is authentic, when authenticity is understood to mean that which is genuine and possessed of an intimate singularity. I am troubled by the assumed authenticity of spontaneous interpersonal influence as it may too quickly solve the limits of knowing, or more precisely foreclose the necessity of unknowing that I believe to be vital to analytic exchange. I am troubled by the ways in which the analyst's employment of projective identification qua empathy may easily morph from authenticity into authority.

I am troubled because I believe that in our modern theorizing of psychotherapeutic action we run the risk of idealizing elasticity and privileging spontaneity, open expression, and interpersonal influence while failing to recognize the necessity and pacing of the patient's and the analyst's contemplation—contemplation that brackets spontaneity, precedes open expression, unfolds through intersubjective entanglement, negotiation, and infuses interpersonal influence.

I am troubled because all of this relating is killing us, as it places an untenable demand on both patient and analyst alike, and risks crowding out the dreamy leisure of reverie and the co-creation of a fantastic life through which patient and analyst may come alive as otherwise.

I am troubled because our emphasis on enactment and exchange has eclipsed other modes of analytic work and therapeutic address, modes and means of practice that are alive and ongoing, not simply routines that bracket the spontaneous lynchpin or serve as handmaidens to negotiation and the investigation of enactments.

In speaking of these other modes, I am speaking specifically about the following practices: containing, waiting, associating, soliciting the patient's associations, wandering into reverie, wandering back out, dreaming, debating, practicing what one might say, silently interpreting, consciously contemplating, bridging, linking, cataloging, pacing, being lost, tolerating being lost, sequencing, listening, listening through hovering attention, listening more acutely, listening with the ear of theory, inquiring, moment-arily stepping out of the bond, taking a break, remaining silent, debating silence, considering when and/or if to bring a feeling or a thought forward, at what point in the hour, at what point in the week.

Psychotherapeutic action

Polyphonic thick narration of clinical process, including dense description of these interimplicated listening and contemplative private practices as they join forces to build and foster psychotherapeutic action, is not possible. There is simply too much at hand and too much that is out of hand and mind. Arguably, that is the point of analytic process. To riff on Freud (1930), therapeutic life, as we know it, is too hard for us. It is too much, and as such, it escapes narration. Given the surfeit of the analytic situation, we tend to pull on one thread of the weave: interpersonal influence, enact-ment, spontaneity, dreaming, symbolization, transference, counter-trans-ference, projection, containment, or knowing, to name but a few.

Perhaps this tendency to privilege certain aspects of our engagement follows on what Thomas Ogden (2012) means when he speaks of analytic "style" versus "technique." Ogden's bid for the freedom that style affords is inviting, especially when it can be put on with the kind of polyglot panache that Ogden can muster. I think of Ogden's (2012) recent book, *Creative Readings,* where he brings together Freud, Isaacs, Fairbairn, Winnicott, Bion, Loewald, and Searles, as the party I want to attend. That said, I think there are important debates to be had, in particular about the function of the analyst's authority that Ogden stylishly skirts.

In a similar comparative exercise, Donnel Stern (2013b, 2013c) has begun to chart the epistemological frames that have developed the idea of the "analytic field"—an idea, following on field theory that is currently enjoying the airing out of discourse. Field theory rests on the necessary consideration of coexisting facts. The state of any part of the field depends on every other part of the field.

In an act of noteworthy historical synthesis, Stern tracks the idea of the co-created field from Sullivan's (1940, 1953) interpersonal field through Bion's (1959, 1962), Ferro's (1999, 2002, 2006), Ferro and Basiles (2008), and Baranager and Baranger's (2008) bipersonal or intersubjective field, to the modern relational field as matrix, following largely on his own work (Stern, 1997, 2010), and on Benjamin (1997, 2004), Bromberg (1998, 2006, 2011), Hoffman (1998), and Mitchell (1988, 1995, 2003). Stern compares and contrasts the epistemologies that guide therapeutic action for Bion and his followers with ways of knowing that inform the practices that build relational technique. Stern, like Ogden, takes up analytic techniques as akin to styles, although Stern does not use that word. Unlike Ogden, and importantly, in my view, Stern speaks directly to the analyst's authority. (Stern is perhaps the cousin at the table who is willing to speak to Uncle Antonio's ethical, affective, and political dispositions. And yes, I want to be at that party as well.)

As Stern makes clear, the analyst's authority rests on how she occupies the "here" in the "here- and-now" of the clinical situation. We come then to a significant distinction between Bion and his followers, especially Ferro and the Barangers, from relational theorists and clinicians. Ferro speaks symbolically, privileging unconscious phantasy and his goal to live each hour as a dream (following on Bion). Ferro's efforts are aimed at speaking from inside the inner world of the patient to the internal objects that live therein. He posits a co-created field, yet not one that is equally co-created. He mostly speaks from his private-dreaming-containing position within the field. He hovers within the dream-hour made with his patient. And from his hovering-containing-perpendicular position, he speaks, speaks symbolically, and speaks as the one who knows.

As Stern points out, relational clinicians speak primarily in an interpersonal register: conscious person to conscious person. Relational clinicians court the border territory between inner and outer worlds as they come alive in inner/outer moments of co-created enactment and association. This stance reflects the belief that inner and outer cannot be distinguished, as well as the belief that the unformulated can only come alive in the formation of relational bonds. The authority upon which the relational analyst relies is found in person, not in symbol.

We might say that relational authority is sought in the relational here-and-now, whereas Bionian authority is sought in the dream here-and-now.

Reading along with Stern as I was undertaking my own rereading of Bion and Ferro and an introductory reading of the Baranagers, I found myself betwixt and between, somewhere between the relational position and the course charted by Bion's followers. It is this betwixt position that has led me to try to resurrect the analyst's private space within relational discourse. I believe my position follows on my training as a child analyst. I move forward to lean into that work to better elucidate my position, and in turn why that position leads me to advocate for the reinvigoration of he analyst's private space with particular emphasis on the necessity of that space in building and sustaining potential space and the work of play.

Ritual as self-care

My interest in thinking about the analyst's contemplation and listening practices follows on the fact that I am often confused, both unwittingly and with intent. Hour by hour, I feel myself to be enveloped in a polyphonic field, and I struggle to get my mind into and around the excess. Adding to my confusion, I often court it, indulge it, and mine it to see where it may lead.

I experience this confusion with all of my patients, but it is given particular expression in my work with children, wherein I am often genuinely lost in the potential space of psychic equivalence. I find myself suspended as I am caught in the vista of a child's vision and led toward a *life suspended playing in reality*, playing in a fantastic zone of psychic equivalence, moving as children are wont to move between material reality and psychic reality.

One of the pleasures of working with children is that one gets to work in the land of psychic- equivalence, a liminal space where being hangs suspended between the material and psychic. A spoon is a spoon is a shovel is an evil shovel-monster-man who speaks with an English accent and is set upon devouring the world. Symbols, objects, and characters meld in the alchemy of psychic equivalence. Play is spoken and played with symbols and objects. Characters manifestly take to the field. As the analyst, one speaks within the play sometimes as symbol, sometimes as object, sometimes as character; if you don't speak thus, you are not playing.

When children show up at my office, they are rarely—almost never—looking for someone with a lot to say. They are looking for someone to be done to. One's function as a doer is parsed to the millimeter. Children are looking for someone who can follow them and someone who they occasionally let speak from inside the game about the dynamics at hand. But, most often, my speeches are scripted. In other words, I am almost always told what to say. Too much talking is akin to wind drag. One runs the risk of being a gasbag. And one is promptly told to "Shut up." Given the squeeze, I often think that my best interventions are monosyllabic: oh, ah, ou, ick, euw, oops, yes, no, wow, ouch.

Most of the time, in ways that I can only call enigmatic, I think my child patients are right. The game thinks us in a way that echoes what Joyce Slochower (2006) spoke of when she referred to holding and containing as doubling as figure and ground. Although given the frequent fixity of play and the ways that fixity brings object relational figures and relationally inflected defenses onto the field, I am left with little room but to comment from a perpendicular position, coming at the play, or at the character, not from within the game but from on high. In a similar vein, because symbols and object relations bloom in psychic equivalence, I am also sometimes given the opportunity to speak in a more symbolic register. The spoon-shovel-monster-man speaks the Father's No (capital F, capital N), and he can sometimes be named as such. These perpendicular modes of address generally follow on long contemplation and consideration. As well, they rest on containing a wide variety of affects and thoughts, both within any given hour and in my recollection and rumination that collects any treatment.

As I stumble across the potential spaces I build with children, I confusedly try to speak with the characters that pop up there. I attempt to follow their fantastic instructions and to respond in accord with the ways they live between psychic reality and material reality. I work to decipher the ways in which their internalized object worlds come alive through our fantastically inflected interpersonal experience. I struggle to not only sort out who they are but in what way they wish to be addressed. I look to greet these object/characters as having an identity of their own and as having the capacity for thinking and feeling that is as real within the liminal world of the game as those of any objects in the outer world (following here on Fairbairn, 1943, 1944, 1952; Isaacs, 1943, 1952; and Winnicott, 1971).

I enter the field expecting to act and to be acted upon. I expect to construct a network of fantasy and to be pulled into that construction by the patient's internalized world. I try my best to wander. I try my best to be aware of what I have up my sleeve. But mostly, I fail.

Working with children has taught me to keep present with the other, where this keeping present has an unexpected relationship to the limits of knowing. I strive to stay one step behind and lean into what I think of as an instructive uncertainty, a mode of unknowing. I am not so much concerned with the content of what is being thought per se or the interpersonal conversation as pace. I am more concerned with ferreting shifts between affects and thoughts, as these shifts do or do not allow for constructing and sustaining potential space. The position of constructive uncertainty is not equivalent to negative withholding or holding back, as it has sometimes been construed; rather, it is an active, if not quite affirmative *something*: a containing-searching, a potential, and a mode of mutuality that may or may not be simultaneous.

I parse what Benjamin (2004) called the "confusing traffic of two-way streets," and in keeping with her elucidation of intersubjective relatedness, I work to build and speak through various shared thirds (p. 5). I occasionally move toward direct "you-me-us" interpersonal exchange. But I am more likely to seek the congress of play, imagination, and reverie, and the you-me-us that unfurls therein. Here I draw a distinction between the potential space of play and the dream space that Ferro courts and the interpersonal field on which Sullivan lived. Play is neither a dream nor predominately interpersonal. It is potential, the liminal space created between the material and the psychic.

It is difficult to capture the temporal strangeness of play and the floating (real/unreal) peculiarity of psychic equivalence. It is similarly difficult to capture communication within a fantasmatic register. I am thus refracted and thus confused. In my confusion, I am always moving within the field toward my own private space in an effort to hold my confusion and the flood of feeling and information that compose the game.

I believe that our attempts to capture play and potential space offer us valuable insight into the synthesis of spontaneity and ritual, and the grounding necessity of the analyst's private space. Within that space, I have my habits. To the extent that habits are an attempt at order or the effort toward sequencing, they then are one form of ritual. To the extent that they are an effort to find a pace or re-find a route, they are a form of ritual. Indeed, ritual derives from late seventeenth-century French for route or road. I move forward to illustrate my ritual ceremony of deconstructing children's play scenarios and how I employ that task to fall into a blended mode of conscious contemplation and reverie.

Rituals not only order confusion. They contain it and sustain it. To the extent that rituals allow us to stay in a polyphonic register, to stay in a refracted and littered field/archive, and to stay within the uncertain zone of psychic equivalence, they are, in my view, a mode of self-care. When we think about self-care, we tend to think of practices or pleasures that happen outside the hour: yoga, walking, swimming, cashews, chocolate, coffee. While not diminishing these necessary tools, it is surprising to think of how little we think about self-care within the hour, or hour by hour.

"Hey, wait a minute, where are we?"

Five-year-old electively mute Laura sets about to make an elaborate design out of LEGOs on the floor of my office. I watch and admire the formal clarity of her design, the tonality, the sequence, and the balance. (I think the LEGO color palette must offend her. She would prefer a subtler range.) At first I think the design might be a maze, but it is not a puzzle. The pathways, if they can be called that, are clear. Then I think perhaps it is a mandala, a meditative form. Laura takes the stalwart black and white cow and begins walking the perimeter. I take up the golden retriever and follow. We walk in circles for a while.

Then before I know what I am doing/have done, I stand up and open the window. It is the dead of winter. The radiator is turned off. The office is not overheated. As I sit back down, I say, "I can't breathe." As the retriever, I ask the cow if she can breathe. She falls down. I follow suit. We lay there for a while.

Eventually, I get up. I say, "We must go on." The cow pulls herself up and walks into the design, careful not to disturb the order. The retriever follows. He stumbles. A block falls. Laura quickly sets it right. The retriever says, "Oops!" The cow does not respond. She makes her way to the center, where she stops.

The retriever freezes, he says, "Hey, wait a minute, where are we?" The cow stands her ground. After a while, the retriever says, "Hey, Cow, my ears are buzzing." The cow stands her ground. After another while, the retriever tries again, "Cow, the quiet is loud. And it is cold. Cold loud." The cow stands her ground. I laugh and say, "Silly words." The retriever says, "Cow, I am freezing. Are we being punished?" The cow stands her ground.

At that, I get up and close the window. Suddenly, or so it seems, we slip into "the thickness you can't get past called *waiting*," as Jorie Graham (1991) would have it (p. 66). After six silent minutes, the hour ends.

I walk Laura to the waiting room, I say good-bye to her and her mother. I walk back to my office. The cow stands her ground, and there I am in the freezing, buzzing, aftereffects.

I do not ask children to pick up the toys they use or the materials they make. One of my habits is the deconstruction of the scene coupled with the ruminative recollection of the hour. I often wish I had a similar material task/ritual to undertake after every hour with an adult patient.

I began by picking up the LEGOs, again marveling at the beauty of their arrangement even in its careful rigidity. I thought about mandalas, the ways they are employed as an aid in meditation and trance induction. I pondered the trance of mutism and thought about how Laura's mutism tranced our relationship, stuck in the muted fortress of the mandala: "Hey, wait a minute, where are we?"

Various animals had been considered prior to the cow. I put them away and thought about how the cow is the most stolid of the animals. The elephant and the dinosaurs suggest more menace and might, but the cow is stubborn and constant. I put the retriever away and thought back to Laura handing him to me. I was always the retriever, no matter the game. I was not much smarter than the cow but capable of speech, and the rogue moment. I thought about how the retriever knocked a LEGO over and how quickly Laura corrected his lapse.

I thought about how the cow stopped after the block fell. Mistake, error, loss stopped the game. Or was the cow already headed toward the muted fortress? I recollected, as I had many times, that Laura's mother gave birth to a "stillborn" child. Laura fell mute soon thereafter. I was always struck by the resonance of "stillborn," not only with Laura's silence but also with the ways in which her silence hindered our capacity to join her growth, her mind, and her affects as they were borne.

I wondered if there was a presentiment to the block-falling moment, when the cow fell in response to my comment that I could not breathe. Fallen, were we stillborn? Were we suffocated? Or were we exhausted with going on being? I recall practicing how I might formulate a comment about death within the game. But it was a theme, or what I took to be a theme, that had just recently appeared in our work, and I thought it best to let Laura elaborate. At this point I was cataloging and trying to stay close to the immediate exchange.

But why did I press on, doing some bad Beckett imitation? I laughed at myself when I recognized that I had been rereading Beckett and made the link with Laura. I was also rereading John Ashbery, and I can see now that I was looking for the tone, and the language game that matched Laura's play. I press us to "go on," but in hindsight I could see that I anxiously got us up and moving when the dead object joined the game. Simultaneously flatfooted and fleetfooted, I allowed the dead little heed and pressed on. I linked my push with the ways in which many people, including Laura's parents, anxiously responded to the dead and to the death in her world. I understood through this accumulating faltering that I must work to find a way to name not only the death but also the fear that was silencing death.

I paused over how I voiced what would become the game's end: "Hey, wait a minute, where are we?" I believe it was my way of noting a shift in our states, a shift from the activity of "Oops!" to the privation of dissociation. But it seems likely that my comment may have been only in keeping with my own state. This thought led me to once again consider how I had been hypo-manically pushing the hour. I don't believe my question about our location met Laura. She was already there, dissociation having already set in.

The retriever, though, persisted in reinstating the game, no matter that the cow refused to throw the ball. This dynamic and state were by now familiar in my work with Laura. Perhaps in light of its familiarity, I could pause long enough to say as much, speaking my "silly" futility and naming the stopping silence. But in so doing, I could also see that I was punishing. I wanted to play, not be shut out. So, I turned the table and froze us: You want silence. I will give you ice. I will give you the cold anger that greets death.

Grasping my intent, I named the punishment. But by that time, one wonders if the counter-ice of Laura's response had already won out. Should I have found a way to say something more about the freezing silence, especially in the final six minutes? Yes. Should I have found a way to greet death, give it a name? Yes. But I wish I could say that it felt communicable. Instead, I felt like a cow. Slow. Heavy. Tranced. I venture we both dissociated part of that time. We must have. But those minutes also had, at least for me, the feeling of containment, and the necessity of unknowing. If only hazily, I could feel something about rage that I had yet to glimpse. And on yet another register, I was pondering the hour, the course of my work with Laura, and beginning to think about the role of death, even as it left us deadened.

I also wish I could say that I moved into a mode of productive reverie within the silence. But I did not. As I put the boxes on the shelves, I thought again about the moment the LEGO fell: one small spontaneous silent plunk. And how it set in play a surfeit of affects that Laura had to fend off with all of her beautiful and stolid might. And how I was left, the scrambling retriever. The foolish optimist with little to say other than, "Oops!" But then again, I thought it might have been the best intervention of the hour, even as it muted us and left us with the still unsaid and unformulated, the unheard and repressed. "Oops!" voiced the fall, the gap, the impossibility of speech, the unknowing.

When I began to recognize the retriever in the mother's hypo-manic greeting (blond, sunny, prompt, anxious), I worked my way back to the punishing enigmatic transfer (the injunction to recognize the loss of the stillborn child—though not fully—and to only feel so much about the loss, lest one feel too much). I also began to track the trapped rage, the punishing silence and guilt, lest speech and feeling erupt. I slowly found my way to speaking the dead baby no one could name as dead. I worked toward speaking about the fear that too much feeling was at hand, the melancholic too-much-ness, and how we took to the shadow/fortress to hide.

About five months following the session I recount here, when a child took a toy from Laura at her preschool, she said, "No. Mine." And so it was with protest and possession that Laura began once again to speak— first at school, then at home, and finally in therapy. When she began speaking with me, she told me therapy was a place where she could "quiet be." I nodded and said, "Yes, sometimes we need be quiet in order to figure things out. But sometimes we can also talk and figure things out. Right?" She looked at me with a wry smile as if to say that she knew a recruiter/retriever when she saw one.

Laura and I finished up at the end of the school year, about a year from when we had started our work. I thought the ending was premature, but the family was going to be away for six months, and it seemed best to find a way to end. Laura was regularly talking at this point. Remaining quiet, she nevertheless readily answered questions, could say the things she could not say before; and with speech, came more animation.

At our final meeting, Laura brought me a gift, a refrigerator magnet in the shape and image of the ruby slippers from *The Wizard of Oz*. At first, I was charmed that a young girl would buy me something that had caught her eye. I liked the nod to play, even camp. But the association that stayed with me was the fact that Dorothy possessed the ruby slippers because she took them from a dead witch. Dorothy's magic shoes came from the dead. They would carry her back to the present, and out of the fantastic world where she had been living for a while.

References

Baranger, M., & Baranger, W. (2008). The analytic situation as a dynamic field. *The International Journal of Psycho-Analysis*, 89, 796–826.

Bass, A. (1996). Holding, holding back, and holding on: Commentary on paper by Joyce Slochower. *Psychoanalytic Dialogues*, 6, 361–378.

Bass, A. (2007). When the frame doesn't fit the picture. *Psychoanalytic Dialogues*, 17, 1–27.

Benjamin, J. (1997). *The shadow of the other*. New York,: Routledge.

Benjamin, J. (2004). Beyond the doer and done to: An intersubjective view of thirdness. *The Psychoanalytic Quarterly*, 73, 5–46.

Bion, W. R. (1959). Attacks on linking. *The International Journal of Psycho-Analysis*, 40, 308–315.

Bion, W. R. (1962). The psycho-analytic study of thinking. *The International Journal of Psycho-Analysis*, 43, 306–310.

Bromberg, P. (1998). *Standing in the spaces: Essays on clinical process trauma and dissociation*. Hillsdale, NJ: The Analytic Press.

Bromberg, P. (2006). *Awakening the dreamer: Clinical journeys*. New York: Routledge.

Bromberg, P. (2011). *The shadow of the tsunami: And the growth of the relational mind*. New York: Routledge.

Cooper, S. (2010). *A disturbance in the field: Essays in transference-countertransference engagement*. New York: Routledge.

Corbett, K. (2001). More life: Centrality and marginality in human development. *Psychoanalytic Dialogues*, 11, 313–335.

Ehrenberg, D. (1992). *The intimate edge: Extending the reach of psycho-analytic interaction*. Hillsdale, NJ: The Analytic Press.

Fairbairn, W. R. D. (1943). Reply to Mrs. Isaac's "The nature and function of phantasy." In: P. Kind & R. Steiner (Eds.), *The Freud-Klein Controversies, 1941–1945* (pp. 358–360). London: Routledge.

Fairbairn, W. R. D. (1944). Endopsychic structure considered in terms of object-relationships. *The International Journal of Psycho-Analysis*, 25, 70–92.

Fairbairn, W. R. D. (1952). *Psychoanalytic studies of the personality*. London: Tavistock.

Ferro, A. (1999). *The bi-personal field*. London: Routledge.

Ferro, A. (2002). Superego transformations through the analyst's capacity for reverie. *The Psychoanalytic Quarterly*, 71, 477–501.

Ferro, A. (2006). Trauma, reverie, and the field. *The Psychoanalytic Quarterly*, 75, 1045–1056.

Ferro, A., & Basile, R. (2008). Countertransference and the characters of the psychoanalytic session. *The Scandinavian Psychoanalytic Review*, 31, 3–10.

Freud, S. (1914). Remembering, repeating and working-through (further recommendations on the technique of psychoanalysis II). *Standard Edition*, 12, 145–156.

Freud, S. (1930). Civilization and its discontents. *Standard Edition*, 21, 57–146.

Graham, J. (1991). *Region of unlikeness*. New York: Ecco.

Grossmark, R. (2012). The unobtrusive relational analyst, *Psychoanalytic Dialogues*, 22, 629–646.

Hoffman, I. Z. (1998). *Ritual and spontaneity in the psychoanalytic process: A dialectical-constructivist view*. Hillsdale, NJ. The Analytic Press.

Hoffman, I. Z. (2006). Forging difference out of similarity: The multiplicity of corrective experience. *The Psychoanalytic Quarterly*, 75, 715–751.

Hoffman, I. Z. (2009). Therapeutic passion in the countertransference. *Psychoanalytic Dialogues*, 19, 617–637.

Isaacs, S. (1943). The nature and function of phantasy. In: P. King & R. Steiner (Eds.), *The Freud-Klein Controversies 1941–1945* (pp. 264–321). London: Routledge.

Issacs, S. (1952). The nature and function of phantasy. In: J. Riviere (Ed.), *Developments in Psycho-Analysis* (pp. 62–121). London: Hogarth Press.

Mitchell, S. (1988). *Relational concepts in psychoanalysis: An integration*. Hillsdale, NJ: The Analytic Press.

Mitchell, S. (1995). *Hope and dread in psychoanalysis*. Hillsdale, NJ: The Analytic Press.

Mitchell, S. (2003). *Relationality: From attachment to intersubjectivity*. Hillsdale, NJ: The Analytic Press.

Ogden, T. H. (2012). *Creative readings*. London: Routledge.

Slochower, J. (2004). *Holding and psychoanalysis: A relational approach.* Hillsdale, NJ: The Analytic Press.

Slochower, J. (2006). *Psychoanalytic Collisions*. New York: Taylor & Francis.

Stern, D. (1997) *Unformulated experience: From dissociation to imagination in psychoanalysis.* New York: Taylor & Francis.

Stern, D. (2010). *Partners in thought: Working with unformulated experience, dissociation, and enactment.* New York: Taylor & Francis.

Stern, D. (2013a). Relational freedom and therapeutic action. *Journal of the American Psychoanalytic Association*, 61, 227–255.

Stern, D. (2013b). Field theory in psychoanalysis, Part 1: Harry Stack Sullivan and Madeleine and Willy Baranger. *Psychoanalytic Dialogues*, 23, 487–501.

Stern, D. (2013c). Field theory in psychoanalysis, Part 2: Bionian field theory and contemporary interpersonal/relational psychoanalysis. *Psychoanalytic Dialogues*, 23, 630–645.

Sullivan, H. S. (1940). *Conceptions of modern psychiatry*. New York: W. W. Norton.

Sullivan, H. S. (1953). *The interpersonal theory of psychiatry*. New York: W. W. Norton.

Winnicott, D. W. (1958). The capacity to be alone. *The International Journal of Psycho-Analysis*, 39, 416–420.

Winnicott, D. W. (1971). *Playing and reality*. New York: Penguin Books.

Chapter 8

The unobtrusive relational analyst and psychoanalytic companioning

Robert Grossmark

Introduction

The relational turn ushered in a new era of psychoanalysis. We now comfortably regard psychoanalytic process as a mutual and egalitarian endeavor. While this mutuality is not symmetrical (Aron, 1996) the contemporary relational psychoanalyst now uses expressions of his or her own subjectivity with a freedom and creativity and is not silenced by the arbitrary constraints of "abstinence" and "neutrality". No longer regarded as situated on a perch outside of the interaction (D.B. Stern, 1997) with a "view from nowhere" (Nagel, 1986), the contemporary analyst gains insight and fosters the analytic process from a position that allows him or her to be "seen, moved, disrupted and reconfigured" within the treatment process (Wright, 2015). No longer wedded to a view of the human mind as both unitary and sealed, the current psychoanalytic process is viewed as hinging on the interaction of the subjectivities of both psychoanalyst and analysand and as embedded in complex social and historical contexts.

In addition to the classical psychoanalytic focus on transference and its resolution as the fulcrum of the psychoanalytic cure, the relational turn has privileged the centrality of enactments that involve both analyst and analysand and the progress of many relational treatments, as represented in case studies, often hinges on the emergence and resolution of these enactments.

Overall the rapid growth of interest in relational psychoanalysis and its widespread impact on the world of psychoanalysis and psychotherapy in general would seem to suggest that many analysts and patients alike find a more free and welcoming space within relational theory and practice, and I would count myself among them. Relational theory seems to have picked up a climate change in contemporary psychoanalytic and psychotherapy culture that yearns for more human and egalitarian relatedness between patients and analysts, and a view that sees such relatedness as integral to psychoanalytic cure rather than as a contamination of a scientific process.

While all these transformations have enabled so many of us to breathe more easily as psychoanalysts and work with creativity and engagement, we have also come to ask about the patients who are not so able to engage in a dialogic interaction and who barely recognize another self or subjectivity in themselves or in any others including the analyst (Director, 2009; Grossmark, 2012a, 2013). Such patients have gained much attention in the object relations and contemporary Freudian literature and perhaps less in the relational literature. These are patients for whom there is little or no self or object constancy, for whom there are few alternatives to merger and the loss of self in human interaction, for whom sadomasochistic object relations predominate their every interaction and for whom space, time and reality are simply not experienced in a cohesive ongoing manner. Such patients have chronic experiences of emptiness and fears of relational impingement (Bach et al, 2014).

I am also referring here to patients who may have areas of the self that are more developed and may present with, and be able to engage in, what can appear to be intersubjective vitality. The relational embrace of the multiple and decentered self allows us to consider that many patients who present in this way also harbor self-states that contain earlier undeveloped and unspeakable parts of themselves. Such states, as Bromberg (1996, 2006) has so forcefully described, are sequestered and encrusted due to unbearable shame and envy. I would add that patients also harbor empty, unformulated and undeveloped parts of themselves that can find no expression in language. I would suggest that such areas of the self or self-states are much less likely to be reached by dialogic engagement. Such self-states are often chased underground, as it were, by a psychoanalytic treatment that puts a premium on relatedness, thought and dialogic exploration.

In this chapter I will outline some thoughts as to how a relational psychoanalyst might work with these patients in the areas of un-relatedness, psychic deadness and the non-symbolizable. I will outline an unobtrusive yet deeply connected register of psychoanalytic engagement that foregrounds the patient's unique idiom and signature, and respects the need for a transformational space within which the patient and analyst can find meaning together, via mutual regression, in non-alive and non-representable psychic spaces.

The unobtrusive relational analyst

Much relational psychoanalytic treatment privileges the value of the analyst's sharing of his or her subjectivity with the patient. These interventions are generally guided by the idea that the unformulated (D.B. Stern, 1997) and dissociated affect or self-states (Bromberg, 1996, 2006, D.B. Stern, 1997, 2008) find expression in the treatment interaction, including the analyst's experience. By paying attention to the "snags" and "chafings" (D.B. Stern, 1997) within his or her own experience the analyst can pick up the disowned and dissociated aspects of the patient and can then most profitably help the patient by bringing these experiences to the attention of the patient. This outline of entering into and then resolving enactments that emerge in the treatment dyad is for many the *sine qua non* of relational treatment (Bass, 2003). The resolution of enactments in this manner would seem to rely on the ability of the patient to participate in this process and to respond to, and join with, the analyst's question: 'What's going on around here?" (Levenson, 1983). I suggested (Grossmark, 2012a) that this is not the only way that a relational treatment might proceed nor is it the only register within which a relational analyst can utilize his or her own subjectivity within a treatment.

As I have mentioned, for patients who are compromised in the areas of reflective self-awareness (Bach, 1994, 2006), mentalization (Fonagy et al, 2005) and symbolization (Levine et al, 2013), participation in this exploratory process may be asking too much, or will call forth the more related and symbolizing self, at the expense of the more regressed and undeveloped self. In looking for a way to work with such patients, I found much that is useful in the work of the British Middle School, in particular the work of Michael and Enid Balint, who, along with their colleagues, were interested in these more undeveloped parts of the self, "before I was I" (E. Balint, 1993). Michael Balint observed how the recommended treatment of his era placed great premium on the giving and receiving of interpretations (Balint, 1968) and he lamented that many patients did not seem to benefit from this approach. He noted how for many patients it was the relationship itself that was paramount for the treatment to progress and furthermore observed that regressed patients seemed to require a form of relatedness that was "more primitive than that obtaining between two adults" (p. 161) wherein words do not function denotatively. He recommended that the analyst "recognize and be with the patient" (p. 172) and be "unobtrusive and ordinary" (p. 173). By creating and maintaining a treatment environment in which the patient can experience a benign regression, the parts of the patient that we would now call "unformulated" (D.B. Stern, 1997) or non-represented (Levine, et al, 2013) can find expression and reside within the treatment space. To interpret too precipitously or to try to describe the relationship with the patient would be to steal or otherwise obtrude on this very unique nascent experience of self. Balint was explicit that such experiences "cannot, need not, and perhaps must not, be expressed in words" (p. 174). The treatment becomes the "human place in which the patient is becoming whole" (Ogden, 2005, p. 96). I would suggest that for fragmented patients who do not have a sense of self and object constancy, such forms of ongoing relatedness can allow the emergence of an indwelling of the self (Winnicott, 1960), a floating in one's own subjectivity (Bach 2006) and the capacity to be alone in the presence of another (Winnicott, 1958).[1]

The core of Balint's unobtrusive position seems to be "recognizing and being with the patient" (Balint, 1968, p. 172). The orientation of the analyst is to create a space, a relationship that the patient can utilize, mold and expand in his or her own idiom and psychic language. The analyst lends him or herself to the patient's primal process and allows the patient to regress and to use the treatment and the analyst in the most primal and unrelated manner, if need be; to be the object that the patient's regressed self requires developmentally, to "be the analyst the patient needs you to be" (Grossmark, 2012, p. 637). Balint describes how a patient may utilize the analyst and the setting as a "primary object" (p. 69), a primary substance such as water or earth. A patient may float in the realm of the treatment as a person may float on water. In such states the patient has "no concern or consideration" for the object whose work is to "have no separate interests from the individual's" and "simply be there and" be "taken for granted" (p. 69). Such processes can only be disrupted by attempts to understand or talk about the interaction or by acknowledging the analyst as a separate subject, by simply reminding the patient that there is another human being in the room. This position would seem to offer a dimension of treatment that might be obscured by the relational embrace of dialogic intersubjectivity. For instance, Bass has suggested that it is inevitable that the analyst's experience "is unlikely to go undetected by a sensitive patient" (Bass, 1996, p. 373) and Aron foregrounded the need to make conscious the analysand's experience of the analyst's subjectivity (Aron, 1991). The registers of treatment and self-states addressed in this chapter such as Balint's primary object relating, do not assume a sensitive, related and inquiring subject.

Psychoanalytic companioning

I would here like to revisit Winnicott's insights about the intersubjective processes that enable the infant to develop a sense of self, of the other and of reality itself, and the contemporary developmental literature that addresses the development of the infant's subjectivity. The emphasis here is on the value of illusion and the process of shared subjectivity and companionship.

Winnicott emphasizes that the mother and young infant come into meaningful relation with each other when "the mother and the child *live an experience together*" (his italics) and this experience promotes the "first tie the infant makes with an external object" (Winnicott, 1945, p. 152). This is the crucible in which relatedness and the comprehension of external reality grows. Crucial to this relatedness is the mother's unobtrusive understanding that the infant creates an illusion that the breast/mother is his or her unique creation. When the mother and baby are harmoniously in synchrony there is a moment of illusion – "a bit of experience which the infant can take as *either* his hallucination *or* a thing belonging to external reality" (p. 152). The mother does not challenge the illusion, but unobtrusively lives *within* the illusion with the baby. The thrust of Winnicott's argument is that the baby finds his or her way to reality and relatedness through living in the illusory world *with* the mother. I emphasize the words "within" and "with" to foreground how the mother companions the baby in this world that is both illusion and reality.

By living within the illusion with the baby the mother can "enrich" the illusion rather than dispel it. Much like Balint's images of primary substances and the object that is taken for granted, Winnicott suggests that in this illusory world:

> the object behaves according to magical laws, i.e. it exists when desired, it approaches when approached, it hurts when hurt. Lastly it vanishes when not wanted.
>
> (Winnicott, 1945, p. 153)

The mother lends herself totally to this process and is the infant's companion in the illusion. I take from this that the analyst must be prepared to live in the world of illusion with the patient and *not* intrude the coarse reality of the external world or of the "reality" of the relationship. In this vision, the analyst, like the mother, need not challenge this illusion and can live within the illusion unobtrusively. Winnicott placed great value on the states of psychotic unintegration that characterize the infant's early life. They have their place in normal development and likewise they also have their place in psychoanalytic work with primitive patients. To me, his ideas seem to support the sense that we must allow the work to enter the darkness, the unintegrated states, and not hurry the patient out of them into states of greater integration and relatedness.

This vision of psychoanalytic work might seem to pose a challenge to the relational vision of the patient as always aware of and responsive to the analyst's subjectivity (Aron, 1991; Bass, 1996) and the relational appreciation of the real relationship. To state it as paradoxical questions: how do we allow the analytic space for this kind of relating, or non-relating, and remain relational and present in our subjectivity? How do we honor the patient's need to live safely within illusion and un-reality while being present and adhering to the needs and constrictions of the various realities that comprise the treatment?

In grappling with these paradoxes I have turned to Winnicott's description of the mother and infant as "living an experience together", and have found resonance in the contemporary literature on the development of intersubjectivity. Colwyn Trevarthen (2001) draws on a multitude of studies to illustrate the ways that mothers and infants mutually regulate and join together in what he calls a "joint consciousness in companionship" and "cooperative intersubjectivity" such that the infant learns what it is to be a "person in relation to others" (p. 112). This seems to harmonize so well with Winnicott's observations. There is an emphasis on the vocal and rhythmic companionship between mother and infant. Daniel Stern (1993, 2010) talks of "relational emotions" that anticipate contingent rhythms and sympathy from others; Trevarthen (2001) talks of the rhythmic mirroring of vocal and gestural expression and Brazelton (1993), some years back, had observed "proto-conversations" of rhythmic vocal mirroring and expressive movements.

Infants, Trevarthen observes, develop social awareness and meaning in purposive action primarily by *sharing* and *companioning* with their carers. It is the sharing and *being with* infants in the rhythmic, vocal and motoric registers that enables them to grow as humans, not the telling them how to be. Here I recall Winnicott's perspective that reality and relatedness are gained by not intruding upon the infant's illusion, but by "living an experience together", the sharing of experience and illusion.

I would suggest that here we have the outline of an unobtrusive companioning register of psychoanalytic engagement. It is a vision that integrates the primacy of the patient's unintegrated, non-representable states and embraces illusion, without suppressing or otherwise denuding the analyst's subjectivity.

Regression: a relational concept

The idea of regression was central to the British Middle School. Winnicott, Balint, Khan and their colleagues were known at the time as "regression analysts" (Hopkins, 2006). Along with other core Freudian concepts, (I mentioned the demise of neutrality and abstinence) regression has been deconstructed and critiqued in the relational turn. The original concept of regression suggested that the patient would regress to early levels of psychosexual organization (Freud, 1905) in response to the analytic environment, the couch, a dimly lit space and the abstinent analyst (Etchegoyen, 1991). Winnicott (1954) embellished on this psychic landscape suggesting that in the analytic space the patient would gradually surrender the protections offered by the false self and regress to a more primal and developmentally earlier level of dependence and hence afford the growth of the true self. There is much to be gleaned from these formulations, but the relational analyst will feel that such phenomena suggest a one-person process observed by a removed analyst conducting the treatment from outside of the action.

Aron and Bushra (1998) seem to have saved the baby of regression as the bathwater was dispensed with. They suggested regression can be regarded as a relational event, a mutual experience and they emphasized that regression involves a shift into altered *states*. Both patient and analyst enter and reside in altered and perhaps unsettling states. I have found this perspective both useful and true to my experience in many treatments. It casts regression as a mutual and companioned experience, and echoes Trevarthen's "joint consciousness in companionship". I place great value on this mutual regression and suggest that the core of many treatments hinges upon the accompanying of the patient into these often terrifying, confusing and shame-saturated states. So many of our patients have never had the experience of being accompanied in these painful and often unspeakable areas of themselves. Rather than being a response to the setting, from this perspective "the patient comes with his regression, his illness is his regression" (Etchegoyen, p. 553). The analyst can be unobtrusive to this mutual process and the work involves *not* explaining or inquiring about this process in the moment or asking the patient to step out of these states so as to observe and understand. Rather it is to unotrusively companion the patient in these areas, and to allow the organic growth of the "potential space", the transitional area of illusion where the patient can grow. I have described this as "accompanying the patient into the darkness" and "psychoanalytic companioning" (Grossmark, 2013). There is an evocation here of Ogden's perspective when describing Bion's thoughts about "waking dreaming" that analytic work must provide a setting in which the conscious can become unconscious rather than making the unconscious conscious via interpretation (Ogden, 2005) or premature understanding. So often this work can bring great discomfort and disequilibrium for the analyst and one can crave the safety of a discussion or interpretation that gives words and context to this experience. I would suggest that often this is in the service of protecting the analyst from discomfort and fear of breakdown, rather than furthering the analytic work. Pizer (1998) describes how the analyst's use of authoritative interpretations and explanations of the patient and the analytic interaction can "eclipse the internal space wherein the patient might arrive at his own construction of personal meanings" (p. 31) and "assemble" his own personal experience. Similarly, one might say that a relationally informed treatment that tilted too strongly to the dialogic can similarly eclipse these delicate and deeply internal processes.

Hermeneutic regression and the flow of enactive engagement

Relational psychoanalysis is a profoundly hermeneutic and creative endeavor. It is a psychoanalysis that embraces the idea that when two or more people come together new meaning is created. Many relational analysts have spoken from this position, none more so than D.B. Stern and Donna Orange. They draw upon the philosophy of H.G. Gadamer (Orange, 2010, 2011; D.B. Stern, 1997) that embraces the idea that meaning emerges in conversation and in connection rather than from the examination and study of phenomena in a neutral scientific manner, from the outside. In this conception meaning is vibrant, often illusive and always moving, it emerges rather than is static, waiting to be found. Meaning is *lived* rather than found.

I would suggest that when an analyst accompanies the patient in an unobtrusive manner into the worlds of inchoate pain, emptiness, darkness and illusion, new meaning is continually emerging. Regression, the mutual kind, is a hermeneutic phenomenon. The patient and the analyst often *live* the new meaning together before it is clear to either what that meaning might be. The analyst can flow with the patient into new realms and not foreclose the process by asking about it or pulling for dialogic understanding of what is happening. The hermeneutic process is mutual and both participants surrender to it. Both subjectivities are involved.

I have called this mutual process the "flow of enactive engagement" (Grossmark, 2012b), which builds and embellishes on Freud's ideas about free association. Like neutrality, abstinence and regression here is another classical psychoanalytic idea that may have been prematurely retired from the psychoanalytic team. While relational analysts might happily agree that free association is simply not possible in the manner in which Feud envisaged it (Hoffman, 2006), we might also recall that Freud was looking for a method that would facilitate the revelation of what the patient could not possibly tell the analyst in ordinary talk, because the patient simply did not know what it was that he or she knew or was yet to know. In other words: the unconscious. Freud, you will recall, asked his patients to:

> act as though, for instance, you were a traveller sitting next to the window of a railway carriage and describing to someone inside the carriage the changing views which you see outside.
>
> (Freud, 1913, p. 135)

Describing the changing views from the carriage was the work of free association. This to our ears might appear to be a very one-person and somewhat stilted endeavor. However, if we preserve the idea that in psychoanalysis there is a tremendous opportunity for the surrender of one's ordinary self and everyday psychic protections to a mutual and accompanied process we can "relationalize" the free associative goal, so to speak. The patient and analyst together surrender to the regressive process that emerges between them and can flow together into psychic and emotional territory that offers new and often surprising meaning. Rather than Freud's metaphor of a solitary subject reading off the images that pass by the train window, we now have a contemporary relational metaphor of an intersubjective and shared endeavor where both participants sit *side by side* on a roller coaster and hold on as they are taken by a process that they both constitute and are constituted by, into realms neither could have foreseen. The analyst is along for the hermeneutic ride, so to speak. Unobtrusiveness is essential for this hermeneutic process to freely unfold. From this perspective, understanding and meaning are emergent and are *lived* together, rather than cognitively arrived at: a true Gadamerian conversation in which narrative is a relational event and surely a version of Trevarthen's "cooperative intersubjectivity".

The field of treatment and the oneiric perspective

I will draw here on the work of the River Plate Group (e.g., Brown, 2010; D.B. Stern, 2013, 2014 ; Zimmer, 2010). Madeleine and Willy Baranger (2009), French analysts who settled in Uruguay after time in Buenos Aires, outlined the theory of the "field" of an analysis. In brief, from their perspective the field is comprised of the conscious and unconscious realms of both analysand and analyst. In every analytic relationship both participants develop powerful unconscious fantasies of the nature of the dyad as it unfolds and the nature of the cure that is wished for and feared. At any given moment, the analyst can understand what is happening in the treatment according to the current state of fantasies about the relationship. These ideas have been adapted and expanded by many contemporary writers, most notably Ferro (1992, 2002, 2009) and Civitarese (2008, 2013), who provide numerous examples of how they understand the treatment process in terms of a constant message from the unconscious of the dyad as to the state of the relationship. The rather decentering idea here is that the message comes from the field, rather than from either participant. The field, constituted by both participants' conscious and unconscious fantasies and fears, their worlds of internal object relations and the transferences that ensue, develops and takes on a transformative and generative quality of its own. Narratives and worlds are generated that are more than the sum of their parts—that is, the internal and intersubjective worlds of the patient and analyst.

While these writers can offer dense and sometimes mercurial explanations, I recognize this as an ordinary, everyday phenomenon. It seems commonplace that a relationship develops a quality or climate that is more than the contribution of the constituent members. It is perhaps an ordinary, yet unremarked quality of relationships that one experiences oneself as living *inside* a relationship, or a family for that matter, that shapes and forms the states and functioning of the participants as if it has a mind of its own. From my own perspective, as a psychoanalyst who practices group psychoanalysis as well as individual treatment, the theory of the field is organic and very familiar. The group therapy community has, for many years, paid attention to the idea of the phenomenon of the group-as-a-whole (Agazarian, 2006; Anzieu, 1984; Bion, 1961) and the irrationality of groups and organizations (Cytrynbaum & Noumair, 2004). The group-as-a-whole has its own presence and is more than the sum of the interpersonal and intersubjective relationships in the room. Indeed, anyone who has been a part of a large crowd or mob or worked in an organization (or who follows politics) will attest to this phenomenon.[2]

From my perspective there is much convergence here with relational ideas. Among some of Steven Mitchell's more invigoratingly transgressive ideas (Mitchell, 1988, 2003) was his elaboration of Sullivan's idea that we do not find the unconscious inside the mind of one individual even as he or she interacts with another. In a different language the suggestion is that unconscious meaning emerges in the field that is generated in the interaction and unfolding of the treatment. The Barangers' ideas quite seamlessly seem to expand such a perspective. More familiar to many relational readers will be relational theorizing about the "analytic third" (Aron, 2006; Benjamin, 2004; Ogden, 1994). Space does not allow for a more thorough discussion of the different conceptions of the analytic third that these writers offer, but simply put, these would seem to be articulations of the idea that when two or more people come together, something more than an interaction emerges in an area that is beyond the confines of the minds of the individuals involved.

From my perspective, I regard the analyst's surrender to the unfolding of emergent meanings in the flow of enactive engagement as the creation of the space within which the field itself can flow and find meaning. As the analyst and patient both take this "hermeneutic ride" together, the field is allowed to unobtrusively express itself. *The analyst is unobtrusive to the unfolding of the field.* The field affords the emergence of unformulated and non-represented meanings that cannot be articulated in language, but are *lived through* together (Joseph, 1989).

As well as bringing the Barangers' work on the field to our attention, the contemporary Bionians such as Ferro, Civitarese and Neri (2009), have also championed the oneiric mode of psychoanalytic engagement. This mode offers us another window into what is not known or formulated and cannot be accessed by conscious engagement. Rooted in the Greek word for dreams, *oneiros,* oneiric refers to the dream-like quality, or in neo-Bionian terms the waking dream register, of all clinical (and indeed human) interaction. Beautifully explicated by Ogden (2005) waking dreaming refers to the Bionian understanding of the emergence of thought and experience from the bits and fragments of sensory engagement with the world. Dreaming is the waking process whereby the mind dreams experience and self out of mere fragmented sensation. The analyst's primary access to this register of the analysis is via his or her reverie. Among the sublime attractions of this attitude to our experience is the shifting of the boundary between sleep and wakefulness and the unique imprint of each individual's experience of their worlds.[3] From this perspective the flow of enactive engagement is not only regarded as a flow into and out of enacted experience, but also the flow into, and the shared living of, a waking dream. In the simplest possible terms, one can access the field and the unconscious, non-represented register of the analytic relationship by asking oneself: "what if this were a dream?" In other words, I might relate the session to myself as if it were a dream. To offer the crudest example: a boring session, in which the patient arrives late and talks repetitively with little vitality about a difficulty with a computer program he is trying to utilize at work. I feel exhausted and my mind wanders. The whole scene changes when I say to myself: "I had a dream that Mr. X came into the session late and talked about his relationship with an inanimate, unwilling and inaccessible object and I felt numb and dissociated". We are living a dream together and the field is narrating the oneiric register. From the unobtrusive position, one is to live in this world with the patient. We might say that via this shared, lived dream, the field is narrating both the original relational trauma – a mother who fell into inanimate unreachable states – along with a commentary of the treatment (that the treatment is mechanical and non-human, or that I am encountering the inanimate non-human part of the patient, and so on) as well as a cry from deep within the patient for the kind of object relationship that he requires to grow as a self. We could spell out more potential meanings, but the point is that rather than seeing such a patient and such a session as lifeless and the patient as non-related, the oneiric register of the field opens up the idea that the patient is *deeply* related, but in his regressed and very particular register. The patient cannot tell a story in words of, for example, a "dead mother" (Green, 1986), but can only show it, and it can be known via this shared hermeneutic regression, by the flow of this enactive engagement.

I often hear supervisees and students describe cases such as this where the patient is described as not engaging or even not ready for psychoanalytic treatment. I would suggest that these patients are using the analytic setting in the only way they can. The analyst can be unobtrusive to this, the patient's register, not attempt to bring the patient to a more satisfying register of expression (for the analyst), and to surrender to the meaning that is unfolding that cannot possible be narrated in words. This applies, I find, to phenomena that are often regarded as breaks in the boundary of the treatment or even assaults on the analysis. I would include here all the elements of treatment that rely on continuity, time and space. For instance, late arrival for sessions, missed sessions, confusions around time and payment, physical movement in the session and replacing or moving the objects and structure of my office or the waiting room. I must stress that I do not propose that "anything goes", but I am attuned to the idea that a boundary need not be a barrier (Pines, 1998) and our work is to unobtrusively provide the boundaried and safe space within which the oneiric hermeneutic mutual regression of the flow of enactive engagement can unfold. So, again, in the simplest formulation, I regarded a patient who missed many sessions of a multiple-times-per-week analysis with no warning or explanation, not as resisting or avoiding psychoanalytic communication and engagement, but deeply communicating an un-knowable area of profound absence and dread. It is by listening to the field and knowing that I am living a dream with the (absent) patient that I came to know this area of the patient that, I believe, could have found no other incarnation in the treatment. Bach (2011) and Symington (2012) have offered us the helpful advice that the treatment is ongoing regardless of whether the patient is in the room at the required time. I am suggesting that such primal and non-represented phenomena are unlikely to be accessed by addressing the lateness or absence with the patient, as is commonly recommended. Or the contemporary relational analyst may seek to explore the experience by offering his or her own experience of the absence or lateness or inquiring about the analysand's thoughts about the analyst's response to these events. From my perspective exploration itself calls forth the knowing self. The patient cannot describe a regression to, for instance, primary relatedness. I would suggest that it is the unknowing self of both patient and analyst that are likely to offer most access to the yet-to-be-known meanings that the field holds at such times. Engaging in exploration can very easily tilt the patient into his or her knowing, thinking and related self. Accompanying the patient in these primary, regressed states offers the holding and containment that can lead to the growth of self, a "joint consciousness" (Trevarthen) of non-representable experience, a shared waking dream.

Narrative and enactive witnessing

From this hermeneutic perspective a relational story is always being told by the field, a narrative is always unfolding in the treatment. Put another way, beyond the clear denotative meaning of words spoken, patients are always telling their stories. The patients and states I am addressing in this chapter tell and narrate in ways that are very much not in awareness. Such patients tend to show rather than tell. The showing is not with conscious intention and is often in the realm of the physical or behavioral (or rhythmic and motoric). A patient who misses a session or who refuses to engage in the treatment and causes anguish and fear in the analyst is telling a story with little or no access to the self who is doing the telling. The field is doing its narrative work. The analyst's unobtrusive position is to be aware that he or she is part of this oneiric unfolding narrative, and that the analyst's work is to set and maintain the frame such that the participatory narrative can emerge. It is via the flow of enactive engagement that the analyst and patient together bear witness to trauma and non-represented and non-symbolized registers of the patient's being. This enactive witnessing (Reis 2010b, 2010b) is a witnessing from the inside, rather than a legal witnessing that focuses on events viewed in space and time. Enactive witnessing implies a shared experiencing by both patient and analyst together. In the hermeneutic spirit it is not static and does not refer to the registration of information outside of the self (Reis, 2010a, 2010b).

Let me offer a brief clinical example that pulls some of these threads together. Matt Aibel (2014) described a very challenging treatment with Paul, a man who would aggressively reject any form of input from the analyst. The patient would bully the analyst and insist on dominating the sessions, refusing to engage the analyst. The analyst increasingly felt that he was unable to think and that he was losing his mind in sessions. Aibel says that he was "unable to explore, interpret or link" and found himself "reduced to merely a listening function", only able to "mark time" in sessions (Aibel, p. 146). He worried that the treatment was "stalemated" (Aibel, p. 150). A supervisor urged Matt Aibel to confront and explore this experience with the patient. The patient talked over him when he tried to do this and Aibel found himself unable to speak at moments of potential exploration. In my commentary on this case I suggested that the analyst was "not reduced to a listening function. He was *elevated* to a listening function, to being with and in (the patient's) world, the signature of which is to be reduced and diminished" (Grossmark, 2014, p. 165). Paul's unwillingness to explore what was happening can be seen as a silent scream from a self-state that could only be non-verbally communicated and would have been lost in the related world of verbal exchange. Living within this patent's world was excruciating to Aibel and he describes finding himself narcotized, unable to stay awake in sessions. The patient talked about mesmerizing people in his life and dreamed of being in a coma. Ultimately after a particularly soporific session Aibel lay on the couch and fell into a deep, coma-like sleep himself for exactly 45 minutes. In my commentary I suggested that the mutual regression in the flow of this awfully difficult enactive engagement revealed the areas of the patient that could not possibly have been articulated or explored by the patient. In other words, Aibel was witnessing from the inside and participating in a psychoanalytic narrative that the patient was unable to tell. One might also say that he was living within an illusion, a field that was containing this non-representable realm of pain and emptiness that resided deep within Paul. Behind the aggressive, dominating presentation there was a man who did not experience himself as alive. He was like a zombie who was neither alive nor dead (Reis, 2011). From my perspective, Aibel, in deep unspeakable joint consciousness with his patient, was witnessing the patient's yet to be experienced upbringing wherein his parents offered little vitalization and recognition and in many ways psychically killed him. Hence the patient was in the grip of this un-experienced non-alive state that only came to be enactively narrated and lived via Aibel's unobtrusive participation in the flow of enactive engagement. Aibel was present in his own subjectivity, yet could find no purchase in the exploratory and verbal mode. He found himself companioning the patient in the creation of a narrative that could only be expressed in the realm of joint motoric and physical consciousness. I would suggest that this mode offered the patient an accompanied pathway to the integration of self and ultimately to relatedness.

The unobtrusive psychoanalytic register, holding and the analyst's subjectivity

The conceptualization of unobtrusiveness allows the analyst to not be shackled by the arbitrary constrictions of "neutrality" and "abstinence". While placing primacy on the analysand's internal world and idiom, it enables the analyst to be sincerely and personally present even as he or she lends his or her subjectivity to the psychic world emerging in the treatment. It also privileges this work of mutual regression and companioning in the darker and less formulated reaches of the patient's inner worlds.

Slochower (1996, 2006, 2013) has been the primary relational psychoanalyst to address work with patients "whose sense of self is especially vulnerable to external assault" (1996, p. 62) and recommends periods where the analyst "brackets aspects of her own complex emotional experience" (1996, p. 1). There is much convergence with Slochower's position and the unobtrusive relational perspective outlined here. Slochower (2013) explains:

> There are limits to the clinical value of intersubjective work. Some patients cannot tolerate or integrate evidence of the analyst's otherness without prolonged derailment that shuts down (rather than opens up) the therapeutic process. Analytic holding is a useful clinical response to this kind of vulnerability.
>
> (p. 609)

Further, Slochower embraces the idea that dependence is the expression of a needed relationship rather than purely defensive, "because early need was real and needed repair" (Slochower, 2013, p. 607). Much akin to my thoughts above about being the analyst the patient requires you to be, she recommends that the analyst "remain within *whatever affective frame* [Slochower's italics] a patient anticipates and needs" (Slochower 2013, p. 609) such that "the patient may become able to identify, perhaps amplify, aspects of a nascent, unarticulated, or only partially articulated experience" (Slochower, 2013, p. 613): all sentiments that cohere fully with the unobtrusive relational register.

However, the unobtrusive and companioning register that I am articulating here does seem to diverge in some of its emphases from Slochower's "holding position". Slochower seems to pose the holding mode as a strategy to utilize when she fears that any evidence of her subjectivity will "derail" the treatment. This might suggest that the "holding mode" can be seen as a way-station toward the analytic work of reflection, confrontation and interpretation and suggests that change is what happens once the analytic couple can engage in more related and exploratory work.

Certainly, I take much from Slochower's recommendation to not bring her subjectivity to the patient who cannot use it, or will be disturbed by its expression. But I do see the unobtrusive position as engaging in a hermeneutic joint consciousness with the non-representable, unsymbolizable and disobjectalized (Green, 1999) forms of non-relatedness that emerge in the field of the treatment and the dyad. Hence, I regarded Aibel (above) as unobtrusively holding his patient Paul and the treatment. But there was more: a narrative emerged in the treatment comprised of Aibel's experience of the narcotized obliteration of his mind together with Paul's inability to consider another subjectivity. The work of psychoanalysis for this patient, I would argue, was being accomplished as the joint consciousness of the analytic couple lived and survived the experience and illusion of psychic obliteration together.

Slochower stresses the world of affect, recommending (above) that the analyst stay within whatever "affective frame" the patient anticipates and needs. Dispelling the familiar misconception that "holding" involves softer and gentler emotions, she tells us: "I also hold states like self-involvement, rage and contempt." (2013, p. 609). Certainly, this coheres fully with the unobtrusive relational register, but in addition to affect, I also foreground multiple and altered *states* of joint consciousness that offer a somewhat different register of analytic engagement.

Perhaps one might say that while holding, as explicated by Slochower, forms a necessary part of the register of the unobtrusive relational analyst, it is not the whole of what I am describing. The unobtrusive position suggests an emotionally present and companioning psycho-analyst who, guided by the patient's state, may or may not decide that it is the moment to talk about his or her experience or to ask anything of the patient. The emphasis is on companioning the patient into their worlds of experience, fragmentation, non-being and non-relatedness. As Winnicott and Trevarthen have underlined, each in his own inimitable way, the development of self and self-other relatedness grows out of entering into shared illusion or joint consciousness. The shift here is from holding to unobtrusive *companioning* (Grossmark, 2013). I am more inclined to allow a companioned regressive flow with and into the patient's more vulnerable and less integrated states and would regard *this* as the psycho-analytic work itself.

Many relational analysts following Steven Mitchell have cautioned against the withholding of the analyst's subjectivity and have suggested that the analyst's subjectivity is always a presence in the room. To not address this is to deprive or to withhold from the patient, and at worst will compound the patient's dysfunctional relational patterns. Bass (1996) suggests that to not offer our subjective experience of the patient is to "elude and obscure" rather than "to explore with genuine interest and concern" (p. 364) and that our "personal responsiveness as it emerges in our work with our patients represents the deepest source of our analytic gift" (p. 378). I would suggest that the unobtrusive companioning of patients into their darkest and least representable states involves a deep offering of the analyst's subjectivity. It is a profound provision of one register of the analyst's subjectivity rather than a withholding. It is a subjectivity that is proffered to the process of mutual regression, a process that by its very nature is not available to be "explored" in the moment. Exploration suggests calling upon the more related symbolizing self of the patient, the self that is conscious and participatory. This is the very self-state that is often dedicated to not permitting the expression of the more regressed, unformulated and empty states, "unlife" as a patient said to me just this morning.

I would suggest that the way we have talked about using and offering the analyst's subjectivity in the relational literature has too often emphasized the knowing and exploratory aspects of one's subjectivity; the expression of subjectivity that aims to help develop the dialogic and reflective aspects of the patient. Our case studies are replete with accounts of the resolution of enactments after an intelligent and sincere expression of the analyst's understanding of what has transpired in the treatment relationship. Indeed, a presentation of my own (Grossmark, 2009) would be a case in point. I am suggesting here that there are many other registers of the analyst's subjectivity that the analyst can choose to offer in the course of treatment and there are treatments with the kinds of patients that I am describing where a different register of the analyst's subjectivity is required. They may not be exploratory but I would argue that they are certainly expressions of the analyst's subjectivity. The register of unobtrusive accompanying in mutual regression involves the presence of a subjectivity whose signature is surrender (Ghent, 1990), responsiveness, receptivity and unknowing.

Conclusion

I have outlined a register of relational psychoanalytic work that involves an expansion of the use of the analyst's subjectivity so as to work with patients and states that are not accessible to reflection and exploration in the verbal and related realm. The unobtrusive relational register allows access to unformulated, non-represented and unspeakable realms of the patients experience and emphasizes the sometimes quiet and deeply engaged accompanying of the patient. Primacy is given to the patient's idiom, psychic signature and illusion. The analyst is interested to embrace and accompany the patient into inner darkness, emptiness, wordlessness and deadness rather than seeking to move the patient into more related and dialogic registers. The analyst lends his or her subjectivity to the growth of the transformational space of the treatment and both analyst and patient reside within the emergent and oneiric field of the treatment. The analyst's task is to hold and protect the space, to allow the mutual flow of enactive engagement that emerges and to not obtrude by drawing the analytic couple into the verbal and dialogic realm when there is still benefit to be gained from the mutual journey into the unknown and non-symbolizable realms of the treatment. Treatment is characterized by a mutual hermeneutic regression where both analyst and patient find and make meaning as regressed states are lived through together in "joint consciousness in companionship".

Notes

1   I do wonder if such coming together internally in the quiet, connected presence of another speaks to a register of psychoanalytic work that was more familiar to the British Middle Group, and perhaps more compatible with a British poetic sensibility where solitude and silent companionship are more highly valued (Storr, 1988) than the American cultural/philosophic environment built on pragmatism and the valorization of emotional expression (*Psychoanalytic Dialogues*, Symposium, 2004).
2   There is a tradition in group therapy technique that limits therapist interventions to only addressing the group-as-a-whole, for example, Agazarian (2006), and the Group Relations/Tavistock approach (Hayden & Molenkamp, 2004). The group analyst would only address an individual member of the group as a container or "role" for a piece of the group-as-

a-whole's dynamic. See Rizzolo (2014) for a relational critique of this technique.

3   See Ogden's work for a fuller and fascinating exploration of waking dreaming.

References

Agazarian, Y. (2006). The invisible group: An integrational theory of "group-as-a-whole". In: Y. Agazarian (Ed.). *Systems-Centered Practice: Selected Papers on Group Psychotherapy* (pp. 105–130). London: Karnac Books.

Aibel, M. (2014). Being railroaded: A candidate's struggle to stay on track. *Psychoanalytic Perspectives*, 11, 140–163.

Anzieu, D. (1984). The group and the unconscious. *International Library of Group Psychoanalysis*. London: Routledge.

Aron, L. (1991). The patient's experience of the analyst's subjectivity. *Psychoanalytic Dialogues*, 1, 29–51.

Aron, L. (1996). *A Meeting of Minds: Mutuality in Psychoanalysis*. Hillsdale, MI and London: The Analytic Press.

Aron, L. and Bushra, A. (1998). Mutual regression: Altered states in the psychoanalytic situation. *Journal of the American Psychoanalytic Association*, 46, 389–412.

Bach S. (1994). *The Language of Perversion and the Language of Love*. Northvale, NJ: Aronson.

Bach, S. (2006). *Getting From Here To There: Analytic Love and Analytic Process*. Hillsdale, NJ: The Analytic Press.

Bach, S. (2011). *The How-To Book for Students of Psychoanalysis and Psychotherapy*. London: Karnac.

Bach, S., Grossmark, C. & Kandall, E. (2014). The empty self and the perils of attachment. *The Psychoanalytic Review*, 101, 3, 321–340.

Balint, E. (1993). *Before I Was I: Psychoanalysis and the Imagination*. Edited by J. Mitchell & M. Parsons. New York and London: Guilford Press.

Balint, M. (1968). *The Basic Fault: Therapeutic Aspects of Regression*. New York: Bruner/Mazel.

Baranger, M. & Baranger, W. (2009). *The Work of Confluence: Listening and Interpreting in the Psychoanalytic Field*. London: Karnac Books.

Bass, A. (1996). Holding, holding back and holding on: Commentary on paper by Joyce Slochower. *Psychoanalytic Dialogues*, 6, 3, 361–378.

Bass, A. (2003). 'E' Enactments in psychoanalysis: another medium, another message. *Psychoanalytic Dialogues*, 13, 657–675.

Benjamin, J. (2004). Beyond doer and done to: An intersubjective view of thirdness. *Psychoanalytic Quarterly*, 73, 5–46.

Bion, W. (1961). *Experiences in groups*. London: Basic Books.

Bromberg, P.M. (1996). *Standing in the Spaces: Essays on Clinical Process, Trauma and Dissociation*. Hillsdale, NJ: The Analytic Press.

Bromberg, P.M. (2006). *Awakening the Dreamer: Clinical Journeys*. Mahwah, NJ: The Analytic Press.

Brown, L.J. (2010). Klein, Bion and intersubjectivity: Becoming, transforming, and dreaming. *Psychoanalytic Dialogues*, 20, 6, 669–682.

Civitarese, G. (2008). *The Intimate Room: Theory and Technique of the Analytic Field*. London, New York: Routledge.

Civitarese, G. (2013). The inaccessible unconscious and reverie as a path of figurability. In: H. Levine, G.S. Reed, & D. Scarfone (Eds.). *Unrepresented States and the Construction of Meaning: Clinical and Theoretical Contributions*. London: Karnak Books, pp. 220–239.

Director, L. (2009). The enlivening object. *Contemporary Psychoanalysis*, 45, 1, 120–141.

Etchegoyen, R.H. (1991). *The Fundamentals of Psychoanalytic Technique*. London: Karnac Books.

Fonagy, P., Gergely, G., Jurist, E. & Target, M. (20015). *Affect regulation, mentalization and the development of the self*. New York: Other Press.

Freud, S. (1905). Three essays on the theory of sexuality. *Standard Edition of the Complete Psychological Works of Sigmund Freud* VII. London: Hogarth Press, p. 125.

Freud, S. (1913). On beginning the treatment. *Standard Edition of the Complete Psychological Works of Sigmund Freud* XII. London: Hogarth Press, p. 135.

Ghent, E. (1990). Masochism, submission, surrender. *Contemporary Psychoanalysis*, 26, 169–211.

Green, A. (1986). The dead mother. In: A. Green (Ed.). *On Private Madness*. London: Karnac.

Green, A. (1999). *The Work of the Negative*. London: Free Association Books.

Grossmark, R. (2009). The case of Pamela. *Psychoanalytic Dialogues*, 19, 1, 22–30.

Grossmark, R. (2012a). The unobtrusive relational analyst. *Psychoanalytic Dialogues*, 22, 6, 629–646.

Grossmark, R. (2012b). The flow of enactive engagement. *Contemporary Psychoanalysis*, 48, 3, 287–300.

Grossmark, R. (2013). The Register of Psychoanalytic Companioning. Paper presentation. New York University Postdoctoral Program in Psychoanalysis, Relational Track Colloquium, November 2013.

Grossmark, R. (2014). The flow of enactive engagement: Commentary on Matt Aibel's "Being railroaded: A candidate's struggle to stay on track". *Psychoanalytic Perspectives*, 11, 164–172.

Hayden, C. & Molenkamp, R. (2004). Tavistock primer II. In: S. Cytrynbaum & D. Noumair (Eds.) *Group Dynamics, Organizational Irrationality and*

Social Complexity: group relations Reader 3 (pp. 137–157). Waldorf, MD: McArdle Printing.

Hoffman, I.Z. (2006) The myths of free association and the potentials of the analytic relationship. *IJP*, 87, 143–62.

Hopkins, L. (2006) *False Self: The Life of Masud Khan*. New York: Other Press.

Joseph, B. (1989). Transference: The total situation. In: M. Feldman & E.B. Spillius (Eds.). *Psychic equilibrium and psychic change; Selected papers of Betty Joseph* (pp. 156–167). London: Routledge.

Levenson, E. (1983). *The Ambiguity of Change*. New York: Basic Books.

Levine, H., Reed, G.S. & Scarfone, D. (Eds.). (2013). *Unrepresented States and the Construction of Meaning: Clinical and Theoretical Contributions*. London: Karnak Books.

Nagel, T. (1986). *The View From Nowhere*. New York: Oxford University Press.

Neri, C. (2009). The enlarged notion of the field in psychoanalysis. In: A. Ferro & R. Basile (Eds.). *The Analytic Field: A Clinical Concept* (pp. 45–80). London: Karnac Books.

Ogden, T.H. (2005). *This Art of Psychoanalysis: Dreaming Undreamt Dreams and Interrupted Cries*. London: Routledge.

Orange, D.M. (2010). *Thinking for Clinicians: Philosophical Resources for Contemporary Psychoanalysis and the Humanistic Psychotherapies*. New York: Routledge.

Orange, D.M. (2011). *The Suffering Stranger: Hermeneutics for Everyday Clinical Practice*. New York: Routledge.

Pines, M. (1998). *Circular Reflections: Selected Papers on Group Analysis and Psychoanalysis*. London: Jessica Kingsley Publishers.

Pizer, S. A. (1998). *Building Bridges: The Negotiation of Paradox in Psycho-analysis*. Hillsdale, NJ and London: The Analytic Press.

Reis, B. (2010a). Enactive fields: An approach to interaction in the Kleinian-Bionian model. Commentary on paper by Lawrence J. Brown. *Psychoanalytic Dialogues*, 20, 695–703.

Reis, B. (2010b). Performative and enactive features of psychoanalytic witnessing: The transference as the scene of address. *International Journal of Psychoanalysis*, 90, 1359–1372.

Reis, B. (2011). Zombie states: Reconsidering the relationship between life and death instincts. *Psychoanalytic Quarterly*, Vol. LXXX, 2, 269–286.

Rizzolo, G. (2015). Rethinking Tavistock: Enactment, the analytic third and the implications for group relations. In: R. Grossmark & F. Wright (Eds.). *The One and the Many: Relational Approaches to Group Psychotherapy* (pp. 215–241). New York, London: Taylor & Francis.

Slochower, J. (1996). *Holding and Psychoanalysis: A Relational Perspective*. Hillsdale, NJ and London: The Analytic Press.

Slochower, J. (2006). *Psychoanalytic Collisions.* Hillsdale, NJ: Analytic Press.

Slochower, J. (2013). Psychoanalytic mommies and psychoanalytic babies: A long view. *Contemporary Psychoanalysis*, 49, 4, 606–628.

Stern, D.B. (1997). *Unformulated Experience: From Dissociation to Imagination in Psychoanalysis.* Hillsdale, NJ: Analytic Press.

Stern, D.B. (2010). *Partners in thought: Working with unformulated experience, dissociation and enactment.* New York: Routledge.

Stern, D.B. (2013). Field theory in psychoanalysis, Part 2: Bionian field theory and contemporary interpersonal/relational psychoanalysis. *Psychoanalytic Dialogues*, 23, 6, 630–646.

Stern, D.N. (2010). *Forms of Vitality: Exploring Dynamic Experience in Psychology, the Arts, Psychotherapy, and Development.* Oxford: Oxford University Press.

Storr, A. (1988). *Solitude: A Return to the Self.* New York: Ballantine Books.

Symington, N. (2012). The Essence of psychoanalysis as opposed to what is secondary. *Psychoanalytic Dialogues*, 22, 4, 395–409.

Symposium (2004). Symposium on what's American about American Psychoanalysis? *Psychoanalytic Dialogues*, 14, 163–286.

Trevarthen, C. (2001). Intrinsic motives for companionship in understanding: Their origin, development, and the significance for infant mental health. *Infant Mental Health Journal*, 22, 1–2, 95–131.

Winnicott, D.W. (1945). Primitive emotional development. Reprinted in D.W. Winnoctt. *Through Pediatrics To Psycho-analysis.* New York: Basic Books, 1975.

Winnicott, D.W. (1954) Metaphysical and clinical aspects of regression within the psycho-analytic set-up. In: D.W. Winicott. *Through Pediatrics to Psycho-analysis.* London: Basic Books, 1958.

Winnicott, D.W. (1958). The capacity to be alone. In: D.W. Winnicott. *The Maturational Processes and the Facilitating Environment.* New York: International Universities Press, 1965.

Winnicott, D.W. (1960). *Playing and Reality.* London: Routledge.

Wright, F. (2015). Being seen, moved, disrupted and reconfigured: group leadership from a relational perspective. In: R. Grossmark & F. Wright (Eds.). *The One and the Many: Relational Approaches to Group Psychotherapy* (pp. 27–37). New York, London: Routledge.

Zimmer, R. (2010). A view from the field: clinical process and the work of confluence. *Psychoanalytic Quarterly*, 89, 1151–1165.

Chapter 9

The things we carry

Finding/creating the object and the analyst's self-reflective participation[1]

Steven H. Cooper

Relational theory has generated interest from analysts with theoretical relationships/allegiances to interpersonal, self psychological, object relations, and Freudian psychologies. I will suggest in this paper that as relational theory developed it became more a general, overarching theory, a metatheory combining elements of a clinical sensibility and critique of other clinical theories. What it has gained in breadth in terms of this sensibility it may have lost in terms of some of its unique contributions to the development of object relations theory.

In my view, Mitchell's contributions to object relations theory were substantial and are still unrealized in terms of the ways that his mind occupied a seam at the border of internalized objects relations and interpersonal experience. His definition of psychoanalysis as a process marked by the analyst's self-reflection brought more directly into play the understanding and dedication of the analyst to the notion that we are always participating in one way or other with the patient's internalized object world. Understanding that internalized object world is in many ways the deepest element of our personal participation.

It's my impression that in recent years branches of relational theory that emphasize the importance of internalized object relations as a construct (e.g. Cooper, 1998; 2000; 2010; Cooper & Levit, 1998; Davies, 2004; Davies & Frawley, 1992; Mitchell, 1994; 1995; 1997; Slochower, 1996; Stern, 2010) have been less theorized than those emphasizing interpersonal theory, self psychology, and attachment theory.

I will suggest that a dedicated attention to internal object relations is part of the analyst's attention to the reciprocally influencing relationship between object relations and interpersonal phenomena, one of the unique elements of early relational theory. I think of object relations theory as fundamentally a theory of unconscious internal object relations in dynamic interplay with current interpersonal experience. This definition is consistent with Ogden's (2012) recent definition of object relations theory as "a group of psychoanalytic theories holding in common a loosely knit set of metaphors that address the intrapsychic and interpersonal effects of relationships among unconscious internal objects, that is, among unconscious split-off parts of the personality" (p. 11–12). The analysis of internal object relations centers upon the exploration of the relationship between internal objects and the ways in which the patient feels reluctant and resists the prospect of changing these unconscious internal object relations in the face of current experience.

I will also suggest that the patient's and analyst's need for privacy and more importantly, the illusion of privacy in the presence of the other, hallmarks of Kleinian, Independent, and Bionian object relations theories, has always been somewhat under-theorized within relational theory (Cooper, 2008). If I am correct in this assessment, it is likely related to an emphasis within relational theory on the patient's read on the analyst and their mutual influence on each other. However, I do not believe that there needs to be a dichotomy between the analyst's needs for the illusion of privacy to think and dream and Mitchell's s essential contribution to the notion that there's no place to hide in analytic process. The analyst's need for the illusion of privacy is part of what allows him to work in slower tempos, to 'think slow' (Kahneman, 2011) to use reverie, clinical imagination, and our self-reflection about our participation to make connections to the ways that our patient's inner lives are peopled.

I would like to suggest a major caveat to this paper as a "critique" of relational theory. My focus in this paper is really very much on my own very personal clinical sensibility, which is substantially influenced by Freud, Bion, Klein, Mitchell and particularly Winnicott. Thus I do not suggest that I speak for relational theory and what it should or should not represent. I write as an author who was excited about Mitchell's work and the promise that it held for integrating object relations theory and interpersonal theory. My critique issues forth from the point of view of how relational theory developed that promising area and how it has not.

Leaving and not leaving home and the importance of the construct, 'internal object'

We never entirely leave home. Psychoanalysis allows us to eke out the freedom derived from the awareness of this fact and to avail ourselves of the opportunity for new experience. I like to think about psychoanalysis as in line with what Money-Kyrle (1968) referred to as a psychic base or Spezzano (2007) referred to as a "home" for the minds of the patient and analyst, including a home for the patient's mind in the mind of the analyst. It is in that home that patient and analyst strive in a process to make sense of what the patient conveys about himself that he doesn't know he is conveying and how their interaction is informed by these communications.

What has been on offer from contemporary psychoanalytic theory in general, and relational theory in particular, is that we can never be entirely satisfied with sharply differentiated determinations about the extent to which our patient is elaborating his relationships to unconscious internalized objects or elaborating more conscious perceptions and experiences of the other within the interpersonal setting of analysis. I liken the ambiguity about what is inside and what is outside to the interfused and permeable boundaries in the magnificent oil paintings of Richard Diebenkorn. Elements of subjectivity emerge and are not easily placed as belonging clearly to one container or another. As Ferenzci (1932) put it, pain is not a point in time and space. We are always trying to somehow help the patient establish: "Where does this belong and come from? What do I do with it?"

Indeed, it might be said that psychoanalysts are a kind of boundary artist. For those analysts who make very active use of object relations theory as well as the analyst's personal participation in their developed theories of therapeutic action, the ambiguity about interiority versus what is outside is lived with rather than "resolved."

In this essay I want to reflect about and emphasize the interaction between an interest in the analyst's dedicated attention to the patient's internal object relations, his "irrevocable condition" and the analyst's self-reflective participation. Our stops and starts of attention to the patient's internal objects and our own is in some sense one of the most important elements of our *personal participation*. I wish to make explicit, to underscore ways of thinking about object relations in the context of relational theory.

The analyst's dedicated attention to internal objects and his self-reflective participation as clinical ideals: metatheory versus clinical theory

Psychoanalysts who consider themselves as holding a relational sensibility are extraordinarily theoretically diverse in their influences (Harris, 2011). I am very much in agreement with Tublin (2011) who in a broad ranging, cogent critical appreciation of relational theory, emphasized the importance of each analyst to be explicit about their theories of mind and therapeutic action – to, as Ghent (1989) put it, lay out their credo.

I have never thought of relational theory as either a theory of technique or obviously a psychoanalytic metapsychology such as Freudian theory, ego psychology, self psychology, and Kleinian or Bionian theory. There is an important, implicit but not necessarily articulated debate within relational theory about whether it is a clinical theory versus a kind of psychoanalytic meta-theory (Bass & Cooper, 2012; Cooper, 2010; Tublin, 2011). Traditional psychoanalytic theories suggest particular methods or guidelines for working and understanding the patient in analysis. As a meta-theory, however, relational theory would essentially stand outside the matrix of theories of psychoanalysis that offer a metapsychology or a specific body of technique. As a meta-theory, a relational perspective suggests an overarching set of principles that guide clinical thinking and clinical sensibility and might accompany analysts from a variety of schools to approach patients in understanding the analytic process.

I think of relational theory as an overarching clinical model, a meta-theory at a different level of theoretical discourse than theories such as self psychology or ego psychology, a theory productively used by many different kinds of analysts. How else might we understand the enormous differences in technical choices that we see among analysts who describe their work as informed by relational theory?

I would suggest that the guiding clinical precept at the heart of a relational sensibility lies in Mitchell's emphasis on the importance of the analyst's dedicated interest in his self-reflective participation at the heart of analytic process. Some of the other overarching principles related to relational theory involve the analyst's awareness of tensions between discipline and spontaneity, the analyst's participation as an old and new object, and our sliding and moving awareness of mutual impact and participation. Many of the other overarching principles of relational theory were well summarized by Harris (2011) in a far-ranging essay that included various points of clinical focus and epistemology within a relational perspective. In my view, implicit in many of these ideals is that of helping patients to experience and see new modes of expressiveness as they escape (often for nanoseconds in protean expressions) from the bondage of internalized objects along with the analyst's self-reflective participation in aiding and obstructing this process.

It is difficult for me to understand the patient's forward movement, his efforts at growth as well as his attempts to stay the same, without keeping in mind some concept of the internal objects that keep the patient company and provides him with self—continuity and stability. Internal object relations are akin to private poems that have been mysteriously written and are in the process of being expressed in the public arena of dyadic communication within the psychoanalytic process. Here an appreciation of the ubiquity of repetition is at play, background to whatever forward movement is being expressed through a patient's and analyst's experiences in the analytic process (Bromberg, 1998; Loewald, 1960; Russell, 1978). I have to know who is attacking the patient, the "internal saboteur" (Fairbairn, 1952) in order to engage creatively in understanding what is being communicated through the system of saboteurs. I am aiming to listen as Frederic Lanzmann, the film director of "Shoa," described when he termed his film, "a fiction of the real." Lanzmann said that he "was imagining himself as much into the minds and the souls of the killers as of the victims" (2012). Each analysis is a fiction of the real that our patients are narrating through what they remember and the coverings of what they remember.

My point is that we each have to arrive at a new relationship to the patient's most apparently destructive internal objects that are part of what is familiar to the patient's adaptation. *This is where the heart of analytic work lies, in a paradoxical way, partly in the analyst's internal life.* This is why the most paradoxical part of the analyst's personal participation in some ways lies in his dedicated interest to the patient's internal object world. I have a very personal participation, a very personal relationship with the patient's internal objects.

Along these lines, Ogden (1994) also suggested that interpretation is a form of object relationship and each object relationship carries a sense of the analyst's understanding of the latent content of the interaction with the object. I am particularly drawn to this way of putting things because I believe it conveys not only the ways that we inevitably convey elements of our subjective participation but also how, when we are able, we convey what we have done with our patient's internalized experience through the filter of our own subjective lenses about how we participate with our patients.

I view internalized object relations as always associated with particular affective states that move in and out of our awareness. I find helpful the BCPSG's way of thinking about introjects as implicitly encoded emotional memories that are not easily available to verbalization and which are expressed or known when enacted in a relational context that prompts their retrieval. Seen from this perspective, the relationship between analyst and patient consists of the interaction and intersection of the patients and analyst's internalized object relations.

I believe that relationally oriented analysts are so attuned to the here and now elements of reciprocal influence that perhaps we think too dichotomously of old experience, the things that we carry, as an avoidance of here and now interaction. Slochower's (1996) work and beyond is notable for the way that she is constantly describing her attempts to hold and contextualize the patient's internalized objects in order to make contact with the parts of the patient that are most accessible. Framing the past elements of internalized object relations involves the patient's dialogue with past relationships in the present for particular reasons but does not mean that we as analysts are not involved in the "creation" of the object as well (Bromberg, 1998, p. 213). Bromberg puts it beautifully when he describes objects not as static structures but as components of a dynamic structure. He notes that even though the patient's need to perceive elements of the other is strongly motivated, it doesn't mean that the analyst doesn't have a role in creating the object. I agree with Bromberg that to understand another person's interiority requires that we understand our own in their presence. This makes the understanding of another person's internal objects a fundamentally relational activity.

I have had the sense that relational theory's focus on mutual influence (Aron, 1996) and mutual containment (Cooper, 2000) has sometimes led to an unnecessary kind of theoretical incompatibility with formulations about how we are recruited to fight with these internal saboteurs (Fairbairn, 1952) and internalized objects (Sandler, 1976). I see no need to view mutual influence between patient and analyst and the patient's recruitment into internalized scenarios as dichotomous and incompatible dimensions within the analytic situation. It is true that formulations about recruitment can easily be used to absolve the analyst of his participation but it doesn't mean that the patient isn't unconsciously doing this at times. I find indispensable the contemporary Kleinian concept elaborated by Feldman (1997) that the patient is often projecting internalized objects on to the analyst and at some level psychically working to make the analytic situation congruent (familiar) with the patient's internalized world. Greenberg (1995) has also made this point by emphasizing that in each "interactive matrix" we are often more likely to observe places where there is an incongruity between the patient's way of seeing and our own. However, understanding this tendency is only a part of engagement with patients and does not address the patient's conscious and unconscious experience of the impact of internal objects of both patient and analyst on the patient. Indeed, the analyst's personal participation involves curiosity about our influence on the patient as well as seeing obstacles to helping a patient observe how he is expressing something that he doesn't know that he is expressing. As Bass (personal communication) has pointed out, the importance of mutuality is always at play in that the analyst is also often expressing things that he doesn't know that he is expressing.

Experiences of those we carry are always being communicated in dialogue with the other for multiple reasons that are rarely best understood strictly in relation to recruiting us to participate with these internal experiences in prescribed roles. Ricoeur's question about why we are being told a past story in the present begs many questions that relate to what is happening between the patient and analyst that threaten old attachments. Another way to put this is that the communication of internal object relations is not always communicative of simply "old object" experience but is often conveyed in the new experience of the analytic situation. Just as we are often invited to participate on the old object continuum, it is easy to minimize the ways that patients are unconsciously expressing internal objects in the present and by so doing, testing the waters about whether something new can be integrated (or often enacted) with the analyst. Patients seek an "exit from unending, futile wanderings in their own internal object world" (Ogden, 2004, p. 193) or as David Foster Wallace put it, an escape is sought for those who are "marooned in our own skull" (2014). A tension is held in the best of circumstances by patient and analyst that includes the more concrete and literal experience of old internalized object relations and the here and now of the analytic situation in which the patient may be probing new modes of experience and integration.

Psychoanalysis is fundamentally dialogic in nature, and the telling of what is inside us, some of which we are aware of as patients and some not, is always changing in dialogue with another. The meaning is always changing within us as well, as we reveal the coverings of what we remember and focus on (Ferenczi, 1932). Psychoanalysis aims to change the meaning of our internalized voices and relations as these coverings are explored.

Thus a dedication to understanding the patient's internal objects often works in a complementary way with an appreciation of clinical ideals associated with relational theory. The relationship between the analyst's personal participation and internalized objects has been repeatedly advanced, particularly in the writing of Bass (2009), Bromberg (1998, 2011), Davies (2004), Davies and Frawley, (1992) and Stern (2010), and I hope in some of my own work. In the tradition of some this writing, the analyst's personal participation has been framed as an attempt to understand all of those inside the patient and analyst with whom we are conversing.

In the language of self-states that has dominated recent writing from relational theorists, it is easy to overlook that self-states arise in relation to internalized experiences with important others who live inside us.

Dedication to understanding the pervasive influence of the patient's internal objects does not imply that there is value in unearthing these object relations as reified structures, nor is it synonymous with believing that all that occurs in analytic work is exclusively determined by the patient's internal world. The analyst's use of the construct of internalized object relations that we are unconsciously communicating to others about does not mean that all meaning is pre-formed but instead emerges in the dialogic context of psychoanalysis (e.g. Bass, 2001).

The elaboration of the pervasive influence of internal object relations is best accomplished through appreciating a tension between the often concrete ways that these internal experiences are held by the patient and a figurative relationship to internal objects that we are trying to show the patient. Our way of speaking of internal objects is through the translation of private experience, of the private condensed poems that our patients are expressing. We do so with a kind of "as if" quality through the use of metaphors that exist in dynamic tension with respect for the patient's literal meaning, what Bion would call its concrete and material meaning for the patient. Metaphors are our border language at the border of what is inside and outside.

Analyst and patient differ in their relationships to each other's internal world. The analyst is dedicated to understanding the patient's internal objects as well as to reflecting on his own participation with his patient. The patient does not truck in dedicated understanding of the analyst's internal objects even though he is influenced by them and often curious about them; the analyst cannot help but convey his internal object world because it is intrinsic to human communication. The patient is, however, motivated by his curiosity, his wish to make attachments, his fears, his wish to be gratified, his wish to be understood, and to express many sexual and aggressive feelings. The patient gets to know much about our internalized objects (often without naming them) and the patient is forced or enabled to work with them as imaginatively as possible (e.g. Davies, 2003). In fact, unfortunately, some of our patient's "shells" (Bromberg, 1991), described well by Winnicott's (1971) false self, Balint's (1968) basic fault, and Modell's (1963) cocoon, allow them to be gifted at working with the analyst's internal objects at the expense of their own capacities for enlivening and imaginative relatedness.

In my own experience as both analyst and patient, treatments worth their weight involve the analyst becoming deeply familiar with parts of the patient that are rigidly influential, troubling, and refractory to insight. These parts of the patient become animated in treatment as a collection of characters with whom we regularly visit and communicate. Some of these features in response to internalized object relations are almost like atavistic features from the perspective of the analyst but feel like vital elements of self for the patient. The analyst's participation is always framed in the shadow of these forces, including our most improvisational and creative activities as analysts. In a sense, I think of what we do by coming to understand the patient's internalized world and his adaptation as a kind of animating the atavistic. We try to bring it into the world now and know it with the patient in contrast to its anachronistic origins in which it was the best the patient had at that time. We come to know it because fundamentally analytic work lies, in a paradoxical way, partly in the analyst's internal life.

Thinking fast and slow (Kahneman, 2011): the analyst's needs for the illusion of privacy and self-reflection

One paradoxical element of deeply valuing the analyst's personal participation as an essential element of understanding his patient is that it often takes some privacy or the illusion of privacy for self-reflection about these matters. I have used the word privacy (Cooper, 2008) to refer to a place for the analyst's self-reflective activity. The fact that it is a private place as conceived by the analyst does not imply that the patient doesn't read and experience us in a variety of ways. Just as the patient's private space is never entirely private in the analytic setting, the analyst's private space is also never entirely private. *Instead, patient and analyst share illusions about privacy.* The analyst and patient's privacy and illusory privacy exist in their individual imaginations and are a shared part of the psychical field. In a fascinating paper, Foehl (2011) suggests that psychological distance is well understood as a phenomenon that is fundamental to the nature of experience, a way of understanding how we are, at once, fundamentally connected and private.

Illusions and the capacity to use illusion are essential to our well-being and capacity to function in all regards as humans – as romantic partners, parents, children, and certainly as analysts. To some extent what makes analysis productive is the capacity of a patient and analyst to work with their illusions about knowing and being known and about what is private and shared. The privacy I want to draw attention to is the analyst's need for self-reflection, not for privacy's sake, though our experienced needs for both personal privacy and self-reflection also differ in relationship to each patient.

The analyst's illusion of privacy is something that he will hold in many different ways and with various feelings and conflicts associated with these needs, and these needs obviously vary from analyst to analyst. He may be relatively comfortable with these needs because he has found that he has able to help patients through the use of his mind in this space. He may feel guilty about needing privacy or be avoidant or even somewhat dissembling about his need for this space. Perhaps this particular place of reflection for each analyst (and each analyst is also probably different with each patient) may also be usefully regarded as another form of self-care (Harris, 2009) that the analyst requires.

Our privacy or need for privacy doesn't contradict the basic understanding that we are readable to our patients and that they are keen observers of us. Yet it is easy to conflate our awareness that there's no place to hide in analytic work from the question of how much we as analysts value our place for self-reflection and reverie just as we promote our patients' efforts to tell us what they feel and think.

A "home" for the minds of the patient and analyst (Spezzano, 2007) involves an assemblage of various characters comprised of the internal objects of the patient and analyst. I try to maintain a dedicated attention to this assemblage of characters, and in order to do so, the place for my own capacity for feeling and thinking is indispensable.

I want the patient to be able to develop a sense and a home for self-reflection about what they are saying that they do not already know that they are saying and for them to see that I need a space for the same. In fact, to this point, our understanding of particular enactment evolves over time in the privacy of the analyst's imagination (Cooper, 2009) while at other times it occurs through the analyst's capacities to think aloud in less formulated ways about what they might be saying together (e.g. Bass, 2001; Stern, 1983, 2010).

The seminal contributions of analysts over the last thirty years that have emphasized the importance of the analyst's personal participation have created room for analysts to be open to spontaneity, improvisation, unformulated experience, and thinking aloud with their patients. Yet within the development of relationally influenced clinical theory, there has been less discussion of the analyst's need for privacy. When I wrote a paper several years ago about my own use of reverie (Cooper, 2008) and the analyst's needs for the illusion of privacy to advance self-reflection about his participation, I was unable to find a paper explicitly about the use of reverie within the relational literature. I suggested that within the relative literature it would be useful to provide more explicit elaboration of the private analytic space for self-reflection and more transparency about the analyst's need for privacy. My use of my associative processes overlaps a great deal with that of Ogden except that I am likely to share a bit more directly about what I thought about that leads me to the understanding I am putting forward. I see a great deal of overlap also with Stern (2010) who has repeatedly tried to address how he uses his associative processes and how he communicates elements of these to his patients.

This relative absence in the relational literature is striking because self-reflection, after all, was at the heart of Mitchell's descriptions and characterizations of the analytic process. He suggested that psychoanalysis itself is defined as a process between two people in which the analyst's engagement is guided by his own capacity for self-reflection about the quality of engagement with the patient. He stated:

> The intention that shapes my methodology is a self-reflective responsiveness of a particular (psychoanalytic) sort. In putting it this way, I am suggesting that my way of working entails not a striving for a particular state of mind, but an engagement in a process.
>
> (Mitchell, p. 193)

Here Mitchell might be construed as saying that in not "striving" for a particular state of mind he is eschewing the analyst's seeking a place for reverie. In my own experience, reverie happens. Our clinical imaginations are always in motion and when they are seemingly not we are seeking ways to get our minds to think about why they are not. So I agree with the idea of not striving for a state of mind that allows reverie but I am striving for a kind of openness to what Ogden (2004) termed a "motley" collection of what I am thinking and feeling.

I would hasten to add that Mitchell's (e.g. 1991) case examples are filled with examples of internal work, hard work that he put toward understanding the nuances of countertransference responsiveness in relation to what the patient was conveying. He was constantly asking himself questions such as why does this sound like this now, while it sounded like something else earlier in the process? For Mitchell, though, even more than for Racker (1952) and Searles (1979) before him, self-reflection occurs in a kind of public discourse, either as work with a patient or in analytic writing with us as readers; the privacy of his clinical imagination is never conceptualized as entirely private and a part of his entire clinical and theoretical project was to redefine what is personal and private. He wanted to insist, and I agree, that there is no such conceptual category as an isolated intrapsychic structure of one person defined as entirely separate from the sensibility of the person who is perceiving and receiving the patient. It is important, however, to not conflate this seminal clinical insight at one level of theoretical discourse about personal and private with an overly concrete and thus degraded version of practice in which the analyst might dispense too much with the articulated need for self-reflection about his patient.

Reverie itself has always implied a relatively more quiet analytic space, in which the analyst is allowing himself periods of silence to reflect on what he is hearing. I think that the concrete and degraded version of reverie is the construction of a space in which the analyst sits for long periods of silence while thinking about what he is hearing (Cooper, 2008). So while I see no need to concretely equate reverie with long periods of silence, I view the opportunity to think and feel a precondition for some analytic work. I value the notion of psychic reality as it emerges in the analytic field that was explored by Andre Green (2005) and Ogden's (1994a, b) intersubjective analytic third; these phenomena result from the exchange of the patient's and analyst's reverie, a third subjectivity that is unconsciously generated by the analytic pair. It has been my sense that some field theorists may tend to too easily presume a collapse of the analytic third that results from the dyadic focus on interpersonal exchanges more frequently described by relationally influenced analysts (e.g. Levine, 2013).

The analyst's self-reflection is embedded in a framework that incudes his interest in the patient's affective experience and internalized object relations. It is easy to conceive of an interest in both internal objects and self-reflective participation in narrow and concrete ways. All of us who are deeply interested in internalized object relations need to keep in mind that we misrepresent reality when we think that what is inside the patient determines what happens in the analytic situation (Baranger, 1993).

Concluding remarks

For analysts who aim to be deeply attuned to their personal participation as inevitable and crucial in understanding the unconscious mind of the patient, it is possible to concretize the meaning of personal participation – in essence a form of resistance on the part of the analyst to understanding the patient's unconscious experience. In my view, a very large part of interpersonal engagement with the patient, interaction if you will, is with internal attachments to objects that the patient holds and that constitute the formation of an analytic intersubjective third, a view described with various terminology by a range of analysts (Aron, 2006; Benjamin, 2004; Bromberg, 2000; Cooper, 2010a, b; Ferro, 2005; Foehl, 2010; Ogden, 2004; Russell, 1978; Slochower, 1996; Spezzano, 2007; and Stern, 2011).

Relational theory may, like many theories, have a particular kind of fantasy associated with its central tenets. Fantasies are productive to the extent that they guide direction and carry hope. In fact, one could argue that all therapeutic exchanges are partly bound by and through fantasy, in dynamic relations with individual characters and psychoanalytic theories, ideologies, institutions and cultures. Fantasy is also potentially problematic if it excludes complexity about helping our patients and understanding our patients. The fantasy that may be a part of relational theory is that we could ever "authentically" be present with a patient or know ourselves well enough, including our dissemblance from self and other, to make such a claim. A strength of relational theory has involved the effort to not add to the mystification of analytic work. But mystery is not mystification, and mystery is a part of that which makes analysis so powerful. As Friedman (2007, p. 829) put it so well, "a consistent treatment will be an opaque treatment." In this comment he is honoring and providing respect for the ways that psychoanalysis is a work situation and a situation involving intimacy, and that knowing in psychoanalysis is a very particular kind of knowing and being known. Privacy and the illusion of privacy that the patient and analyst need both honors and provides self-care for the analyst to reflect on the element of the mysterious.

Put still another way, I find myself wondering about a question about the existential center of analysis and relational thought. If Freud and his followers in the first eighty years of psychoanalysis taught us anything, it is that there is something in human relatedness that constantly mitigates our ability to be with one another and ourselves. In psychoanalysis, successful as we may be at finding deep emotional resonance with our patients, we are also to some extent always isolated, as so profoundly demonstrated in the work of Winnicott and Bion. There is something of what the Japanese refer to as "mono no aware" translated as a "slender sadness" that informs this poignant and ironic aspect of analytic work. This is indeed part of the platform from which I am trying to expand Relationalists' attention to the more solitary, private part of our participation in our analytic relationships.

I think of the analyst's self-reflection as a process of trying to be curious about helping a patient in very unusual circumstances – those in which we aim to learn with the patient something that he might not know in advance that he is saying. So too, our reflections issue from the understanding that patients come to know parts of us that we are not always aware of feeling or expressing. It is in this self-with-other and self-reflective space that we breathe in the psychoanalytic process.

Notes

1   Some portions of this paper were published in the journal article 'The Things We Carry: Finding/Creating the Object and the Analyst's Self-Reflective Participation', *Psychoanalytic Dialogues*, 24:6; pp. 621–636, 2015 and in Steven Cooper's, 2016 book *The Analyst's Experience of the Depressive Position: The Melancholic Errand of Psychoanalysis* (Routledge). Reprinted by permission of Taylor & Francis.

References

Aron, L. (1996). *A Meeting of Minds: Mutual Influence in Psychoanalysis*. Hillsdale, NJ: The Analytic Press.

——, (2006). Analytic impasse and the third: Clinical implications of intersubjectivity. *Int. J. Psycho-Anal.*, 87:349–368.

Barranger, M. (1993). The mind of the analyst: From listening to interpretation. *Int. J. Psychoanal.*, 74:15–24.

Baranger, M, Baranger, W. and Mom, J (1983). Process and non-process in analytic work. *Int. J. Psycho-Anal.*, 64:1–15.

Bass, A. (2001). It takes one to know one: Or, whose unconscious is it anyway? *Psychoanal. Dial.*, 11:683–703.

——, (2003). "E" enactments in psychoanalysis: Another medium, another message. *Psychoanal. Dial.*, 13:657–675.

——, (2009). An independent theory of clinical technique viewed through a relational lens. *Psychoanal. Dial.*, 19:237–245.

Bass, A. and Cooper, S. (2012). Relational Psychoanalysis. In: *Psychoanalytic Terms and Concepts*, ed. Auschincloss, E. and Samberg, E. *The American Psychoanalytic Association.*

Benjamin, J. (1988). *The Bonds of Love: Psychoanalysis, Feminism, and the Problem of Domination.* New York: Pantheon

——, (2004). Beyond doer and done to: An intersubjective view of thirdness. *Psychoanal Q.*, 73:5–46.

Bion, W. (1959). Attacks on linking. *Int. J. Psychoanal.*, 40:308–315.

——, (1963). *Elements of Psychoanalysis.* London: Heinemann

Bromberg, P. (1978). Interpersonal theory and the concept of regression. *Contemp. Psychoanal.* 15:647–655.

——, (1991). On knowing one's patient inside and out: The aesthetics of unconscious communication. *Psychoanal. Dial.*, 1:399–422.

——, (1995). Resistance, object usage, and human relatedness. *Contemp. Psychoanal.*, 31:163–192.

——, (1998). *Standing in the Spaces: Essays on Clinical Process, Trauma, and Dissociation.* Hillsdale, NJ: The Analytic Press.

Coates, S. (2012). The child as traumatic trigger: Commentary on paper by Laurel Moldawsky Silbur. *Psychoanal. Dial.*, 22:123–128

Cooper, S. (1997). Interpretation and the psychic future. *Int. J. Psychoanal.*, 78:667–681.

——, (2000). *Objects of Hope: Exploring Possibility and Limit in Psychoanalysis.* Hillsdale, NJ: The Analytic Press.

——, (2000). Mutual containment in the psychoanalytic process. *Psychoanal. Dial.*, 10:166–189.

——, (2004). State of the hope: The new bad object and the therapeutic action of psychoanalysis. *Psychoanal. Dial.*, 14:527–553.

——, (2008). Privacy, reverie, and the analyst's ethical imagination. *Psychoanal. Q.* 77:1045–1073.

——, (2010). *A Disturbance in the Field: Essays in Transference-Countertransference.* London: Routledge.

——, (2012). Exploring a patient's shift from relative silence to verbal expressiveness: Observations on an element of the analyst's participation. *Int. J. Psycho-Anal.*, 83:97–116.

Cooper, S. and Levit, D. (1998). Old and new objects in Fairbairnian and American relational theory. *Psychoanal. Dial.*, 8:603–624.

Corbett, K. (2001). Faggot = Loser. *Studies in Gender and Sexuality*, 2:3–28.

——, (2009). Boyhood femininity, gender identity disorder, masculine presuppositions. *Psychoanal. Dial.*, 19:353–370.

Davies, J. (2004). Whose bad objects are we anyway?: Repetition and our elusive love affair.*Psychoanal. Dial.*, 14:711–732.

Davies, J. M. and Frawley, M. (1992). Dissociative processes and transference-countertransference paradigms in the psychoanalytically oriented treatment of adult survivors of childhood sexual abuse. *Psychoanal. Dial.*, 2:5–36.

Faimberg, H. (1988). The telescoping of generations – genealogy of certain identifications. *Contemp. Psychoanal.*, 24:99–117.

Fairbairn, R. (1952). *Psychoanalytic Studies of the Personality*. London: Routledge.

Feldman, M. (1997). Projective identification: The analyst's involvement. *Int. J. Psycho-Anal.*, 78:227–241.

Ferenczi, S. (1988). *The Clinical Diaries of Sandor Ferenczi*, ed. J. Dupont, Cambridge, MA: Harvard University Press.

——, (1909). Introjection and transference. In: *Contributions to Psycho-Analysis*. New York: Basic Books, 1950, pp. 35–93.

Foehl, J.C. (2010). The play's the thing: The primacy of process and the persistence of pluralism. *Contemp. Psychoanal.*, 46:48–86.

——, (2011). A phenomenology of distance: On being hard to reach. *Psychoanal. Dial.*, 21:607–618.

Foster Wallace, D. (2014). A conversation with David Foster Wallace, 2000. *The Hudson Review*, December 2014.

Friedman, L. (2007). The delicate balance of work and illusion in psycho-analysis. *Psychoanal. Q.*, 76:817–833.

Ghent, E. (1990). Masochism, submission, surrender: Masochism as a per-version of surrender. *Contemp. Psychoanal.*, 26:108–136.

Green, A. (2005). *Key Ideas for Contemporary Psychoanalysis: Misrecog-nition and Recognition of the Unconscious*. Hove, UK & New York: Brunner-Routledge.

Greenberg, J. (1986). Theoretical models and the analyst's neutrality. *Contemp. Psychoanal.*, 6:87–106.

——, (1995). Psychoanalytic technique and the interactive matrix. *Psychoanal. Q.*, 64:1–22.

Harris, A. (2009). You must remember this. *Psychoanal. Dial.*, 19:2–21.

——, (2011). The relational tradition: Landscape and canon. *J. Amer. Psychoanal. Assn.*, 59:701–735.

Hoffman, I. (1996). The intimate and ironic authority of the psychoanalyst's presence. *Psychoanal. Q.*, 65:102–136.

——, (2009). Therapeutic passion in the countertransference, *Psychoanal. Dial.*, 19:619–637.

Kahneman, D. (2011) *Thinking Fast and Slow*. New York: Farrar, Strauss, and Giroux.

Knoblach, S. (2011). Contextualizing attunement with the Polyrhythmic wave: The Psychoanalytic Samba. *Psychoanal. Dial.*, 21:414–427.

Lanzman, C. (2012). The man who stood witness for the world. *The Guardian*, March 3, 2012.

Levine, H. (2013). Comparing field theories. *Psychoanal. Dial.*, 23:667–673.

Mitchell, S. (1988). *Relational Concepts in Psychoanalysis.* Cambridge, MA: Harvard University Press.

——, (1991). Needs, wishes and interpersonal negotiation. *Psychoanal. Inq.*, 11:147–170.

——, (1997). *Influence and Autonomy in Psychoanalysis.* Hillsdale, NJ: The Analytic Press.

Modell, A.H. (1963). Primitive object relationships and the predisposition to schizophrenia. *Int. J. Psycho-Anal.*, 44:282–292.

Ogden, T. (1994a). The analytic third: Working with intersubjective clinical facts. *Int. J. Psycho-Anal.*, 75:3–20.

——, (1994b). Psychoanalysis and interpretive action. *Psychoanal. Q.*, 63:219–245.

——, (1997). Reverie and metaphor. *Int. J. of Psycho-Anal.*, 78:719–732.

——, (2004). The analytic third: Implications for psychoanalytic theory and technique. *Psychoanal. Q.*,73:167–196.

——, (2012). *Creative Readings: Essays on Seminal Analytic Works.* London and New York: Routledge.

Racker, H. (1968). *Transference and Countertransference.* New York: International Universities Press.

Ringstrom, P.A. (2001). Cultivating the improvisational in psychoanalytic treatment. *Psychoanal. Dial.*, 11:727–754.

Sandler, J. (1976). Countertransference and role-responsiveness. *Int. J. Psycho-Anal.*, 3:43–50.

Searles, H. (1979). *Countertransference and Related Subjects.* Madison, CT: International Universities Press.

Seligman, S. (2005). Dynamic systems theories as a metaframework for psychoanalysis. *Psychoanal. Dial.*, 15:285–319.

——, (2014). Paying attention and feeling puzzled: The analytic mindset as an agent of therapeutic change. *Psychoanal. Dial.*, 24, 6:648–662.

Slavin, M. and Kriegman, D. (1998). Why the analyst needs to change: Toward a theory of conflict, negotiation, and mutual influence in the therapeutic process. *Psychoanal. Dial.*, 8:247–284.

Slochower, J. (1996). *Holding and Psychoanalysis.* Hillsdale, NJ: The Analytic Press.

Stern, D (1997). Unformulated Experience. In: *Dissociation to Imagination in Psychoanalysis.* Hillsdale, NJ: The Analytic Press.

——, (2010). *Partners in Thought: Working with Unformulated Experience, Dissociation and Enactment.* New York: Routledge.

Tublin, S. (2011). Discipline and freedom in relational technique. *Contemp. Psychoanal.*, 47:519–546.

Winnicott, D. (ed.) (1969). The use of an object and relating through identifications. In: *Playing and Reality.* New York: Basic Books, 1971, pp. 86–94.

Chapter 10

Relational theory in socio-historical context

Implications for technique

Lynne Layton

Those of us who read widely in contemporary theory will surely be struck by the fact that just about every discipline, theoretical or practical, and certainly most forms of critique, have committed themselves to a relational ontology in the past 25 years or so. Indeed, I've begun to notice that not just here, in the concept that informs this volume, but in various other high theory fields, relational ontologies are just beginning to be critiqued – often for not putting enough emphasis on the singularity of the individual. Here, I take a step back from critique in order first to focus on some of the features of contemporary social life that may account for the popularity of relational ontologies in general, and relational psychoanalysis in particular. I then explore the implications of this approach for expanding the boundaries of relational technique.

From the time I began to train in clinical psychology, in the early 80s, through my time teaching feminist psychoanalytic theory and then finally training as an analyst in the 90s, I have been attracted to relational theories because they feel "true" to me. Because of my own family and cultural history, Freud has never spoken to me in quite the same way as Ferenczi, Kohut, the British Independents, and US relational theory. I have shunned theories that divorce the individual from social context, that commit to an ontology of innate forces that will manifest no matter what the environmental situation might be, that do not question authority or take into account the analyst's influence, both pernicious and benevolent, on treatment. But, even more than that, what I mean when I say that I am committed to a relational ontology is that I favor a poststructuralist and Bourdieusian sense that individual psyches are embedded in and forged in the context of history and in social relations that themselves exist in fields permeated by power differentials. I believe that identities are in some important psychic senses collective – not just defensively so but facilitatingly so. For example, I have argued (see Layton, 1998/2004), against poststructuralist conceptions of identity categories as solely oppressive, that identifications with social categories can facilitate change, as seen very clearly in social movements such as feminism. In turn, I also believe that individual and group psychic phenomena, including fantasy and other forms of unconscious and conscious process, participate in the forging of new historical contexts, new social relations, new collective identities, new fields.

My commitment to a relational ontology means that I understand individual and group identity formation as occurring always in relation to other culturally available identity positions. I believe that cultural ideals of what it means, for example, to be a "proper" white middle-class female, emerge in relation to and confrontation with cultural ideals not only for white middle-class males, but for non-white middle-class females and both white and non-white working-class females. Psychologically, these identity-forming relational fields require identifying and disidentifying with certain ways of being and loving. The splitting, projections, and dissociations that go into both identifications and disidentifications create symptoms, defenses and character structures that permeate what happens in the clinic. What relational theory has enabled me to do, particularly relational theories that center on the analyst's conscious and unconscious contribution to what transpires, is to develop a theory of the ways in which cultural inequalities of race, class, sex, gender enter into what happens in the clinic. My focus has been on the ways that cultural inequalities are at times unconsciously and performatively reproduced (Layton, 2002, 2004, 2006). Thus, I am a relationalist in what I would call a broad sense, that is, I try always to think not only about the individual and family context of patients and therapists, but also about how cultural forces and power differentials shape those contexts. And yet, like all psychoanalysts, my clinical focus is on the singularity of the patient. For example, if a patient is a white working-class female, I want to know how this particular person has lived and is living both the facilitating and constricting aspects of class, sexuality, gender, and race. I think about these categories as existing intersectionally; for example, the way that gender is lived is always marked not only by gender relations but by class, sexual, and racial relations.

What relational theory has not enabled me to do is to conceptualize what the consequences of thinking this way about identity might be for re-working or adding to relational ideas about technique. While many relational thinkers have proposed theories about how the psyche is shaped by culture, I can think of few who have extended that thinking into the realm of technique (as an exception, see Samuels, 1993; 2001). Attempting both a historical and a forward-looking approach to evaluating the impact of relational theory, I want first to place relational theory into its historical and social context. I ask what has happened culturally, politically, historically that might help us understand why so many of us have found relational theories compelling (I focus here on the US context) and why they feel so "true" to us. Second, I want to begin to think about what technical innovations might be necessary to enable us more fully to elaborate a relational ontology that includes relations beyond the family.

Relational theory in socio-historic perspective

In *The Lonely Crowd*, David Riesman (1950), a sociologist influenced by the "culture and personality" anthropological school prominent in the mid-twentieth century, argued that every culture produces a dominant character type that insures the efficient functioning and reproduction of that culture. The close connection between psychoanalysis and sociology in that period/school is attested to by the fact that Riesman was analyzed by, and remained a close colleague of, Erich Fromm, who himself was one of the founders of the Frankfurt School critical theory sociology tradition, as well as an analyst working in the interpersonal tradition. While Fromm's ideas about social character focused on individual and collective "escapes from freedom" (1941), and, later, on what he called the "marketing personality" (1947), Riesman's concern was with what he saw as a shift in the dominant form of social character in the post-WWII U.S.: from "inner" to "outer-directed." The "inner-directed" character arose in the late nineteenth century, spanning the period in which entrepreneurial capitalism was oriented toward production. The "outer-directed" character, consonant with a consumer society, is primarily oriented toward the various relational matrices in which it finds itself. Unlike the "inner-directed," this character needs social approval for its achievements, seeks recognition, and becomes adept at understanding the emotional nuances of what goes on in the relational worlds of work and home. The autonomy precious to the inner-directed character type is mediated by a greater value on, and anxiety around, what others think of you. Riesman was one of the first sociologists to describe a social reality in which meaning-making and the internal experience of the self are rooted in our multiple and contradictory relational matrices. It is in such conditions that a relational theory staple such as the need for "recognition," for example, becomes key to psychological health. As we look further at the social context within which the popularity of relational analytic theories emerges, we might keep the implications of Riesman's work in mind: psychological theories both reflect and shape broader cultural changes that change the ways that people experience life and what is meaningful (see Cushman, 1995, for more recent reflections on the connection between social change and psychological theories).

Once the culture and personality school fell out of favor, few academic works sought to combine sociology and psychology; in fact, mainstream sociology became rather hostile to psychology. In the past 25 years, however, several prominent sociologists have argued that, in what they refer to as "late modernity" (post-World War II), sociology and psychology are "bound up in a direct way" (Giddens, 1991, p. 33). Among these sociologists, a relatively recent consensus has emerged that one cannot grasp the objective social circumstances of late modernity without a deeper and more nuanced understanding of subjectivity and intersubjectivity. As Giddens (1991, pp. 140–142) writes, for these sociologists "the real meaning of modernity is the construction of the self," beginning to say *I*. At the same time, Giddens (UK), Beck and Beck-Gernsheim (2002; Germany), Touraine (2009; France) and others describe dilemmas of contemporary subjectivity that relational theory is perhaps particularly well suited to address.

Individualization, reflexivity, and risk society

A patient spent most of a session talking about how a visit from her sister-in-law had "unnerved" her. The sister-in-law seemed so happy with her life, so content with her choices. While noting that something about her seemed "not real," my patient was nonetheless very self-critical about her own dissatisfactions with her relatively privileged life. Toward the end of the session I asked her if it was common for her to go through this kind of comparison. I think I was perhaps pathologizing what seemed like shaky self-esteem. She replied, "Doesn't everybody?" And then, "I do have the tendency to second guess myself." And then, "Well, I'm aware there are a lot of different ways to do things, and I think that's positive. And that can be unsettling." Indeed, the patient's plight is captured in several relational tenets, well summed up in many of Hoffman's principles of dialectical constructivism (1998): for example, the assertion of the ambiguity and indeterminacy of much of reality; the "principle of uncertainty" that requires respect for the differing convictions put forth by patient and analyst; the multiplicity of possible "good" options for living the good life; the ambiguities of truth that demand continuous reflection on previous choices; the urgent feeling about choices we make as we search for what for us will be the good life; the changing truths that the process of reflection upon choices itself brings to the fore; the questions that the patient's plight raises for the "expert" analyst. My patient exemplifies what the sociologists refer to as a "reflexive" subjectivity that exists within a socio-historically particular "architecture of choice" (Illouz, 2012). She presents a major dilemma of life in our times: at least among the privileged, never before has there been so much opportunity for the uniqueness of the individual to emerge and to discover what, for him or her, the good life might be. At the same time, rarely before have there been so few traditions or such little cultural consensus to appeal to for guidance–nor so much conflicting expert advice telling us what's best for us to do.

Sociologists concerned with subjectivity refer to the postwar period in which this patient and her analyst dwell variously as "late modernity" (Giddens, 1991) and "second modernity" (Beck & Beck-Gernsheim, 2002). For Beck and Beck-Gernsheim, late or "second" modernity is marked by "institutionalized individualization," a result of the disembedding of individuals from any of the traditional frameworks that once provided an anchor for knowing how to live: nation-state, class, ethnic group, kinship ties, community, religion, or any other authority. While this loss can dispose us to "radical doubt" (Giddens, 1991, p. 181), it is also true that institutionalized individualization produces the possibility for many of living "a life of one's own" for the first time, the opportunity (and demand) to create a "do-it-yourself biography" (which is not to be confused with the ideology of individualism). This condition is the very one that relational theory describes as normative, and from which many of its theoretical and technical innovations have emanated.

Individualization processes have been at work since the urbanization and industrialization of the late eighteenth and nineteenth centuries in the West, but they have rapidly accelerated since the end of WWII. These processes include not only the disembedding from tradition but also the construction of legal frameworks that aim more at insuring individual freedom than at protecting collective life. Social movements such as feminism and civil rights have also played a role in individualization, widening the opportunity in the middle classes – beyond the world of privileged white men – to live for oneself rather than solely for others. "What is historically new," as Beck and Beck-Gernsheim assert, "is that something that was earlier expected of a few – to lead a life of their own – is now being demanded of more and more people and, in the limiting case, of all" (2002, p. 8). "In modern life," they write,

> the individual is confronted on many levels with the following challenge: You may and you must lead your own independent life, outside the old bonds of family, tribe, religion, origin and class; and you must do this within the new guidelines and rules which the state, the job market, the bureaucracy etc. lay down. The new element is, first, the democratization of individualization processes and, second (and closely connected), the fact that basic conditions in society favour or enforce individualization (the job market, the need for mobility and training, labour and social legislation, pension provisions, etc.).
>
> (p. 11)

The new ethic becomes enshrined as a duty to oneself; Beck-Gernsheim (2002, Ch. 5, n. 94, p. 80) cites as a prime example Fritz Perls's popular 60s motto: "I do my thing and you do your thing . . . I am not in this world to live up to your expectations, and you are not in this world to live up to mine. You are you and I am I; if by chance we find each other, it's beautiful. If not, it can't be helped."

Perls's words suggest that the individualized self is highly stable and confident. But individualization processes themselves are dialectical: the very forces that open the self to opportunity simultaneously create what the sociologists refer to as a "precariousness" of the self. As an example, we can look at changes in the organization of work. "Flexibility" is the watchword of what Sennett (2006) calls the "new" capitalism (loosely equal to free market or neoliberal capitalism). "Flexibility," which includes short-term contracts, willingness to move from job to job, and so on, emerges largely to guarantee short-term profit for corporate shareholders. It has heralded a major change for a workforce that in the recent past often stayed in the same job for entire careers. For a mobile elite, "flexibility" seems to work well and seems to offer freedom of choice, particularly in good economic times. But for the non-elite, and for everyone in times of downsizing, outsourcing and the imposition of other demands of global capital, flexibility can create enormous insecurity and anxious feelings of disposability (Layton, 2009, 2010, 2014a, b; Stein, 2000). Indeed, part of what Beck and Beck-Gernsheim mean by "institutionalized individual-ization" is a historical, political and legal situation in which institutional structures are conceptualized around individual rights and duties and not around the interests of collectivities. The decline of unions as a source of collective support is a symptom of institutionalized individualism as it intersects with neoliberalism.

An important aspect of second modernity that simultaneously has existential, psychological, and social ramifications is what Beck (1999) refers to as "risk society." In his model, first modernity, the period of industrialization, was marked by the sense that society could calculate and insure against risks by socializing and collectivizing them – for example, workmen's compensation, social security. Second modernity, on the other hand, is marked by the unforeseen risks and "manufactured uncertainties" produced by first modernity, for example, nuclear threat, genetic engineering, and ecological destruction. These dangers cannot be insured against and many of them threaten not just local populations but the whole world. To live in "risk society" we have to be able to keep in the background of consciousness our awareness of the potential disasters that could occur; yet we must also be able to face and deal with those dangers that, if denied or only selectively attended to, could destroy all life as we know it.

Risk society encompasses both the manufactured uncertainties produced by first modernity and the precarious corporate work world described by Sennett. Risk society and institutionalized individualization have been intensified by the dominance of neoliberal economic and political principles, which devalue dependency and deny the ways in which we are interdependent (Hollander, 2017; Layton, 2009, 2010, 2014a, b). Neoliberalism requires individuals to be enterprising selves in competition with other enterprising selves (du Gay, 2004; Rose, 1989). Neoliberalism's offloading of formerly public responsibilities onto individuals, which began with the Reagan "revolution" against "big government," contributes to an institutionalized individualization that is primarily individualistic – and thus contributes to the creation of precarious selves (Peltz, 2006; Rustin, 2014).

The psychological requirements of institutionalized individualization

The loss of traditional anchors and the conditions of a "multi-option" society produce "reflexive" subjects, like my patient, who draw on constantly changing and contradictory expert knowledge that they, in turn, shape as they create their individual life narratives (Giddens, 1991, pp. 14–15). In late modernity, Giddens asserts, the question "how shall I live?" has to be answered daily (p. 14). He argues that if the hysterics of Freud's day experienced symptoms of a sexually repressive society, the self-hating, self-punishing patient of today expresses symptoms of a society in which the coherence of the self and trust in abstract systems are absolutely necessary to function—because you are on your own in both positive and negative ways. The sociologists of late modernity well describe the fine line we all walk between successful individuation and complete breakdown. As Beck and Beck-Gernsheim assert, "Depending on the economic situation, educational qualifications, stage of life, family situation, colleagues – [the do-it-yourself biography] can easily turn into a 'breakdown biography'" (2002, p. 7). If individuals are to thrive in the conditions prevalent in second modernity or risk society, that is, if individuals are to avoid breakdown, they need to rely more on inner psychological resources than on the social surround.

Echoing Erikson (1959) and British Independents, Giddens (1991) suggests that to avoid "breakdown," one must establish "basic trust," which, in turn, depends on good-enough early attachments that promote "ontological security." The resulting "protective cocoon" enables one later to have enough trust in abstract systems to function without tremendous anxiety (which also requires bracketing much of what we know, e.g., the threat of "an ending to everything," Giddens, p. 183). But it seems to me Giddens' own work suggests that the constructs "basic trust" and "secure attachment," not to mention other contemporary psychoanalytic mainstays such as "multiple selves," have themselves arisen from a need to make sense of the social realities of second modernity – they are not timeless universal truths describing subjectivity. Rather, they describe what becomes necessary psychologically to navigate modern life. To develop basic trust, for example, attachment and other dependency needs must be attended to, precisely the domains of post-war psychoanalytic "discovery" that have so influenced the development of relational theory (Young-Bruehl, 2011). The literatures on risk and on institutionalized individualization suggest to me that it is no accident that many post-war analytic theorists have found the need for safety and security to be a more compelling explanation of what motivates human behavior than sex and aggression. Nor is it any wonder that, at the very moment in which our collective containers began to abandon us (Hollander & Gutwill, 2006; Layton, 2009; Peltz, 2006), that is, the moment when neoliberal economics and ideology, with their relentless attack on the caretaking functions of big government, became more pervasive (the late 70s to the present), analytic theories foregrounding attachment, dependency and vulnerability, holding and containment began to feel so existentially relevant and "true."

Reflexivity, risk, and the pure relationship

In a world of risk, detraditionalization, and contradictory expert knowledge claims, the capacity to depend on intimate relations crucially replaces the capacity reliably to depend on social holding environments. Indeed, one of the few anchors against existential anxiety available in contemporary life lies in what Giddens calls "the pure relationship" (1991, pp. 88–98). By pure he means that nothing extrinsic keeps such relationships in place (as did, for example, arranged marriages or religious beliefs). For the most part, in the contemporary West, friendships and love relationships are held together largely by psychological gratifications, the "fulfillment of inner needs" (Beck & Beck-Gernsheim, p. 71). Thus, the pure relationship, like the reality that makes it feel so necessary, is itself precarious: since little anchors it but the emotional and psychological satisfactions it brings to the partners, it is constantly subject to question and to possible dissolution: is this right for me? am I happy? Such questions simply were not asked in earlier eras – even as recently as the 1950s – and are still not asked in many cultures. The way we answer those questions in the West is highly influenced by what experts of all kinds write and say (Layton, 2013a, b; Rose, 1989). But the increasing need to have a certain kind of relationship ground us itself creates new definitions of intimacy, new demands, and new problems. Some of the principles of relational theory are in fact consonant with what Giddens claims is required for pure relationships to function well, for example, the openness to the truth of each other's perspective and the vulnerability necessary to establish trust. Indeed, the precariousness of the pure relationship and the pressures of individualization are alleviated by the stability and consistency of the (paid for) therapeutic relationship (see Hoffman, 1998, on the dark side of the analytic frame).

Thus, the conditions of late modernity create particular ways of being human, particular kinds of attachments and attachment needs, particular human struggles, and particular responses to them. Among these responses is the relational analytic practice that has been elaborated in the past 30 years. Relational psychoanalytic theory, influenced by attachment theories, interpersonal theories, self-psychology and the British independent tradition (with its influences from Ferenczi), all of which are concerned with deficits in environmental care, has, I am arguing, developed in tandem with the development of the particular kind of subject demanded by the social forces of institutionalized individualization and risk society. Our work enhances capacities for reflexivity, for determining what for each individual the good life might be. We work to keep the do-it-yourself biography from becoming a breakdown biography. In many ways, too, relational theory and practice counter institutionalized individualization's and neoliberalism's devaluation and denial of dependency and mutual interdependence. At the same time, however, like most analytic theories, relational theory and technique, while making a space in its journals for political critique, tends to collude with institutionalized individualization's demand to neglect the collective components of subjectivity. One of the features that Stern (2013) recently pointed to as distinguishing interpersonal/relational field theories from Bionian field theories was the former's belief that "it isn't possible to be uninvolved in the meanings and ideologies of the world at large, even while you are inside the psycho-analytic session," and its belief "that it is possible to have an impact on the reality of the world and not just on the inner world" (pp. 679–680). Yet, much relational theory and practice do not take into account the impact of the meanings and ideologies of the world at large. Thus, while recognizing that most psychoanalytic theories separate the psychic from the social, I address my critique specifically to relational theory – precisely because its own assumptions challenge that separation. I now turn, then, to consider how enlarging the frame to take into account unconscious and conscious collective identifications and power differentials can lead to an expansion of relational technique, one that I feel is necessary to contest the psychological damage wrought by cultural hierarchies, neoliberal versions of individualism, and institutionalized individualization.

Notes toward a socio-cultural expansion of relational technique

Relational clinicians have contributed greatly to re-thinking questions of technique and drawing out the technical implications of our theories. Our roots in interpersonal ideas about analyst-patient interaction, Ferenczi's (1949) thoughts about professional hypocrisy, Winnicottian ideas on holding have led to respect for, as Mitchell (1988; 1997) put it, the varieties of interaction and their effect on treatment. Relational theorists have deconstructed the authority of the analyst, our particular form of expertise, emphasizing its ironic and dark sides (Hoffman, 1998; 2005); we have explored mutuality and asymmetry (Aron, 1996; Mitchell, 1988) and we have offered profound work on how the analyst's vulner-ability and fallibility implicate us in enactments (Altman, 2000; Cooper, 2000; Grand, 2007, 2013; Hirsch, 2008; Layton, 2006, 2009; Levenson, 1972; Slochower, 2003; Suchet, 2004, 2010, and others too numerous to mention). We have elaborated numerous ways of thinking about enact-ments, along with some technical ideas for recognizing them and disengaging from them (Benjamin, 2004, 2009; Davies, 2004; Stern, 1997, 2010); in this work, the emphasis on dissociation has been crucial (Bromberg, 2001; Davies & Frawley, 1994; Stern, 1997, 2010). We have questioned analytic dogma around neutrality and recognized our role in what has traditionally been understood as resistance (Gerson, 1996; Stein, 2005). Hoffman (2009) has perhaps most persuasively examined and re-valued the role of suggestion, arguing that we ought to take an active role in battling our patients' bad introjects. Crucial to the ethic I hope to elaborate is Benjamin's (2004, 2009) idea of the acknowledgment of harm done, an ethical form of self-disclosure. I consider this to be one of the most important innovations in technique in the relational canon.

Those of us committed to thinking about cultural power differentials and their effects on treatment have been tremendously influenced by all of these theoretical and technical developments. To instances of enactment, we have added the interactional effects of a socially constructed and relational unconscious (Altman, 2000; Bodnar, 2004; Bonovitz, 2005; Botticelli, 2012; Dimen, 2003; the authors in Dimen, 2011; Grand, 2007, 2013; Gump, 2010; Guralnik and Simeon, 2010; Harris, 2005, 2011, 2012; Hartman, 2005; Layton, Hollander and Gutwill, 2006; Layton, 1998, 2002, 2004, 2006; Leary, 1997, 2000, 2012; Straker, 2006; Suchet, 2004, 2010). Andrew Samuels (1993, 2001) has proposed techniques for unearthing what he understands to be an important aspect of development, urging us to take account of our patients' political development. Drawing on all of my colleagues' work on how collective identifications and disidentifications are lived, I elaborated the concept of normative unconscious processes (2002, 2004, 2006, 2013c), that is, processes in which patient and therapist unconsciously collude in reproducing the sexism, racism, and other effects of cultural oppressions that mark the psyche.

In 2014, I began teaching a course in comparative technique. I inherited a syllabus from the previous teachers, and, only at the end of the course did I realize that, as is usual in courses that aren't specifically devoted to culture or gender or sexuality or race, there was not one paper on the syllabus that reflected anything cultural. Determined to add papers to the syllabus that take culture into account, I was struck by a short paper by Rozmarin (2014) written at the height of the Israel-Gaza summer-2014 war. Here, Rozmarin makes the absolutely correct claim that most analysts have neglected to attend to the collective dimensions of subjectivity. It is in this way perhaps that we most clearly collude with institutionalized individualization and the culture of neoliberalism, particularly when we frame socially-generated pathologies (e.g., racism) in terms of intrapsychic pathology (see Eng & Han, 2000).

Rozmarin writes that his Israeli expatriate patients, when speaking about a war in which they feel deeply and intimately implicated, "are not only enacting personal dramas, although they invariably do. They are also wondering, sometimes desperately, how one ought to live in this world as one of many, as a social, ethical being with collective identities" (p. 1). One thing that struck me deeply in reading this was a conviction that, in fact, all patients, at all times, wonder how to live in the world as one of many, as social and ethical beings with collective identities. At times of war, as Rozmarin says, the wondering is explicit. But what about at other times? Are collective identities, our implication in our own and others' suffering, our quest to be ethical beings, not operating all the time? Might it be the case that an absence of such wondering would reflect not the state of nature but rather something about the way our culture radically separates the individual from the social?

Rozmarin goes on to say that when his patients talk about the war, they are also "talking about belonging and alienation, about conforming and resisting, about our place in a collective that has its own history and conflicts, and anxieties and madness" (p. 2). As he says, "We should be able to address this register of human experience in our work." But how? Rozmarin goes on to talk about the effects of ideology on collective identities and how to make those effects conscious, and I think that here he begins to adumbrate the kind of technical innovation that I have in mind.

Rozmarin notes that, in his experience, because of an "inherent need of and therefore surrender to collectively, politically and ideologically generated narratives," "questioning collective identifications is often harder, more troubling, than doing so in the context of one's relations with one's family" (p. 2) (see, also, Rozmarin, 2009, which emphasizes the damaging effects of collective identities and argues that our job is to resist colluding with them when they are damaging). I agree, although I do not see the two as mutually exclusive. For one thing, those of us in the U.S. who were born into an era of institutionalized individualization are not even aware of our collective identifications until there is some threat to them (see Volkan, 2004, on conditions in which large-group identity becomes salient, and Aviram, 2009, on prejudice and the large-group mind). This works in the service of neoliberalism's denial of the ways we are mutually implicated in each other's lives and histories. Rozmarin suggests that it may be questionable to challenge people on unconscious ways in which their identity has been organized, noting (ironically) that "After all, it is not my role to unsettle what makes my patients feel secure" (p. 3). Actually, that is precisely our role, isn't it? Why do we hesitate to recognize that it is just as much our role to unsettle unconscious facilitating and/or defensive collective identities as it is to unsettle individual identity commitments that might be blinding us to the psychologically damaging ideological cultural work that they are doing?

Within the relational canon (broad tent relational), there has been some important theorizing about collective identities and how they impact treatment. For instance, work on the intergenerational transmission of trauma often addresses collective identity. Davoine and Gaudillière (2004) argue that ruptures in what they call the social link (following Lacan), war, for example, produce quests for restoration of trust that require analysts to give something of themselves, the missing piece of "terra cotta" that will restore trust in a moral social order. Technical suggestions include a deep engagement with both one's own and the patient's social history, for they suggest that there will inevitably be a way in which the two histories intertwine and that the therapist will somehow need to make that known to the patient. To that end, Gaudillière (2012) writes that if he dreams about a patient, he will tell the patient the dream. He insists that the dream is a co-construction of their unconscious process and belongs as much to the patient as to himself. For Davoine and Gaudillière, the small histories revealed in their patients' fragmented narratives and symptoms are inextricably intertwined with the BIG history in which they and their ancestors lived their lives. Thus, intergenerational transmission of trauma cannot be understood or treated without comprehending (and resonating with affectively) the particular ruptures in the social link, in history, that have produced them.

Relational theorists (small tent) who write about intergenerational transmission of trauma have offered gripping narratives of the ways that the conflicting collective identities of patient and analyst often come to the fore in clinical enactments. Like Davoine and Gaudillière, Altman (2000); Bodnar (2004); Gentile (2013; 2017); Grand (2000; 2007; 2013; 2014); Hartman (2005); Leary (1997; 2000); Suchet (2004; 2010), and others, make it clear that analysts need to immerse themselves in learning about the intergenerational cultural history of their patients and themselves in order to understand and find their way out of enactments. Grand, all of whose work integrates the social being that lies at the core of psychic exploration, focuses often on the body clues emerging in the analyst, clues that can lead to a more conscious appreciation of her own unconscious collective identifications. A striking example is her 2013 case in which she came to recognize that her patient was living a collective identity with collective commitments that stood in stark contrast to the individualized ethos of psychoanalytic treatment. The patient was asking Grand precisely the question that I am addressing here: does psychoanalysis have any way of speaking to the collective self? As Grand notes (private communication), patients often are the ones who pose the very questions that psychoanalytic theory and technique must next address.

Guralnik and Simeon (2010) persuasively argue that the symptoms many of us treat (in their case, depersonalization) are disorders produced by the disparity between our longings for recognition and our inter-pellation by the discourses of a social order that recognizes only what conforms to its norms. They theorize that we are humiliated by our depend-ence on recognition from a social order that requires us to yield on our own sense of reality. Further, they recognize that psychoanalysts are, and are perceived by their patients as being, agents of interpellation; thus, analysts are always present as potential sources of shame. Technically, they identify moments of countertransferential confusions and ruptures, particularly ones involving shame, as moments that signal "the presence of mixed and seductive transmissions from the *great big hegemony*" (p. 410), that which dislocates the patient from his/her reality and to which patients unconsciously and repeatedly succumb. They interpret in a frame that enables their patients to understand how their symptoms derive from their social context, how socially allowable discourses are calling into question the patient's counterhegemonic personhood.

Gentile (2017) recognizes that taking account of, and making ourselves accountable for, our cultural positions and positions of power in relation to those of our patients, affects even such a common technical choice as how, in any given moment, we offer our empathic attunement. Describing work with a Latina patient who was lovingly attached to a father who had sexually abused her, Gentile, aware of the father's own complicated history of racial and gender oppression as well as of her own privileged position of whiteness, writes, "Integral to this [holding space for multiple identifications] was sustaining a vigilant awareness of how, when, where I deployed empathy, the power based roots of it, and to what ends" (p. 179). What strikes me as crucially important in such theorizing is the idea that the more aware we become of our own and our patients' cultural embeddedness and collective histories of privilege and oppression, the less likely we are to pathologize our patients' intimate others in the rather concrete and uncomplicated ways we often do. Gentile argues that the way that she responds to her patient must take into account the fact that the patient's father's psyche, too, was formed within a history of racial and gender oppression. And Gentile's own white privilege had to be spoken.

Such self-disclosures have played an important role in the technical tool-kit of those relational theorists engaged in investigating the ways that the ideological underpinnings of collective identifications are enacted in the clinic. One of Bodnar's (2004) vignettes with an African American patient culminates in Bodnar disclosing her envy of her patient's beauty – which opens up the treatment to the unconscious racist assumptions of both patient and analyst. The patient could not imagine a white person being envious of a black person, and yet, it became clear that she had been unconsciously engaged in trying to prove that her analyst was racist (that is, that she could not possibly envy the patient's beauty) by often attending to beauty rituals that caused her to be late for her therapy appointments. Here, collective identifications transmitted intergenerationally, bonds wrought from unconscious racism, were lived as questions of who can be beautiful.

In this case, as well, we learn that the source of an intergenerational transmission of seemingly inexplicable outbursts of anger lies in an emotionally abusive ancestor whose rageful strictness toward his children emerged in good measure from his need to protect his children from the greater abuses likely to befall them at the hands of Jim Crow southern whites. The process of making this history conscious not only makes conscious a source of the patient's outbursts of rage, the symptom, but also locates the symptom in a depathologized collective narrative (or, rather, it relocates the pathology from the black grandfather to the white culture in which he had to make his way). I would argue that the therapeutic action here lies in re-connecting patients with their histories and restoring the broken social link in a way that counters institutionalized individualization and neoliberal denials of embeddedness. As I argued in earlier work (Layton, 2005), colluding with the separation of the individual from the cultural too often leads to producing a subjectivity that we might think of merely as a healthier version of narcissism than the version with which the patient entered treatment.

Bodnar's case suggests to me as well that we not only have to understand the historical dimension of collective identifications but also need to understand the relational field in which current identifications take place. To do this, we have to take note of the intersectionality of identifications. The beauty issue that comes up in Bodnar's case is about gender every bit as much as race, about raced ways of living gender. In a second look at Altman's paper on black and white thinking, I suggested (Layton, 2013d) that along with race and class, the enactment needed to be understood in terms of gender, in particular, male disavowal of need. In that case of a white, Jewish, middle-class male and an African American male who had risen from poverty to middle-class, need was the hot potato that no one seemed to want to hold, and the enactment was very much conditioned by that disavowal. My own set of enactments with an Asian American gay man (Layton, 2006) was conditioned not only by race, but by the way our racial identifications intersected with our gender and sexual identifications. Had I recognized how, for him, masculinity was troubled both by being gay and by being Asian, I likely would not have proposed an interpretation that had the effect of feminizing him. Had I been conscious of how the wounding interpretation then led to his hostility toward my gender position, I might have made explicit in the treatment the way in which these hierarchies and intersections were working.

Intersectionality is a complex concept, but it is rendered even more complex if we think about the psychic costs entailed in inhabiting various collective identifications. My concept of normative unconscious processes (2002, 2004, 2006, 2013c) rests on a belief that those versions of collective identity that garner social approval often require that we split off and project various ways of being human, ways of loving, ways of being in our bodies. An example I used in my biographical work on gender (1998) focused on how capacities for attachment and capacities for agentic activity became split as a result of trying to incarnate what it meant to be a proper white middle-class female in the 50s and 60s. Cultural binaries such as male/female, black/white, straight/gay exist in hierarchical relations conditioned by cultural power differentials, and each side of the binary comes with an array of psychological attributes considered proper to it. If you are a white middle-class female, for example, you are likely to live dependency differently from the way someone raised as a white middle-class male lives dependency. The technical implications of being aware of how ideologically-produced binaries operate, how they require psychological splitting, entail challenging normative ideologies and revealing what options for being have been cut off by one's attachment to binary either/ors (see Aron & Starr, 2013). The challenge probably occurs most frequently when played out between patient and analyst, since the effects of projecting the unwanted, not-me ways of being are generally enacted in sadomasochistic relational scenarios (see Benjamin, 1988; Goldner, 1991).

Where commitments to binary forms of collective identities have been made, analysts can hold fluidity as a challenge to the splitting and projection that keep sadomasochistic relations to self and others in place. Thus, I would suggest that doing analytic work requires understanding the effects on subjectivity of normative and counter-normative ideologies. We need to be mindful of how our identifications and disidentifications are intertwined with hierarchies of class, race, gender, sexuality, nation – and how these are experienced psychologically in ways of being and loving that are differentially valued and are often lived via splitting and projection. As Gentile (2017) argues, making power relations and cultural hierarchies of oppression explicit in our work produces new possibilities for relating that contest the damaging structures of institutionalized individualization and neoliberal forms of individualism.

Conclusion: changing the frame

In her paper, "Who is the Sufferer and What is Being Suffered? Subjectivity in Times of Social Malaise," Nancy Hollander (2017) has offered an important way of thinking about what these new possibilities for relating might look like. Hollander was working with a white upper-middle-class female patient, a corporate lawyer, L, "whose frenetic life leaves little opportunity for her to be with her infant daughter" (p. 644). This situation led to resentment and envy of her child's Latina nanny, which played out in the treatment as a demand for special attention from

Hollander and fears that Hollander would retaliate and reject her. Hollander describes how the working through of the transference/countertransference led to the patient being able more easily to assert herself with the nanny "and to claim her place as her baby's mother" (p. 644). However, as Hollander goes on to note, there was something "uncannily absent in the frame" (p. 645), which did finally enter Hollander's consciousness when the patient said something that reminded Hollander that her patient was paying the nanny less than minimum wage and was requiring of the nanny "excessively long work days and nights" (p. 645). Hollander then realizes that she and her patient, both white, had unconsciously occluded the way that the nanny had been treated as an "other" in their work. When Hollander became conscious that she and her patient had "projected dissociated states of vulnerability" (p. 645) onto the nanny, Hollander "struggled" to find a way to raise this in the treatment. She simply noted, at some point, that they had "not talked much about L's nanny's personal life and experience and [wondered] what that might mean" (p. 645). Her patient was surprised at recognizing this to be true (see Leary, 2012, on the way that race and ethnicity often enter the room in the form of shock and surprise, thus potentially offering what she calls an adaptive challenge to the status quo). Eventually, the patient herself talked about how paying the nanny low wages in fact violated her own social values. And this made her realize that she had been denying how much of her anxiety had been generated by her firm's downsizing policies. Hollander concludes that they came to "understand that her nanny has functioned as the repository for dissociated and denigrated emotional states of insecurity and vulnerability" (p. 646). L had been able to defend herself from her anxious feelings of impotence as a professional employee through her experience of agency in her role as a boss with absolute control over her worker" (p. 646). Hollander is arguing here for precisely the kind of frame change for which I have been arguing: had she not become conscious of how they both had been excluding the personhood of the nanny from the frame, Hollander would have left "intact the neoliberal split between the private individual and the social individual or citizen, a split that hinders the development of empathy and accountability" (p. 645).

As Hollander's work reveals, making our social positionings explicit in our clinical work not only enhances relational technical and theoretical understandings of therapeutic action but also entails a relational ethic that goes beyond the dyad or triad. In my recent work on neoliberalism (Layton, 2009, 2010, 2011, 2013a, b, 2014a, b), I have wrestled with the problem of whether or not explicitly to interpret some of my patients' experience in the context of neoliberalism – that is, like Hollander's patient, several of my patients seem to me to be suffering from symptomatic effects of neoliberalism (decimation of small businesses, disappearance of public institutions of care, housing crises, the severe strains of trying to raise children while both parents are working and where there is no extended family or community on which to rely, alienation from political activity because it doesn't seem to matter, jobs that demand multiple moves and thus interfere with a sense of community, 60-plus hour work weeks). Patients bring in the symptoms, which we are apt to tie to family histories, but, as I have been arguing, those histories themselves are psychosocial, that is, social conditions generate certain versions of gendered, raced, sexed and classed subject positions that are riven with conflict. I have often guiltily felt that supplying such social contexts is "not analytic." I have found some solace in Andrew Samuels' (2006) dictum that today's bad practice may end up being tomorrow's cutting-edge practice. Results, for me, of making connections between a patient's symptoms and cultural inequalities have been mixed – sometimes supplying context has made a patient feel that she has no right to complain. But more often it has helped patients understand more about the choices and ways of being to which they have unconsciously committed, and the constraints within which they have done so (Layton, 2010). Patients who have been trained ideologically to believe that they have a limitless array of choices and only themselves to blame for failure – the neoliberal scenario par excellence – come to recognize that their choices were made within particular psychosocial "architectures of choice." The recognition of the sadomasochism inherent to neoliberal subject formation has, in turn, enabled them to feel more empathy toward themselves and others.

But what happens when the therapist, bathed in the same neoliberal atmosphere as the patient, does not become conscious of the psychic dilemmas neoliberalism generates? As Hollander's case suggests, it is all too common for us unconsciously to collude with the norms of neoliberalism. I offer one last vignette from my own work that suggests how normative unconscious processes generated by neoliberalism can pervade technique (see Layton, 2014a):

A middle-class white female patient had become ashamed of what she felt family members condemned as too much desire for attention. When I began seeing her, she was in fact quite constricted. Sometime during our work together I moved into a home office, which I had decorated in higher style than the office I had been renting. In our first meeting in the new office, the theme of entitlement and selfishness arose. The patient spoke about having just read Barbara Ehrenreich's (2001) book, *Nickel and Dimed*, and said she felt guilty and indulgent about having hired a maid for the first time. I said, "It's hard to acknowledge that you're privileged." She agreed and held out her hands to show me her nails, which she had recently had done in clear polish. She said, "I get my nails done, I have a therapist in Brookline in a place like this." My own privilege having been invoked, I think I felt anxious and did not know what to do with the guilt over privilege, hers, mine, ours. I remember having tried to normalize the privilege, saying something like, "You don't have to feel guilty for having nice things." I think this comment closed down something the patient was trying to say, something that went against the neoliberal grain because it attempted to connect her fortune to the misfortune of others. My first comment had kept the question of privilege open; the second one closed it down. There was something significant to explore here about our mutual discomfort about our privilege and its connection to the lack of privilege all around us, and I would suggest that normalizing privilege is perhaps a neoliberalizing practice that keeps class inequality in place. This example illustrates that technical choices that focus on the individual as separate from the social are quite different from those that focus on the individual as psychosocial.

In conclusion, I would argue that relational work needs to take account not only of the power differentials of race, class, gender, and sexuality, but also of the way that institutionalized individualization has become articulated with neoliberalism and marks conscious and unconscious versions of subjectivity. I believe that changing the frame to address conscious and unconscious social and collective aspects of identity/identifications demands a re-thinking of relational technique, and I hope here to have begun to adumbrate some possible directions this re-thinking might take.

References

Altman, N. (2000). Black and white thinking. *Psychoanalytic Dialogues*, 10(4):589–605.

Aron, L. (1996). *A Meeting of Minds*. Hillside, NJ: The Analytic Press.

Aron, L. and Starr, K. (2013). *A Psychotherapy for the People*. New York: Routledge.

Aviram, R. (2009). *The Relational Origins of Prejudice*. New York: Jason Aronson.

Beck, U. (1999). *World Risk Society*. London: Polity.

Beck, U. and Beck-Gernsheim, E. (2002). *Individualization. Institutionalized Individualism and its Social and Political Consequences*. London: Sage.

Benjamin, J. (1988). *The Bonds of Love*. New York: Pantheon.

Benjamin, J. (2004). Beyond doer and done-to: an intersubjective view of thirdness. *Psychoanalytic Quarterly*, 73:5–46.

Benjamin, J. (2009). A relational psychoanalysis perspective on the necessity of acknowledging failure in order to restore the facilitating and containing features of the intersubjective relationship (the shared third). *International Journal of Psychoanalysis*, 90:441–450.

Bodnar, S. (2004). Remember where you come from: dissociative process in multicultural individuals. *Psychoanalytic Dialogues*, 14:581–603.

Bonovitz, C. (2005). Locating culture in the psychic field. Transference and countertransference as cultural products. *Contemporary Psychoanalysis*, 41:55–76.

Botticelli, S. (2012). Weak ties, slight claims: the psychotherapy relationship in an era of reduced expectations. *Contemporary Psychoanalysis*, 48:394–407.

Bromberg, P. (2001). *Standing in the Spaces*. New York: Routledge.

Cooper, S. (2000). *Objects of Hope*. New York: Routledge.

Cushman, P. (1995). *Constructing the Self, Constructing America*. Reading, MA: Addison-Wesley.

Davies, J.M. (2004). Whose bad objects are we anyway? *Psychoanalytic Dialogues*, 14:711–732.

Davies, J.M. and Frawley, M.G. (1994). *Treating the Adult Survivor of Childhood Sexual Abuse*. New York: Basic Books.

Davoine, F. and Gaudillière, J.-M. (2004). *History Beyond Trauma*. S. Fairfield, trans. New York: Other Press.

Dimen, M. (2003). *Sexuality. Intimacy. Power*. New York: Routledge.

Dimen, M. (ed.) (2011). *With Culture in Mind: Psychoanalytic Stories*. New York: Routledge.

du Gay, P. (2004). Against 'Enterprise' (but not against 'enterprise', for that would make no sense). *Organization*, 11:37–57.

Eng, D. and Han, S. (2000). A dialogue on racial melancholia. *Psychoanalytic Dialogues*, 10:667–700.

Erikson, E.H. (1959; repr. 1980). *Identity and the Life Cycle*. New York: W.W. Norton.

Ferenczi, S. (1949). Confusion of the tongues between the adults and the child – (The language of tenderness and of passion). *International Journal of Psychoanalysis*, 30:225–230.

Fromm, E. (1941). *Escape from Freedom*. New York: Farrar and Rinehart.

Fromm, E. (1947) *Man for Himself: Towards a Psychology of Ethics*. New York: Rinehart.

Gaudillière, J.-M. (2012) Madness as a form of research targeting the historical scotomas in the life and mind of the analyst. *Psychoanalysis, Culture & Society*, 17(4):348–355.

Gentile, K. (2013) Bearing the cultural in order to engage in a process of witnessing. *Psychoanalytic Psychology*, 30(3):456–470.

Gentile, K. (2014) Collectively creating conditions for emergence. In S. Grand & J. Salberg (eds.). *Wounds of History: Repair and Resilience in the Transgenerational Transmission of Trauma*. New York: Routledge, pp. 169–188.

Gerson, S. (1996). Neutrality, resistance and self-disclosure in an intersubjective psychoanalysis. *Psychoanalytic Dialogues*, 6:623–645.

Gerson, S. (2004) The relational unconscious: a core element of intersubjectivity, thirdness, and clinical process. *Psychoanalytic Quarterly*, 73:63–98.

Giddens, A. (1991). *Modernity and Self-Identity. Self and Society in the Late Modern Age*. Stanford, CA: Stanford University Press.

Goldner, V. (1991). Toward a critical relational theory of gender. *Psychoanalytic Dialogues*, 1:249–272.

Grand, S. (2000). *The Reproduction of Evil*. Hillsdale, NJ: The Analytic Press.

Grand, S. (2007). Maternal surveillance: disrupting the rhetoric of war. *Psychoanalysis, Culture & Society*, 12(4):305–322.

Grand, S. (2013) God at an impasse: devotion, social justice, and the psychoanalytic subject. *Psychoanalytic Dialogues*, 23:449–463.

Grand, S. (2014), Skin memories: on race, love and loss. *Psychoanalysis, Culture & Society*, 19(3):232–249.

Gump, J. (2010). Reality matters: The shadow of trauma on African American subjectivity. *Psychoanalytic Psychology*, 27:42–54.

Guralnik, O. and Simeon, D. (2010). Depersonalization: standing in the spaces between recognition and interpellation. *Psychoanalytic Dialogues*, 20:400–416.

Harris, A. (2005). *Gender as Soft Assembly*. Hillsdale, NJ: Analytic Press.

Harris, A. (2011). The relational tradition: landscape and canon. *JAPA*, 59:701–735.

Harris, A. (2012) The house of difference, or white silence. *Studies in Gender & Sexuality*, 13:197–216.

Harris, A. and Botticelli, S. (eds.) *First Do No Harm*. New York: Routledge.

Hartman, S. (2005). Class unconscious: from dialectical materialism to relational material. *Psychoanalysis, Culture & Society*, 10(2):121–137.

Hirsch, I. (2008). *Coasting in the Countertransference*. New York: Routledge.

Hoffman, I.Z. (1998). *Ritual and Spontaneity in the Psychoanalytic Process*. Hillsdale, NJ: The Analytic Press.

Hoffman, I.Z. (2005) Standard dominance versus creation of interludes of equalization of power in the psychoanalytic situation: discussion of case presentation by Joseph Newirth. *Psychoanalytic Inquiry*, 25:328–341.

Hoffman, I.Z. (2009) Therapeutic Passion in the Countertransference. *Psychoanalytic Dialogues*, 19:617–637.

Hollander, N.C. (2017) Who is the sufferer and what is being suffered? Subjectivity in times of social malaise. *Psychoanalytic Dialogues*, 27(6):635–650.

Hollander, N.C. and Gutwill, S. (2006). Despair and hope in a culture of denial. In Layton, L., Hollander, N.C. and Gutwill, S. (eds.). *Psychoanalysis, Class and Politics: Encounters in the Clinical Setting*. New York: Routledge, pp. 81–91.

Illouz, E. (2012). *Why Love Hurts*. Malden, MA: Polity Press.

Layton, L. (1998; repr. 2004). *Who's that Girl? Who's that Boy? Clinical Practice Meets Postmodern Gender Theory*. Hillsdale, NJ: The Analytic Press.

Layton, L. (2000). The psychopolitics of bisexuality. *Studies in Gender and Sexuality*, 1:41–60.

Layton, L. (2002). Cultural hierarchies, splitting, and the heterosexist unconscious. In Fairfield, S., Layton, L., and Stack, C. (eds). *Bringing the Plague. Toward a Postmodern Psychoanalysis*. New York: Other Press, pp. 195–223.

Layton, L. (2004) That place gives me the heebie jeebies, *International Journal of Critical Psychology. Psycho-Social Research*, 10:36–50. Reprinted in Layton, Hollander, and Gutwill (2006). *Psychoanalysis, Class and Politics: Encounters in the Clinical Setting*, New York: Routledge, pp. 51–64.

Layton, L. (2005). Notes toward a nonconformist clinical practice. *Contemporary Psychoanalysis*, 41:419–429.

Layton, L. (2006). Racial identities, racial enactments, and normative unconscious processes. *Psychoanalytic Quarterly*, LXXV 1:237–269.

Layton, L. (2009). Who's responsible? Our mutual implication in each other's suffering. *Psychoanalytic Dialogues*, 19:105–120.

Layton, L. (2010). Irrational exuberance: neoliberal subjectivity and the perversion of truth. *Subjectivity*, 3(3):303–322.

Layton, L. (2011). Something to do with a girl named Marla Singer: capitalism, narcissism, and therapeutic discourse. In: David Fincher's *Fight Club. Free Associations*, 62:112–134.

Layton, L. (2013a). Dialectical constructivism in historical context: expertise and the subject of late modernity. *Psychoanalytic Dialogues*, 23(3): 271–286.

Layton, L. (2013b). Psychoanalysis and politics: historicizing subjectivity. *Mens Sana Monographs*, 11(1):68–81.

Layton, L. (2013c). Normative unconscious processes. In: T. Teo (ed.). *Encyclopedia of Critical Psychology.* www.springerreference.com/docs/html/chapterdbid/307088.html.

Layton, L. (2013d). *Enacting distinction: Normative unconscious processes in the clinic. Keynote address at Turning a blind eye: Working with 'race', culture and ethnicity in practice.* Tavistock Centre, London, Nov. 8.

Layton, L. (2014a). Some psychic effects of neoliberalism: narcissism, disavowal, perversion. *Psychoanalysis, Culture & Society*, 19(2):161–178.

Layton, L. (2014b). Grandiosity, neoliberalism and neoconservatism. *Psychoanalytic Inquiry*, 34(5):463–474.

Layton, L., Hollander, N.C., Gutwill, S. (2006). *Psychoanalysis, Class and Politics: Encounters in the Clinical Setting.* New York: Routledge.

Leary, K. (1997). Race in psychoanalytic space. *Gender & Psychoanalysis*, 2:157–172.

Leary, K. (2000). Racial enactments in dynamic treatment. *Psychoanalytic Dialogues*, 10:639–653.

Leary, K. (2012). Race as an adaptive challenge: working with diversity in the clinical consulting room. *Psychoanalytic Psychology*, 29:279–291.

Levenson, E. (1972; repr. 2005). *The Fallacy of Understanding.* Hillsdale, NJ: The Analytic Press.

Mitchell, S. (1988). *Relational Concepts in Psychoanalysis.* Cambridge, MA: Harvard University Press.

Mitchell, S. (1997). *Influence and Autonomy in Psychoanalysis.* Hillsdale, NJ: Analytic Press.

Peltz, R. (2006). The manic society. In: Layton, L., Hollander, N.C. and Gutwill, S. (eds.). *Psychoanalysis, Class and Politics: Encounters in the Clinical Setting.* New York: Routledge, pp. 65–80.

Riesman, D. with Glazer, N. and Denney, R. (1950; repr. 2001). *The Lonely Crowd.* New Haven, CT: Yale University Press.

Rose, N. (1989). *Governing the Soul. The Shaping of the Private Self.* London: Free Association Books.

Rozmarin, E. (2009). I am yourself: subjectivity and the collective. *Psychoanalytic Dialogues*, 19(5):604–616.

Rozmarin, E. (2014). Talking about Gaza in psychoanalysis. *Public Seminar* 1(2): www.publicseminar.org/2014/08/talking-about-gaza-in-psychoanalysis/#. U-nyIaOodEN. Accessed August 15, 2014.

Rustin, M. (2014). Belonging to oneself alone: the spirit of neoliberalism. *Psychoanalysis, Culture & Society*, 19(2):145–160.

Samuels, A. (1993). *The Political Psyche*. London: Routledge.

Samuels, A. (2001) *Politics on the Couch*. New York; Karnac/Other Press.

Samuels, A. (2006). Response to roundtable: politics and/or/in for psycho-analysis. In: L. Layton, N.C. Hollander, S. Gutwill (eds.) *Psychoanalysis, Class and Politics: Encounters in the Clinical Setting*. New York: Routledge, pp. 202–209.

Sennett, R. (2006). *The Culture of the New Capitalism*. New Haven, CT: Yale University Press.

Slochower, J (2003). The analyst's secret delinquencies. *Psychoanalytic Dialogues*, 13:451–469.

Stein, H.F. (2000). Disposable youth: the 1999 Columbine high school massacre as American metaphor. *Journal for the Psychoanalysis of Culture & Society*, 5:217–236.

Stein, R. (2005). Why perversion? "False love" and the perverse pact. *International Journal of Psychoanalysis*, 86:775–799.

Stern, D.B. (1997). *Unformulated Experience*. Hillsdale, NJ: The Analytic Press.

Stern, D.B. (2010). *Partners in Thought*. New York: Routledge.

Stern, D.B. (2013). Responses to commentaries by Ferro and Civitarese, Carnochan, Peltz and Goldberg, and Levine. *Psychoanalytic Dialogues*, 23(6):674–682.

Straker, G. (2006). The anti-analytic third. *Psychoanalytic Review*, 93:729–753.

Suchet, M. (2004). A relational encounter with race. *Psychoanalytic Dialogues*, 14:423–438.

Suchet, M. (2010). Face to face. *Psychoanalytic Dialogues*, 20:158–171.

Touraine, A. (2009). *Thinking differently*. D. Macey, trans. Cambridge, UK: Polity.

Volkan, V. (2004). *Blind Trust*. Charlottesville, VA: Pitchstone.

Young-Bruehl, E. (2011). Psychoanalysis and social democracy: a tale of two developments. *Contemporary Psychoanalysis*, 47(2):179–201.

Index

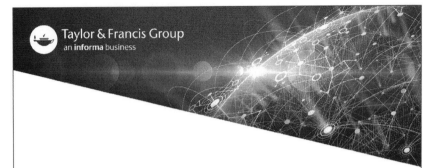